NEGRO SLAVERY IN THE SUGAR PLANTATIONS OF VERACRUZ AND PERNAMBUCO 1550-1680

A Comparative Study

Gerald Cardoso

UNIVERSITY
PRESS OF
AMERICA

Copyright © 1983 by

University Press of America, Inc.

P.O. Box 19101, Washington, D.C. 20036

All rights reserved

Printed in the United States of America

Library of Congress Cataloging in Publication Data

Cardoso, Gerald.
  Negro slavery in the sugar plantations of Veracruz and Pernambuco, 1550-1680.

  Bibliography: p.
  Includes index.
  1. Slavery--Brazil--Pernambuco--History. 2. Slavery--Mexico--Veracruz (State)--History. 3. Plantations--Brazil--Pernambuco--History. 4. Plantations--Mexico--Veracruz (State)--History. 5. Sugar growing--Brazil--Pernambuco--History. 6. Sugar growing--Mexico--Veracruz (State)--History. I. Title.
HT1129.P47C37 1983   306'.362'097262   82-21731
ISBN 0-8191-2926-7
ISBN 0-8191-2927-5 (pbk.)

To the memory of my father
Antonio Maria Moreira Cardoso

The ivy grows best when it grows wild, and the arbutus is most lovely when it grows in some solitary cleft; birds sing most sweetly untaught.

                      -Propertius.

CONTENTS

PREFACE ix

PART I
NEGRO SLAVERY IN VERACRUZ

1. THE DECLINE OF THE INDIAN POPULATION 3
2. THE NEGRO SLAVE POPULATION IN VERACRUZ 9
3. SLAVE LABOR IN THE SUGAR ESTATES 23
4. SOCIAL AND CULTURAL LIFE AT THE PLANTATION 41
5. SLAVE RESISTANCE AND REBELLIONS 51

PART II
NEGRO SLAVERY IN PERNAMBUCO

1. THE INDIAN AND FORCED LABOR 65
2. THE NEGRO POPULATION OF PERNAMBUCO 73
3. SLAVE LABOR IN THE SUGAR ESTATES 89

4. SOCIAL AND CULTURAL LIFE AT THE
   PLANTATION 123
5. SLAVE RESISTANCE AND REBELLIONS 149

PART III

CONCLUSION 167
BIBLIOGRAPHY 191
INDEX 205

PREFACE

Negro slavery was one of the most important features of European colonization in the New World. The availability of what was thought to be cheap and abundant labor proved essential for the orderly development of most colonial economies. It can even be argued that if the African slave trade did not mushroom as it did after the discovery of America, the blossoming of the Spanish and Portuguese possessions in the New World would have been impossible or at best greatly retarded.

Negro slavery touched every aspect of colonial life. In the Spanish and Portuguese colonies it was fundamental to economic survival. It perpetuated a negative concept of labor based on caste, class and color which had its roots in medieval Spain and Portugal. Finally, it helped shape an infinity of mores and attitudes which could only result from the interaction between ruling and subservient groups and between whites and peoples of color under a social system based on forced labor and race.

Being such an integral part of the American experience, it is not surprising that slavery has been the focus of attention by scholars in many fields and from every continent. Over the years a large number of volumes have been published on the subject of Negro slavery. The majority presented a general view of the institution in a particular country such as the United States or Cuba. Others treated specific aspects, such as the Atlantic Slave Trade, the personality of the African slave, or the problem of acculturation and race relations. More recently a smaller group of authors studied slavery from a comparative perspective.

Among authors who chose the comparative approach, the best known compared slavery under the Spanish or Portuguese in Latin America with the slave system as it existed in the United States. Gilberto Freyre and Frank Tannenbaum, in separate works, pioneered the concept that slavery was milder in Brazil than in the American South. Portuguese laws, they argued, were less harsh with the Negroes and the Portuguese colonizer was more flexible on matters of color and race than his Anglo-Saxon counterpart. Freyre and Tannenbaum's theories remained largely unchallenged until the 1970's, when Professor Carl N. Degler disputed their contentions in another comparative study of slavery in Brazil and the United States.

This work departs from the usual comparison of slavery under the Anglo-Saxon versus Iberian colonizer. Instead, it looks at the institution of slavery as it developed in two areas in Latin America under the Spanish and the Portuguese. The specific areas of comparison are the sugar plantations of Veracruz and Pernambuco. The time frame of the study, 1550 - 1680, encompasses the periods when both regions enjoyed considerable economic prosperity generated by the sugar industry.

This account is divided into three parts. The first discusses the many facets of slavery as it existed in Veracruz under Spanish rule. The second examines the same aspects of the institution but in a different setting, the sugar plantations of Pernambuco under the Portuguese. The third and final segment compares and contrasts the total slavery experience in the sugar plantations of the Mexican province and the Brazilian captaincy. Factors which led to the importation of Africans as well as the nature of the slave population in the two areas are examined side by side. Treatment and working conditions under the law and in practice are compared and evaluated. Cultural and social life as well as race relations under the two systems are reviewed. Finally, the Negro's resistance to captivity under either system is made obvious by a discussion of the nature and incidence of slave rebellions.

Preface

It is hoped that this study will shed some light on the nature of slavery in the regions discussed. It is also the author's expectation that it will expose other areas within the general subject of Negro slavery which are in need of further investigation. Despite the vast literature already extant, the topic is far from exhausted and beckons young scholars to make new contributions.

In the preparation of this work I received the generous assistance of dedicated and competent men and women, far too numerous to acknowledge here by name. I would like, however, to register a special debt of gratitude to the following individuals: Professor William L. Sherman, of the University of Nebraska, for his encouragement, guidance, and valuable criticism during all stages of this endeavor; Professor José Antonio Gonsalves de Mello, of the Federal University of Pernambuco, whose advice on the Portuguese archives saved me many days of digging for information in Lisbon; Professor Ralph Vigil, of the University of Nebraska, for the many conversations we had on this topic and for his suggestions, some of which are now part of the text. Because of their help this book is better than it would otherwise have been. They are not to blame, however, for any of its shortcomings. That responsibility is entirely my own.

Brunswick, Maine.   G.C.

PART I
NEGRO SLAVERY IN VERACRUZ

CHAPTER I

THE DECLINE OF THE INDIAN POPULATION

The Spanish conquest of Mexico in 1521 brought unprecedented agony and destruction to the Indians of that region. In less than a century following the first contacts with the Europeans, the native population declined catastrophically and was threatened with extinction. The tragedy followed progressive stages: it began with the early battles of the conquest, gained momentum with the enslavement and overworking of the natives, and reached a climax with the spread of fevers and epidemics.

The epic battles of the conquest and the extensive loss of lives which resulted are too well-known to warrant repetition here. The second phase of depopulation resulted from the enslavement of the Indians and the occurrence of plagues. It came with early settlement and was a consequence of Spanish colonization patterns and exposure to unknown European diseases. Alonso de Zorita saw the rapid decline in population as a direct result of economic exploitation,[1] while the more dramatic Bartolomé de Las Casas accused the Spaniards of having a homicidal plan for the extermination of the Indians.

Given in *encomienda* to the Spanish settlers, the Indians were forced to pay excessive tribute and work in their farms and mines.

Unable to withstand the harsh working conditions and the abuses to which they were subjected, they died in large numbers. In 1549, for example, it was noted that one sugar mill in the province of Chiapas was sufficient to account for the deaths of two thousand Indians a year.[2] These wretched conditions often drove the natives to desperate and extreme measures. Many took their own lives. Others refused to procreate or resorted to abortions and infanticide to save their offspring from following them into servitude. Indians also rebelled in an effort to escape servitude, but such actions invariably led to brutal reprisals by the Spaniards and more Indian deaths.

Another, and perhaps the single most severe cause of depopulation, was the spread of fevers and epidemics. With the coming of the first Spaniards a great many European diseases were brought to the New World. Smallpox, yellow fever, measles, and other pests, found an ideal habitat in the hot and humid areas of Mexico and expedient carriers among the vast armies of mosquitoes which infested them.

Defenseless against these hitherto-unknown diseases, the Indians succumbed by the tens of thousands. Plagues occurred with great frequency, killing Indians of both sexes and of all ages, while the Spanish population remained relatively immune.[3] During the sixteenth century two of these plagues reached widespread proportions. The first occurred in 1545. It struck primarily children, and in one area alone, Tecamachalco, it carried off forty victims a day. The second, and much more severe, struck in 1576. It lasted for one year and killed two and one half times as many Indians.[4] Estimates of the total number of fatalities attributed to the plague of 1576 vary and are sometimes exaggerated. Nevertheless, as many as two million Indians[5] are said to have been claimed by that calamity.

In actual numbers the losses among the Indian population resulting from all of the above factors were staggering. Woodrow Borah and Sherburne Cook rate the Indian population of central Mexico in 1519 at about 25,000,000. In 1532, it was already down to 16,800,000. By 1548, the number of Indians had dwindled to 6,300,000, and towards the end of the century (1595) it has reached a low of 1,375,000.[6]

In the state of Veracruz, however, where the number of Indians since pre-Columbian days had been small, the effects of the massive depopulation were more drastically felt. One of the four areas in the New World which were endemic foci for yellow fever, the hot, humid, and mosquito-infected lowlands of Mexico's eastern coast, were truly a living hell, or what Philip II appropriately called "sepultura de vivos,"[7] or grave of the living. Thousands of Indians died from fevers and overwork, until many areas of the vast territory of Veracruz were virtually depopulated.[8] Cempoala, one of the first villages to have contact with the Spaniards, had at the time of the conquest 20,000 households ("veinte mil vecinos"). By the end of 1580 that pueblo had been reduced to fifty houses ("cincuenta casas"). Other formerly important pueblos, such as Xamloluco, Espiche, and Cotastla, all near the port city of Veracruz, had, according to the same report, no more than twelve or fifteen houses.[9] Jalapa, another important town in Veracruz, had, before the conquest, 30,000 inhabitants. According to some sources this number had dropped to 639 tributaries by 1580.[10] George Kubler paints an even gloomier picture by putting the number of tributaries in Jalapa between thirty-five and fifty by 1570.[11]

The growing exploitation of the Indians by the Spaniards soon became the subject of severe attacks by members of religious orders and Spanish intellectuals.[12] Reacting to the strong criticism, the Crown sought to remedy the situation by issuing a series of laws aimed at protecting the Indian population. Following the New Laws of 1542-1543, which prohibited the future enslavement of Indians,[13] a series of royal decrees banned the use of Indians in occupations which endangered their health and welfare. In a decree dated November 24, 1601, Philip III expressly prohibited the use of Indians in textile and sugar mills because of the high incidence of deaths resulting from these occupations.[14] The combined effect of the sharp decline in the Indian population and the gradual enforcement of the protective laws was a severe labor shortage, particularly in the textile and sugar industries.[15]

NOTES

1. For a more detailed treatment of this topic see Alonso de Zorita, *Breve y summaria relación de los señores y maneras y diferencias que habia de ellos en la Nueva Espana*, in Joaquin Garcia Icazbalceta (ed.), Nueva Colección de documentos para la história de México, 8 vols. (México: Andrade y Norales, 1891), 3:181-82.

2. *Archivo General de Indias*, Sevilla (hereafter cited as AGI), Carta de S.M. a Alonso López de Cerrato (Valladolid: 29 de abril de 1549), Guatemala, legajo 402, libros T-3, folios 27v-33.

3. AGI, Carta de Martin Enríquez a S.M. (10 de diciembre de 1576) México, legajo 19.

4. AGI, Carta de Martin Enríquez a S.M. (19 de octubre de 1577) México, legajo 20, ramo 1. For more detail on this disaster see Francisco de Paso y Troncoso, *Papeles de Nueva España*, Segunda Serie, 7 vols. (Madrid: Geografia y Estadistica, 1905), 4:137, 6:258-59.

5. Francisco Florencia, S. J., "La Peste de 1575," in Ernesto de La Torre Villar, *Lecturas Históricas Mexicanas*, 5 vols. (México: Empresas Editoriales, 1966), 1:574. Florencia erroneously states that the plague occurred in 1575. According to Kubler and Paso y Troncoso, the plague broke out in August, 1576, and lasted until the end of 1577. See Paso y Troncoso, op. cit., and George Kubler, "Population Movements in Mexico 1520-1600," *Hispanic American Historical Review*, hereafter cited as HAHR, Vol. 22 (November, 1942), pp. 606-643.

6. "... Central Mexico may be defined as Mexico from the Isthmus of Tehuantepec to the northern border of the sedentary settlement in 1550. The southern boundary of this area excludes Chiapas but includes the old province of Coatzacoalcos on the Gulf Coast as far as the Laguna de Términos. The northern boundary is a vast semicircle stretching from Pánuco and southern Tamaulipas through the present states of Querétaro, Guanajuato, Zacatecas, Jalisco, and Nayarit, to include southern and central Sinaloa on the Pacific coast." Woodrow Borah and Sherburne F. Cook, *The Aboriginal Population of Central Mexico on the Eve of the Spanish Conquest* (Berkeley and Los Angeles: The University of California Press, 1963), pp. 3-4. Another important earlier study of this topic gives somewhat lower figures. See Sherburne F. Cook and Lesley Byrd Simpson, *The Population of Central Mexico in the Sixteenth Century*. Ibero-Americana: 31 (Berkeley and Los Angeles: The University of California Press, 1948).

7. *Colección de Documentos Inéditos, relativos al descubrimiento, conquista y organización de las antiguas posesiones Españolas de America y Oceanía sacados de los Archivos del Reino y muy especialmente del de Indias*, 42 Vols. (Madrid, 1867. Reprinted at Nendelin, Liechtenstein: Kraus Reprint Ltd., 1966), 23:535, hereafter cited as DII.

8. Luis Chávez Orozco and Enrique Florescano, *Agricultura y Industria Textil de Veracruz, Siglo XIX* (Xalapa: Universidad Veracruzana, 1965) p. 33.

9. Joaquin Ramirez Cabañas, *La Ciudad de Veracruz en el Siglo XVI* (México: Imprenta Universitaria, 1943), pp. 23-24.

10. Paso y Troncoso, *Papeles de Nueva España*, 5:100.

11. Kubler, "Population Movements in Mexico 1520-1600," p. 621.

12. Bartolomé de Las Casas was the most influential among the critics of Spanish abuses. Largely as a result of his indefatigable efforts, early protective legislation, including the New Laws of 1542, were instituted. Other religious figures such as Juan de Zumárraga, and Vasco de Quiroga continued Las Casas' struggle to curb exploitation of the Indians. In Spain, distinguished intellectuals also denounced Spanish policies, and questioned the right of the conquerors to enslave the Indians. For an interesting study of the resulting controversy, see J. H. Parry, *The Spanish Theory of Empire in the Sixteenth Century* (Cambridge: The University Press, 1940). On the same topic see Richard Konetzke, "La Esclavitud de los indios como elemento de la estructuración social de Hispanoamérica," 4 Vols., *Estudios de História social de España*, 1:441-79 (Madrid: Consejo Superior de Investigaciones Cientificas, 1949); and Lewis Hanke, *Aristotle and the American Indians* (London: Hollis & Carter, 1959).

13. AGI, Instrucción dada por S.M. al Virrey de N. España D. Luis de Velasco [1552], Patronato, legajo 181, ramo 26.

14. DII, 19:153-54. "... Porque he sido informado que el trauajo que los yndios an padecido y padecen en los obrajes de paños e yngenios de azucar es muy grande y excesiuo y contrario a su salud, y causa de que se ayan consumido y acabado en el, muchos, prohibo y expresamente Defiendo y Mando que de aqui adelante en ninguna provincia ni parte de esos Reynos puedan trauajar ni trauajen los yndios en los dichos obrajes de paños de españoles, ni en los yngenios de azucar...."

15. There is a considerable debate among scholars as to whether the decline of the Indian population was the central cause of a slump in the Atlantic trade between Mexico and Spain beginning in 1620. Most specialists agree, however, that the decline of the Indian population created a serious labor shortage. The shortage was more severely felt in the sugar plantations of the eastern lowlands where the demand for labor was higher than in the mines and textile mills. Plantation owners in Veracruz often complained about the shortage. In 1599, for example, they petitioned the Crown for permission to use *indios de socorro* on a temporary basis in order to save their harvest. For a detailed discussion of the decline of the Indian population and its consequences see Woodrow Borah, *New Spain's Century of Depression* (Berkeley and Los Angeles: University of California Press, 1951), and J.I. Israel, *Race, Class and Politics in Colonial Mexico 1610-1670* (London: Oxford University Press, 1975).

CHAPTER II

THE NEGRO SLAVE POPULATION IN VERACRUZ

The Spanish economy in the Indies was severely crippled by the sharp reduction in the available work force. The problem was particularly critical in the growing sugar industry, in which large numbers of workers were essential to the successful operation of the plantations. The importation of sufficient quantities of Negro slaves became imperative to alleviate the labor shortage. Negro slaves were common in the Iberian Peninsula even before the discovery of America. As early as 1441, Antão Gonçalves acquired the first African slaves on the shores of the Rio de Ouro and shipped them to Lisbon. After the discovery of the coastal areas of the Gulf of Guinea, Lisbon and Seville became important distribution centers and Negroes began taking over the tasks performed by Moorish slaves since the Middle Ages. Because of the tradition inherited from the days of the Roman occupation which gave slaves a legal position,[1] these Africans were easily assimilated into Spanish and Portuguese societies.

The importation of Negro slaves into the Spanish possessions in the New World was first authorized on September 3, 1501. On this date instructions were given to Nicolás Ovando, Governor of the island of Española, granting him permission to introduce Negro slaves into the island, provided that they had already been converted to Christianity in Spain.[2] According to Perdigão Malheiros by 1503 the first Negroes had landed in Santo Domingo.[3] In his recent study of the slave trade James Rawley states that in 1510, King Ferdinand ordered the Casa de Contratación, or House of Trade, to send two hundred fifty slaves to the Indies. He also argues that the event marks "... the start of the Negro slave trade between the Old and New Worlds."[4] In an earlier work Affonso Taunay stated, more specifically, that the first fifty Negroes to come to the New World as part of the regular traffic were brought to the Antilles in 1511.[5] Two years later the demand for Negroes was so great that the Crown found it expedient to start an import duty. On July 22, 1513, a royal decree required that a license be obtained for the importation of slaves and established a head tax of two ducats for each Negro brought into the New World. To supply slaves in such large quantities, the Council of the Indies authorized Negroes to be brought directly from Africa to the Islands without having to undergo the cathechization period in Spain.[6] For this purpose the Baron of Montinay, Lorenzo de Gumenot (also known as Gouvenot or Garrewood), Governor of Brésa and a favorite of Charles V, requested, and was granted in 1517, a license to introduce four thousand Negroes into the greater Antilles over a period of eight years.[7] The Governor of Brésa immediately sold his license to some Genoese who greatly profited from the transactions. This led to such an increase in the price of Negroes that few of the colonists were able to buy them, and therefore, only a part of the four thousand was brought into the islands. Another contract was granted by the Crown to two Germans, Heinrich Eynger and Hieronymus Sayller, on February 12, 1528. They pledged to introduce four thousand Negroes into the Indies in the shorter period of four years. To avoid abuses it was specified in the contract that the slaves would be sold at no more than forty ducats each. This attempt to satisfy the growing demand for labor also proved to be unsatisfactory.[8]

In New Spain the introduction and expansion of Negro slavery followed a similar pattern. The first Negroes came in small numbers, accompanying the *conquistadores*. Yet between 1519 and 1650 Mexico was to import over 120,000 Africans, or well over half the total of Negroes taken to Spanish America.[9] Hernán Cortés was the first to bring Negro slaves into New Spain. Accompanying him in his expedition were two Africans, Juan Cortés and Juan Garrido. The latter is said to have been the first to plant and harvest wheat in Mexico. Another member of the Cortés expedition of 1519, Juan Sedeño, was also accompanied by a Negro.[10] At least two other African immigrants came to New Spain with the expedition of Pánfilo de Narváez in 1520. One of them contracted smallpox,[11] which quickly spread, killing thousands of Indians.[12]

Gradually more Negroes were introduced as additional settlers began to enter New Spain. Initially, these were brought from the islands, where they had been taken under the contracts of 1517 and 1528. As this arrangement failed to meet the growing demand, Negroes began to be imported from entrepôts in southern Spain under individual licenses granted by the Crown.[13] On March 11, 1531, Juan de Armenta and Hernando Páez were given such an authorization. On March 1, 1535, Rodrigo de Albornoz, royal accountant in New Spain, received a license to import a hundred slaves for his sugar mills and other properties. Later that year another license was granted to Eynger and Albert Coun to bring two hundred Negroes to work in a mining operation.[14] Those who received these licenses and did not wish to engage in the trade themselves often transferred their privileges to others. In 1537, for instance, Doña Maria de Toledo, wife of the Viceroy of New Spain, authorized Melchor de Carrion and Diego de Arana to take three hundred Negroes to the Indies in accordance with a license she had received from the Crown.[15] Later that year, Fernan Sanchez Dalvo paid Doña Maria 1,300 ducats for a license to import two hundred slaves.[16] By 1537, according to Aguirre Beltrán, the slave traffic was well established and large numbers of Negroes were coming in through Veracruz.[17] Also by this time the sudden influx of Negroes was already causing some problems. After plans for a slave revolt in Veracruz had been discovered in 1537, Viceroy Antonio de Mendoza asked the king to halt temporarily the shipment of Negroes to New Spain.[18] By 1553, the number of slaves brought in under these licenses had already reached unexpected proportions. Again the presence of large numbers of Negroes worried the authorities. In a letter to the king, Viceroy Luis de Velasco expressed concern over the fact that there were more than 20,000 Negroes in New Spain and that their increasing numbers could present serious difficulties.[19] It is almost impossible to determine the total number of slaves brought to Mexico under these licenses and partial *asientos*. Huguette and Pierre Chaunu account for licenses for 263 ships between the years of 1551 and 1595, each vessel carrying an average of 138 *piezas de India*, or a total of 36,294 *piezas* for the forty-four year period.[20] Aguirre Beltrán, on the other hand, estimates that 60,000 Negroes entered Mexico during the sixteenth century.[21]

After the plague of 1576, the demand for Negroes to replace Indians in mines, textile and sugar mills, and public works[22] necessitated a more dependable source of slaves. According to Aguirre Beltrán, as early as 1585, slaves were being imported into Mexico directly from Africa under partial *asientos* granted to individuals.[23] In May 1592, a shipment of 140 *piezas de esclavos* brought directly from Cape Verde, arrived in Veracruz according to a license given to the Jaureguis of Seville.[24] These partial *asientos*, however, were merely the precursors of the great *asientos* of the end of the century which granted a monopoly over the slave trade to a single individual.

A more sophisticated organization to provide for an adequate supply of slaves would have to be developed. The union of the Spanish and Portuguese crowns in 1580 greatly facilitated this undertaking by giving the Spaniards direct access to the African factories, a privilege hitherto denied them. At the suggestion of a Portuguese trader, and after prolonged consideration by the Council of the Indies, the Crown decided to embark upon a policy of monopoly concessions for the slave trade.

Accordingly, on January 30, 1595, the Crown and Pedro Gómez Reynel signed the first true *asiento*, that is, the first to be granted by public competition and requiring a large security deposit.[25] By the terms of this contract the *asientista* obligated himself to transport to the New World 38,250 Negroes over a period of nine years at a rate of 4,250 slaves a year. These slaves could be brought from Lisbon, the Canaries, Cape Verde, São Tomé, Angola, Guinea, or Mina.[26] The slaves carried by each ship were to be registered with the Casa de Contratación, and an import tax was to be paid on the number of slaves appearing on the registration certificate. Reynel also agreed to pay the Crown

900,000 ducats, in installments of 100,000 each year, and a security deposit of 150,000 ducats.[27] In exchange, he was to have a monopoly over the slave traffic to the New World and was free to sell his slaves for whatever price he could get. Because of the increased traffic that was to result, specific ports such as Cartagena de Indias and Veracruz were designated as ports of primary entry because of their excellent location as centers of distribution to all parts of the Indies.[28]

Upon receiving the *asiento*, Reynel did not form a company to carry out the transportation of Negroes. Reynel, and the *asientistas* who followed him, merely kept a few licenses for themselves and sold the remainder to captains of slave ships. The contract also gave Reynel the right to have agents known as *factores*, both in the factories in Africa and in the ports of the New World. Both of these practices, though permitted under the contract, led to many abuses which contributed to the termination of the Reynel *asiento*.

First, Reynel sold the licenses for forty-two ducats instead of thirty ducats as specified in the contract. He also allowed the slavers to carry 12 percent more slaves than the number actually registered with the Casa de Contratación, as required in the contract. In the port of destination, Reynel's agents connived with the slavers so that the custom duty of twenty reales would be paid only on the slaves actually registered. Reynel was also able to get some rebate on the slaves introduced by this form of contraband.

Frequent complaints led to a general tightening-up on the part of the custom officials. In July of 1599, four slave ships entering the port of Veracruz under the Reynel *asiento* were found to be carrying at least 186 *piezas de India* in excess of the number declared on the registration certificate.[29] Numerous slaves were taken into Mexico by contraband during the *asiento* period. Exempt from the import duty, and not having to meet the required quality standards, they constituted a most profitable aspect of the slave trade.[30]

Shortly after the July incident, the Reynel *asiento* ended. The illicit trade of which the *asientista* allegedly participated, however, was only one of the reasons for the Crown's action. The decisive factor was the seizure by the Dutch of the island of São Tomé in 1599. This shifted the center of trade from São Tomé, the main source of the Reynel *asiento*, to Angola, where the *asientista* apparently had no agent or jurisdiction.[31]

Coinciding with the great boom in the sugar industry, the importation of Negro slaves into Mexico reached a climax during the first half of the seventeenth century. Between 1595, when the Reynel contract began, and 1640, 88,000 slaves were taken into New Spain.[32] By this time, with the exception of Brazil, New Spain had the highest concentration of Negro slaves in the New World. This was the period of the Portuguese *asientistas*, who controlled the supply areas in Africa not in the hands of Spain's enemies.

The first of these *asientos* signed on May 13, 1601, went to João Rodrigues Coutinho, Governor of Portuguese Angola. The conditions specified in this contract were essentially the same as those of the Reynel *asiento*. Most of the slaves brought in under this *asiento* originated from the Guinea coast. The governor, however, taking advantage of his authority, also exported some Negroes from Angola.[33]

The new *asiento*, like that of Reynel before it, ended before its normal expiration date. In 1603, because of Coutinho's death, the *asiento* passed to his brother, Gonçalo Vaes Coutinho, who had also replaced João as governor. Gonçalo experienced some of the same difficulties his brother had encountered in the Angola trade. Angola was located below the equator, and, therefore farther away from the Spanish possessions in the New World. The greater distance increased the risks of the voyage and the number of deaths during the passage, making the captains of slave ships reluctant to participate in the Angola trade.[34] For instance, of 1,211 Negroes sent to Brazilian ports in 1625, by the Governor of Angola, 583 died during the crossing, and another 68 died shortly after arrival.[35] Veracruz, or Cartagena were, of course, even farther from Angola than Recife or Salvador on the Brazilian coast.

As an incentive to attract the captains, Coutinho allowed them to carry 15 percent more slaves, free of the registry tax, to compensate for those who might die during the crossing. At Coutinho's request, the Crown also permitted his slaves to be taken to the Indies without being registered with the Casa de Contratación. In spite of these concessions, the Coutinho *asiento* proved to be a rather unprofitable venture. In 1609, when the contract expired, the *asientista* was bankrupt.

According to Aguirre Beltrán, Coutinho's failure was mostly due to a continuing decline in the price of slaves since the Reynel *asiento*. Because of saturation in other parts of the Indies, most of Coutinho's slaves were taken to Mexico. The abundant supply produced a corresponding reduction in price. Slaves who before the time of the great *asientos* sold in Veracruz for five hundred pesos, where going for three hundred pesos in 1609.[36]

In view of the failure of the Portuguese *asientos*, the Crown decided to return to the sale of individual licenses without monopoly. In spite of the Crown's efforts, the number of Spaniards interested in the trade was small. While the licenses were few, large numbers of Negroes continued to be smuggled into Mexico. This situation persisted until 1615, when a new *asiento* was granted.

The new contract, signed on September 26, went to Antonio Fernándes d'Elvas. The *asientista* agreed to pay the Crown 115,000 ducats a year and to introduce to the New World 3,500 slaves each year for a period of eight years. Two new features of the trade made their appearance in this contract and became standard in most of the subsequent *asientos*. The first of these gave the *asientista* the right to take from Spain or the Indies, without paying the export tax, goods to barter for Negroes and for their sustenance.[37] The second prohibited the viceroy or the Royal Audiencia of New Spain from interfering in legal disputes involving Negroes.[38] In this contract Cartagena and Veracruz appear as the only ports through which the *asientista* could introduce slaves into the New World. According to José Antonio Saco, this restriction reflected the Crown's distrust of foreigners engaged in the American trade. If this was true, the Crown was the loser. The transfer of slaves from Veracruz and Cartagena to other parts of Spanish America was costly and inevitably increased the price of slaves. The obvious result was an increased market for contraband slaves,[39] and considerable loss of revenue for the Crown.

With the death of the *asientista* in 1622, the Fernandes d'Elvas contract came to an end. In only seven years of operation he had introduced 29,574 Negroes to the New World,[40] a figure larger than the total projected for the eight years the contract was to last.

From 1622 to 1630, the *asiento* was held by Manuel Rodrigues Lamego. In only two provisions did the Lamego contract differ from the previous arrangement. The first of these was a higher fee of 120,000 ducats paid to the Crown.[41] The other was a royal ban on the importation of Filipino and Malay slaves whom the traders from time to time attempted to take into Mexico.[42]

On September 25, 1631, the *asiento* passed to Melchor Gómez Angel and Cristóbal Méndez de Sossa. The new contract was to last for eight years. The number of Negroes to be introduced annually, however, was reduced to 2,500, and accordingly, the payment to the Crown was cut to 95,000 ducats a year.[43] This was the last of the Portuguese *asientos*. In 1640, the Portuguese revolt against Spanish rule disrupted the traffic, and by 1641, the Dutch conquest of São Jorge da Mina and Angola had brought an end to the Portuguese hegemony over the slave trade.[44]

Controlling the most important sources of slaves, the Dutch attempted to secure the Spanish *asiento*. Suspicion of the Dutch traders, however, made the Crown reject their proposals and return to the granting of individual licenses. This practice continued until July 5, 1662, when a new *asiento* went to the Genoese merchants Domingo Grillo, and the brothers, Agustín, Ambrosio, and Franco Lomelín. The new contract called for the introduction into the New World of 24,500 Negroes over a period of nine years and for the payment to the Crown of a fee of 2,100,000 pesos.[45] In spite of the great difficulties encountered, including the killing of Agustín Lomelín by Negro slaves in Mexico, this *asiento* lasted until March 1, 1674.[46]

In the meantime, the Crown insistently tried to interest Spaniards in undertaking the *asiento*. Finally, on December 15, 1674, two merchants from Castile, Antonio García and Sebastián de Siliceo, received the *asiento*. Four thousand slaves were to be introduced annually for a period of five years. For the monopoly the *asientistas* paid the Crown 450,000 pesos a year. This *asiento* was short-lived. One year later the *asientistas* went bankrupt.

On February 23, 1676, a new *asiento* was signed, this time with the *Consulado y Comercio de Sevilla* as the *asientista*. The *Consulado* agreed to bring to the New World ten thousand *toneladas* in the next five years.[47] The *Consulado* fared no better than its predecessors and shortly before the expiration of the *asiento* it petitioned the Crown to transfer to Juan Barroso del Pozo responsibility for six thousand of the original ten thousand tons called for in the contract. On February 28, 1680, this was authorized, and Barroso del Pozo also received permission to import slaves from the Dutch island of Curaçao. From this time until the granting of the *asiento* to the *Companhia Portuguesa de Cabo Verde, Cacheu e Negócio dos Pretos*, on July 7, 1696,[48] slaves brought into Mexico came almost entirely from Curaçao and other Caribbean islands. This involvement with Dutch middlemen in the Caribbean led to a significant increase in the price of slaves. During this time the average price of a slave in the Mexican markets was four hundred pesos.[49]

Mostly under the *asientos*, but also under the individual licenses and through contraband, over 200,000 Negroes entered Mexico during the entire period of the slave trade.[50] The greater part of this total, however, was brought in between 1576-1650, in response to the accelerated decline in the Indian population and the increased economic development of the colony.[51]

By providing a steadier flow of workers, the organized slave traffic, particularly during the *asiento* period, saved the infant colonial economy from certain stagnation owing to the labor shortage. Another contribution of the *asientos* was the improved physical standards of the Negroes. While in the early days of the traffic the slaves brought to New Spain were often old, crippled, and generally unfit for hard work, those brought in under the monopoly contracts, were strong, vigorous, and seldom more than twenty-five years old.[52]

As the traffic drew its slaves from many areas, different types of Africans came to be found in New Spain. Of different cultures, speaking different languages, each group of slaves brought with it distinct characteristics. As these traits proved to be more or less suitable to the interests of the Spaniards, slaves from certain areas were particularly sought after, while those from other lands because of their undesirable disposition, or lack of skills, were increasingly less in demand.

NOTES

1. Frédéric Mauro, *Le Portugal et L'Atlantique aux XVIIe Siècle 1570-1670* (Paris: École Pratique des Hautes Etudes, 1960), p. 147. For a detailed and scholarly study of the Roman law background to Spanish and Portuguese laws see Agostinho Marques Perdigão Malheiros, *A Escravidão no Brasil, Ensaio Histórico-Jurídico-Social*, 2 vols. (São Paulo: Edições Cultura, 1944), Vol. 1. Other interesting books on this subject are two studies by Ruth Pike, *Aristocrats and Traders: Sevillian*

Society in the Sixteenth Century (Ithaca, New York: Cornell University Press, 1972); and *Enterprise and Adventure; the Genoese in Seville and the Opening of the New World* (Ithaca, New York: Cornell University Press, 1966).
  2. Gonzalo Aguirre Beltrán, *La Población Negra de México 1519-1810* (México: Ediciones Fuente Cultural, 1946), p. 5.
  3. Perdigão Malheiros, *A Escravidão no Brasil*, 2:17.
  4. James A. Rawley, *The Atlantic Slave Trade: A History*. (New York: W. W. Norton & Company, 1981), p. 55.
  5. Affonso de Escaragnolle Taunay, *Subsídios para a História do Tráfico Africano no Brasil Colonial* (Rio de Janeiro: Instituto Historico, Imprensa Nacional, 1941), p. 530.
  6. Aguirre Beltrán, *La Población Negra de México*, p. 5.
  7. José Antonio Saco, *História de la Esclavitud de la Raza Africana en el Nuevo Mundo y en Especial en los Países Americo-Hispanos*, 4 Vols. (Habana Cultural S. A., 1938), 1:176. Many historians consider this to be the first *asiento*. Georges Scelle, however, considers that of Pedro Gómez Reynel in 1595 to be the first *asiento* that can be truly used as a model.
  8. Georges Scelle, "The Slave Trade in the Spanish Colonies of America: The Assiento," *The American Journal of International Law*, Vol. 4 (July, 1910), pp. 619-620.
  9. David M. Davidson, "Negro Slave Control and Resistance in Colonial Mexico 1519-1650," HAHR, Vol. 46 (August, 1946), p. 236.
  10. Saco, *Histórica de la Esclavitud*, p. 181.
  11. Aguirre Beltrán, *La Población Negra de México*, p. 8.
  12. Bernal Díaz del Castillo, *The Discovery and Conquest of Mexico* (New York: Noonday, 1968), p. 292.
  13. Aguirre Beltrán, "The Slave Trade in Mexico," HAHR, Vol. 24 (August, 1944), p. 412.
  14. Aguirre Beltrán, *La Población Negra de México*, pp. 10-11.
  15. *Colección de documentos inéditos para la historia de Hispano-América - Catálogo de los Fondos Americanos del Archivo de Protocolos de Sevilla*, Tomo I, Siglo XVI, Excribanía: Alonso de Cazalta. Libro del año 1537 - oficio XV, libro II (10 de noviembre de 1537), fol. 1476.
  16. *Ibid.*, fol. 1726.
  17. Aguirre Beltrán, *la Población Negra de México*, pp. 10-11.
  18. AGI, Carta de Antonio de Mendoza a S.M. (10 de diciembre de 1537), Patronato, legajo 184, ramo 27.
  19. Aguirre Beltrán, "The Slave Trade in Mexico," p. 413.
  20. Huguette and Pierre Chaunu, *Séville et L'Atlantique (1504-1650)*, 8 Vols. (Paris: Librarie Armand Colin, 1955), Table 188, 6:402-403, and text 6:41-42. A *pieza de India* was not necessarily equivalent to

an individual slave. It was rather a measure of potential labor. A *pieza* was a male slave, of a certain age, capable of performing a certain amount of work. Female slaves, youngsters, and the old, were measured according to their ability to work, as half a *pieza*, and other fractions of a *pieza*. The total number of slaves brought into the country, therefore, was always larger than the number of *piezas*. For more detail on this topic see Georges Scelle, *La Traite Négrière aux Indes de Castille*, 2 vols. (Paris: Larose & Tenin, 1906), 2:26-27; and Philip D. Curtin, *The Atlantic Slave Trade, A Census* (Madison: University of Wisconsin Press, 1970), p. 22.

21. Aguirre Beltrán, "The Slave Trade in Mexico," p. 414.

22. AGI, Carta de Martin Enríquez a S.M. (13 de diciembre de 1577), México, legajo 20, ramo 1; AGI, Carta de Martin Enríquez a S.M. (25 de diciembre de 1578), México, legajo 20, ramo 1.

23. Aguirre Beltrán, "The Slave Trade in Mexico," pp. 413-414. As evidence, Aguirre Beltrán quotes from a bill of sale dated 1585: "Francisco de Aguilar, captain of the ship San Cristóbal, anchored in the port of San Juan de Ulúa, with a cargo of *bozal* Negroes fromSan Thomé, on account of and at the risk of His Majesty, Joan Bautista de Rebolasco, and myself..."

24. AGI, Carta de Luis de Velasco a S.M. (18 de mayo de 1592), México, legajo 22, ramo 3.

25. Scelle, "The Slave Trade in the Spanish Colonies," p. 623.

26. AGI, Carta de Pedro Gómez Reynel a S.M. (Madrid, 2 de octubre de 1595), Indiferente General, legajo 743.

27. Saco, *História de la Esclavitud*, 2:91-92.

28. Aguirre Beltrán, *La Población Negra de México*, p. 29.

29. Francisco del Paso y Troncoso, *Epistolario de Nueva España 1505-1818*, 8 vols. (Mexico: Antigua Librería Robredo de Jose Porrua e Hijos, 1939-42), 13:257-58. A more conservative total of ninety *piezas* is given by Manuel B. Trens, *Historia de Veracruz*, 6 vols. (Jalapa-Enríquez Veracruz, n.p., 1944-1950), 2:172.

30. Curtin, *The Atlantic Slave Trade*, p. 23. In addition to the many slaves who lived in the rural areas, Mexico City itself had a large population of Negroes working in urban occupations. In this period, according to Frederick Bowser, the Mexican capital and the city of Lima had the largest concentration of Negroes in the Western Hemisphere. See Davidson, "Negro Slave Control and Resistance in Colonial Mexico," p. 237, and Frederick P. Bowser, *The African Slave in Colonial Peru, 1524-1650* (Stanford, California: Stanford University Press, 1974), p. 328.

31. Aguirre Beltrán, *La Población Negra de México*, pp. 31-32. According to the *asiento*, Reynel was allowed to have agents in

"São Thomé, Cape Verde, Angola, Guinea and all other rivers," but Reynel complained that the Council of Portugal was slow in giving him authorization to employ agents in those localities. It is probable that the Council never granted Reynel the authorization to establish a factory in Angola. See AGI, Pedro Gomez Reynel to S.M. (Madrid, 2 de octubre de 1595), Indiferente General, 743.

32. Oriol Pi-Sunyer, "Historical Background to the Negro in Mexico," *The Journal of Negro History*, Vol. 42 (October, 1957), p. 242.

33. Aguirre Beltrán, *La Población Negra de México*, p. 33.

34. Aguirre Beltrán, "The Slave Trade in Mexico," p. 417.

35. Frédéric Mauro, *L'Expansion Européenne 1600-1870* (Paris: Presses Universitaires de France, 1964), p. 165.

36. Aguirre Beltrán, *La Población Negra de México*, p. 34.

37. For a description of the exchange of slaves for European products see John Barbot, "*A Description of the Coast of North and South Guinea written for the Most Part in 1682,*" in *Churchill's Voyages*, 6 vols. Vol. 5, 3rd ed. (London: n.p., 1744-46).

38. Aguirre Beltrán, "The Slave Trade in Mexico," p. 418.

39. Saco, *História de la Esclavitud*, 2:116.

40. *Ibid.*, p. 134.

41. AGI, Asiento con Manuel Rodriguez Lamego, Indiferente General, legajo 2767.

42. Wilbur Zelinsky, "The Historical Geography of the Negro Population of Latin America," *Journal of Negro History*, Vol. 34 (April, 1949), p. 157.

43. Aguirre Beltrán, *La Población Negra de México*, pp. 38-39.

44. Walter Rodney, "Portuguese Attempts at Monopoly on the Upper Guinea Coast," *Journal of African History*, Vol. 6 (1965), p. 316. For a detailed account of the Dutch seizure of Mina see Gaspar Barléu, *História dos feitos recentemente praticados durante oito anos no Brasil e noutras partes sob o govêrno do ilustríssimo João Mauricio Conde de Nassau* (Rio de Janeiro: Serviço Gráfico do Ministério da Educação, 1940), pp. 56-62.

45. Aguirre Beltrán, *La Población Negra de México*, p. 48.

46. *Ibid.*, p. 50.

47. *Ibid.*, p. 53. "Se estimaba cada tonelada en tres piezas de Indias de la medida ordinaria de siete cuartas, no siendo viejos ni con defectos."

48. Scelle, *La Traite Négrière*, 2:48.

49. Aguirre Beltrán, "The Slave Trade in Mexico," pp. 424-25.

50. Curtin, *The Atlantic Slave Trade*, Table 11, p. 46.

51. Colin Alphonsous Palmer, "Negro Slavery in Mexico, 1570-1650" (unpublished Ph.D. dissertation, Department of History, The University of Wisconsin, 1970), p. 5.
52. Aguirre Beltrán, *La Población Negra de México*, p. 34.

CHAPTER III

SLAVE LABOR IN THE SUGAR ESTATES

Because of their favorable location, Cartagena de Indias and Veracruz had been chosen as ports of primary entry for African slaves coming to the Spanish colonies. One fourth of the slaves to be imported under the Reynel *asiento*, for example, were to be delivered at the port of San Juán de Ulloa.[1] In Veracruz the sugar industry was booming and the demand for labor was great. For these reasons a high percentage of all Negroes brought to Mexico during the colonial period gravitated to the sugar plantations located in the area which now comprises the modern state of Veracruz.

Because of unfavorable conditions, maize and wheat did not grow as well in Veracruz as in other parts of the colony. Very early therefore, the province turned to tropical, plantation type agriculture as the most adaptable to its soil and climatic conditions. Tobacco, cacao, cotton, and above all, sugar cane, became the most important crops in the area.

Sugar cane was introduced to Mexico by Hernán Cortés and other early settlers during the first half of the sixteenth century. As early as 1524, Cortés was growing cane and building a sugar mill in Tuxtla, Veracruz.[2] Cortés' mill at Tuxtla, which began operations in 1534, was the first sugar refinery in the continent[3] and the precursor of an important and valuable industry. From Tuxtla, the cultivation of sugar cane spread rapidly to other parts of Veracruz. Indians began to plant sugar cane to sell to the new sugar mills. By 1571, Indians in Medellín, Cempoala, and La Rinconada were engaged in this activity.

Recognizing the profit to be made from sugar, many Spaniards applied for licenses to build sugar mills. It was not long before several refineries began appearing in many parts of the territory. Even the viceroy himself became interested enough in the new industry to embark on a business venture of his own. About 1542, Don Antonio de Mendoza appropriated some land in the Valle de Ostotipac extending from Orizaba to Aculzingo. In the newly acquired land, near the town of Orizaba, the viceroy established a sugar plantation and a small village which he called *El Ingenio* (the mill). by 1545, the viceroy's plantation had progressed enough to have its own church and priest.[4] On April 16, 1550, the Crown, realizing the potential of the new industry, instructed the Viceroy of New Spain to encourage its development by making grants of land to those interested in the cultivation of sugar cane or the building of mils.[5] That same year five sugar mills were in operation in the jurisdiction of Orizaba: one in Gueguetlán, owned by Francisco Martínez, another in Chietla owned by Maria Cataro, a small mill in Matlala owned by the convent of Los Angeles, and the great sugar mill Orizaba-Tequila owned by doña Melcora de Aberraza, and her son Juán de Vivero y Velasco.[6]

Towards the end of the sixteenth century, sugar cane was widely planted in the jurisdiction of Tuxpan. Jalapa, at the turn of the seventeenth century, had several sugar plantations, and eight mills of different sizes, including the great Santísima Trinidad, which, according to François Chevalier, was the largest sugar refinery in the country at that time.[7] In the Córdoba area there were thirty-three small mills in operation.[8] From Veracruz, sugar cane spread into the warm lands of the interior around Cuernavaca and the Pacific coast at such places as Michoacán, and Oaxaca, and the production of sugar became established as the first processing industry in New Spain. By 1600, according to

Alonso de Sandoval, there were over forty mills in New Spain which represented a large capital investment for that period.[9]

These sugar mills were of different types and sizes. Essentially, they could be grouped in two categories: *trapiches* and *ingenios*. The first were small factories of limited capacity relying as a rule on animals as a source of power. In 1603, Juan Dias Matamoros, for instance, used a horse to power the mill in his *trapiche* near Jalapa. Smaller varieties of the *trapiche* were tiny mills operated by hand known as *trapichillos a mano*, which abounded near Córdoba in the early seventeenth century.

The *ingenios* were much larger operations and constituted the foundation of the sugar industry. They differed from the *trapiches* in that they used a hydraulic wheel usually fed by aqueduct to power their presses. Their industrial equipment usually included a mill house (*casa de ingenio*) where the wheel and a mill with two or three presses were located; a boiler house, furnaces, a purging house, sun decks (*asoleaderos*),[10] and syrup tanks. Orizaba-Tequila, in the valley of Orizaba, and Santísima Trinidad in Jalapa, were two of the largest *ingenios* at the beginning of the seventeenth century. Attesting to its importance, the latter had seven boilers in its boiler house, and two purging houses. Santísima Trinidad was valued at 700,000 pesos and produced an annual net income of 40,000 gold pesos.[11]

The cultivation of sugar cane, like other types of plantation agriculture, depended for its success on the availability of veritable armies of workers. The manufacturing process which was continuous during the season demanded not only many hands, but also imposed great hardships on the workers.

The sugar operations therefore relied heavily on large numbers of Indians and Negro slaves. With the sharp decline in the Indian population and the protective legislation of the second half of the sixteenth century, Negroes began to appear in larger numbers in the sugar plantations of Veracruz and almost exclusively in the refinery process. As early as 1535, the royal accountant Rodrigo de Albornoz imported 150 Negroes for the sugar mill he intended to open in Cempoala.[12] On May 11, 1542, Hernán Cortés entered into a contract with Leonardo Lomelín for the purchase of Negro slaves for his sugar plantations. The Genoese trader agreed to supply Cortés with five-hundred Negroes from Cape Verde in exchange for seventy-six gold ducats. Two thirds of the slaves were to be males and one third female, all between fifteen and twenty six years old.[13] Requiring one third of the slaves in each shipment to be females became a common practice in agreements of this kind. The purpose of this condition was to provide for the replacement of the Negroes who died by breeding the females with the surviving male slaves.[14] Thus, from the very beginning, the Negro was mated not on account of moral or humane considerations but for the purpose of replenishing the stock as it was done with livestock.

Other plantation owners followed suit. In the first decade of the seventeenth century most sugar operations in Veracruz had twenty, thirty, or forty Negroes. Larger and more prosperous plantations had, of course, a larger number of slaves. In 1580, Orizaba-Tequila had 123 negro slaves—seventy-two men, forty-four women, and seven children. An additional number of Negroes were employed in subsidiary tasks.[15] In Jalapa, Santísima Trinidad had in 1606 no less than 200 Negro slaves.[16] By this time Negroes could also be found in the mills at Tuxtla, Izcalpan, Papaloapan, Pánuco, in la Antigua, in the plantations of the coastal areas, and in the Valle de Orizaba.[17]

Initially, Indians and Negroes were used indiscriminately in the fields and in the refining operations. Gradually, however, the Indians proved too weak to withstand the long hours of hard work under the harsh conditions of the mills and boiler houses. Thousands died from overwork and exhaustion. To remedy this situation, royal decrees were issued in 1596,[18] and 1599,[19] prohibiting the use of Indians in the mills. The resulting reduction in the labor supply created great problems for the sugar mill owners. On June 14, 1599, many plantation owners in Veracruz requested and were granted *indios de socorro* to help in the cane fields because they could not acquire enough slaves in time for the harvest.[20]

These Indians were granted in specific cases in order to save the harvest. It was required that they be employed exclusively in field work, and never in the refining process. A system of inspectors (*veedores*) was established to visit the sugar plantations and make sure that Indians were kept away from the manufacturing operation.[21] Severe penalties were imposed when this restriction was not complied with.[22]

Slave Labor in the Sugar Estates

In this manner, some division of labor was attempted. Indians worked in the fields while Negro slaves were, although not exclusively, employed in the more strenuous tasks such as handling the boilers and presses and in other activities in the refining process.[23] Because of his superior performance at these tasks, one Negro was generally considered to be worth as many as four Indians.[24]

After November 24, 1601, when Philip III prohibited the use of Indians in any plantation activity,[25] Negro slaves also replaced the natives in the cane fields. From then on, all stages in the production of sugar, from the seeding of cane to the refining process, depended almost exclusively on the work of Negroes.

The life of the Negro slave in the sugar plantations of Mexico was a hard one. Slaves worked long hours and rarely had a few moments for themselves. Work was particularly strenuous during the grinding season which lasted from September to February and sometimes until May. During this period the mills were in operation twenty-four hours a day, seven days a week, to take care of all the cane being harvested.

The typical work day started at three in the morning and lasted until eleven at night, with most adult male slaves working a full twenty hours each day.[26] Adult males worked primarily in the harvest of cane and in the mills. Women and youngsters between the ages of eight and fourteen worked in the fields, usually in weeding and watering operations.[27] In addition to working as field hands, women performed a number of domestic chores. These included caring for the children, cooking for the gangs, and making bread and tortillas.

In many plantations the day began with the sounding of a bell calling the slaves to work. By four A.M. gangs of men, women, and children were on their way to the field, while other males worked in the mill. Usually at daybreak, those working in the mill had already processed from eight to ten caldrons of cane juice. After that operation was ended, they moved the sugar from the boiler to the purging house, or did odd jobs.[28]

Around noon, all slaves returned home for a meal. The Negroes' diet was similar to that of the Indians. The main staple was maize, usually consumed in the form of tortillas. Each adult received a ration of one *almud*, or 4.6 liters of maize per week. Each child received half that amount. Other items in the slaves' diet were salt, bread, molasses, beef and beans. From time to time, men were also given some tobacco. In most cases food was abundant although lacking in variety. Extra rations were given out as bonuses to slaves and others with special skills.

After the meal, the Negroes returned to the fields and to the mill. In the field, each gang was supervised by an overseer. Male *mandadores* led the male gangs, while in some cases *mandadoras*, or female overseers, supervised the women. These overseers were whites, mestizos, mulattoes, or freed slaves,[29] and received a salary.

Like in other plantations of the New World, the overseers in the plantations of Veracruz were expected to extract as much work from a slave as possible. For this reason, and for fear of rebellions, the overseers strove to keep the slaves constantly occupied.

After the work was completed in the fields the slaves returned to their huts. On their way home the gangs usually sang songs, or in some cases, prayers the priests had taught them. For those working in the mills, work during the grinding season continued through the night.

In addition to slaves and overseers, the mills employed a number of skilled workers. These included ironsmiths, a head carpenter, and a person in charge of livestock. They were mostly mulattoes and mestizos, but in some cases they were also Negro slaves who had learned the trade. According to a contract, these men received a salary in money, and special bonuses in kind such as extra rations of maize, lamb, sugar, and chocolate. In most plantations these men were called *sirvientes* to distinguish them from the rest of the workers.[30]

The most important person in the *ingenio*, however, was the *maestro de azúcar*, a sort of general supervisor of the refinery operation. He commanded great respect because, better than anyone, he knew each and every step in the sugar-making process. In some cases the *maestro de azúcar* was a Spaniard. More frequently, however, he was a Negro slave. When the *maestro de azúcar* was a slave, he received special treatment. In addition to supplementary rations, it was not uncommon for a Negro with such skills to receive each year from his master such items as a smock, a coat, shirts, overalls, a jacket, and a hat.[31] One can easily be led to speculate that some of these skilled slaves, realizing how important they were, quickly came up with all kinds of demands, becoming perhaps true prima donnas of the plantation.

Despite their high cost and short supply, slaves were treated with great cruelty in the *ingenios* of Veracruz. The slave, although recognized within the law was, in practice, considered as an object, or a piece of equipment, devoid of feelings or emotions.

To be profitable, the *ingenios* had to employ a minimum of eighty to a hundred Negroes.[46] Victims of the myth that each of them could do the work of four Indians, these Negroes were forced to work to the limits of their physical capabilities. Often pushed beyond these limits by the demands of cruel and inhuman overseers, many slaves soon became ill or crippled. In addition, the combination of overwork, little rest, and unhealthful working conditions, particularly in the mills and boiler houses, caused a staggering number of deaths.[47]

Deaths were more frequent in plantations where the owner was absent, or in those estates that were rented out. In 1567, the mill of Tepeca in Tuxtla, part of the *Marquesado del Valle*, with all its equipment and slaves, was rented to Diego López Montalván for a period of nine years. This transaction proved disastrous for the *Marqués*. When the *ingenio* was returned to him in 1576, much of its equipment was either missing or damaged. Also because of Montalván's carelessness many slaves died including the valuable *maestro de azúcar*.[48]

For identification purposes slaves were marked, as cattle, with a hot branding iron. In Tuxtla, for example, slaves were branded with the initials of the *Marqués*. In addition to branding, plantation owners registered their slaves by names and number with the town's registry known as "*Caja de Negros*"[49] Slaves also appeared in the plantations' inventories, listed together with farm animals, tools, and equipment.

Even though a number of kind and generous masters must have existed, punishment, as a rule, was frequent and severe. Beating and whipping were common. Age or sex seem to have had little or no bearing upon the severity of the punishment. In 1601, one slave owner was denounced for having tied a slave boy "between sticks with his arms tied and extended and without any cause beat him cruelly."[50] Not satisfied with this punishment, the master dragged

> ...the naked boy through the streets and even took him to hear mass in that condition without having

respect for the church nor the divine acts that were being celebrated, so that there was a great muttering from the natives as well as the Spaniards.[51]

Even while receiving a severe beating the slave was expected to endure the punishment with firmness. If in desperation he cursed his lot, or uttered some blasphemy against God or the Church, he ran the risk of being denounced to the Inquisition. In 1600, a slave named Victorilla was denounced to the Holy Office for having denied "God and all saints and the Virgin Mary" while being brutally whipped.[52] On a later occasion, Juan Villarden, slave of a Gaspar Osorio, was reported for blasphemy for having denied "heaven, God and his saints..." after being beaten with a dagger as a preliminary to being whipped.[53]

Other forms of humiliation, torture, and even mutilation were also commonly used to punish slaves. In 1611, a woman was denounced for punishing her slaves with extreme severity.

> Among the allegations was one where she had placed a nude slave girl in a "sack of coarse cloth like a lunatic, with an iron ring around her neck, hauling her with a chain," and in this fashion took her to church.[54]

There were masters who built private jails in their properties for the purpose of incarcerating their slaves. Others castrated their slaves for serious offenses. This form of punishment was considered ideal to break the slave's "courage and arrogance."[55] Still others went as far as killing their negroes with their own hands. Pedro Marfil, a mine owner in Guanajuato, had a reputation for being extremely cruel with his slaves. In 1572, he was reported to the authorities for having a private jail, murdering some of his slaves and for having castrated Negroes with his own hands.[56] The number of cases of cruelty that were reported was quite large. Nevertheless they represented only a small percentage of the total. The majority of cases of excessive punishment most likely went unreported.

Fugitive slaves were punished even more severely. In addition to the ordinary repressive measures of the plantations, fear of slave rebellions led to a series of royal decrees issued between 1571 and 1574, calling for tighter slave control. According to this fugitive slave code, if a slave was away from his master for more than four days he would be given fifty lashes. For an absence of more than eight days, the penalty was one hundred lashes, "with iron fetters tied to their feet with rope, which they shall wear for two months and shall not take off under pain of two hundred lashes."[57] Slaves absent for six months and over, were to be given the death penalty. In some cases, however, this sentence was reduced to castration.[58]

A number of slaves died as a result of the punishments inflicted on them. So frequent were these incidents that the Crown became concerned with the widespread cruelty and the spiritual welfare of those who died without confession. Towards the end of the sixteenth century the king issued a number of ordinances aimed at improving the treatment of slaves. Among other things the king ordered slave owners to treat their slaves well, to feed and clothe them properly, and not to punish them cruelly or without reason. On this occasion, masters were also forbidden to injure their slaves or to cut their limbs. A master who punished a slave in this manner was required to surrender the victim to the Crown, and to pay twenty pesos to the person who denounced the cruel deed.[59]

Regarding the spiritual welfare of the slaves, the Crown ordered that every plantation which had Negro slaves should have a church in which they could pray each morning before going to work and attend Mass and receive religious instruction on Sundays and holy days. Masters who did not comply with this order were to be fined thirty pesos each time they were caught. In addition, the king ordered slave owners to begin teaching Spanish to their Negroes within six months of the date of purchase, teach them the sacraments and to have them baptized. The penalty for breaking this rule was "one-fourth of the Negro's value the first time..., one half the value of the Negro the second, and the full value of the Negro the third".[60]

As it was often the case with royal decrees of this nature, the ordinances were ignored with impunity by the plantation owners. Slaves continued to be as badly treated as they had been before. In the second half of the seventeenth century reports of cruelty were so frequent that they once again disturbed the royal conscience. In October 1683, the king ordered the Audiencias to investigate cases of extreme cruelty by slave owners. If found guilty of cruelty, a slave owner should be punished, and should be forced to sell his slaves. Once again the Crown emphasized that slaves should be well treated and instructed in the Catholic faith.[61]

Nevertheless, the discrepancy between the law and actual practice continued. "In the lowlands sugar was king,"[62] and the laws, therefore, carried little if any weight in the remote plantations of Veracruz. Excessive cruelty remained a common feature of Negro slavery in New Spain during the rest of the colonial period.

Other laws and plantation regulations also contributed their share to make the slave's lot a miserable one. Slaves were not allowed to carry any kind of offensive or defensive weapons. During the first half of the sixteenth century a Negro carrying a knife or any other weapon without specific authorization was punished with castration. Later this penalty was reduced to 100 lashes in the public square for the first offense. If caught with a weapon a second time, the slave would be given 200 lashes and was to have one hand nailed to the flogging pole at the square for a period of two hours.[63]

Certain manifestations of female vanity were brutally discouraged. Negro women were not permitted to wear dresses made of silk from Castile. Such adornments as pearls, and gold or silver jewelry, were also forbidden. Any female slave caught wearing such embellishments received one hundred lashes and had the garment or jewelry confiscated.[64]

For fear of rebellion, fraternizing among the slaves was kept to a minimum. On April 2, 1612, a decree was issued prohibiting Negroes to assemble, in public or in private, by day or by night, and for whatever reason, in numbers larger than three. Infringement of this rule carried the penalty of two hundred lashes per slave present in the gathering.[65] Even in mourning the slave could not find solace in the company of a large number of friends and relatives. At a slave's funeral no more than four Negroes and four Negresses were allowed to congregate to mourn the dead or to pay their respects. Those who dared to disobey received two hundred lashes.[66] Oftentimes, the Negro was not even given the dignity of a Christian burial. Many slaves, particularly those who died without baptism, were simply thrown into the river. This practice was so common in the city of Veracruz that it soon became a health problem for the community. To protect the population from the foul smell and the many diseases which proliferated from the decomposed bodies, the city council in 1574 prohibited the throwing of dead Indians, Negroes and "other filth" into the river.[67]

Another source of humiliation was the slave's appearance. For lack of care slaves always looked their worst. In some plantations the slaves were given a set of clothes once a year, usually at Christmas. In many others, however, slave owners made no effort to provide any covers for their slaves. In these plantations Negroes, both male and female, went around in rags, and more often, completely naked. So widespread was this practice that on December 2, 1672, the Crown, "para evitar las ocasiones de pecados" ordered slave owners to provide their slaves with appropriate clothing, under the penalty of fine or imprisonment.[68]

Living under such miserable conditions, it was only natural for the slave to yearn for his freedom. Slaves therefore tried by all available means to gain their freedom and that of their children. In theory slaves could purchase their freedom. But, while the hope might have made their burden a little easier to bear, the instances in which this was actually accomplished were few and far between. Voluntary manumission, although encouraged by the Crown and the Church, was also a rare occurrence.[69]

More frequently and more successfully slaves attempted to gain their freedom by marrying into the free Indian population or by rebelling against their owners. In the first instance, slaves who married free persons received their freedom according to the laws of *Las Siete Partidas*. Because many slaves were seeking these unions, and because of the obvious effect this would have on the colonial economy, as early as 1538 Charles V issued a decree denying the Negroes their freedom through such marriages. Since slaves, according to the Roman tradition, followed the condition of their mothers, Negroes continued to marry free Indian women hoping to save if not themselves, at least their children from the terrible condition in which they lived.[70] The last and most dangerous avenue to freedom was to escape. Despite the risks such alternative was frequently chosen. In desperation, many Negroes rebelled against their masters and escaped to the mountains. Finding safety in the valleys and mountains of Veracruz they joined other fugitive slaves and formed their own communities, many never to return to their owners' plantations.

Like plantation systems everywhere, the plantations of Veracruz depended for their success upon a large supply of slave labor. With the decline in the Indian population, and because of legislation restricting and finally prohibiting the use of Indians in the sugar plantations, African slaves gradually replaced the natives in the refineries and in the cane fields.

Costly and scarce Negroes were forced to work long hours under most unfavorable working conditions in order to justify their price. More adaptable to hard work and considered physically superior, the Negro was expected to produce a great deal more than the Indian. Throughout the colonial period this myth of Negro superior strength was used to justify the exploitation of the Negro under a harsh and inhuman slavery system.[71]

Like all human beings Negroes resented living in captivity. Finding few other alternatives to obtain their freedom, many slaves rebelled against their masters and fled into the mountains. Considering the severity of the punishment they would receive if caught, the large number of slaves that chose to escape is perhaps the best indication of the harshness and cruelty of the slave system in the Veracruz plantations.

NOTES

1. AGI, Carta de los Oficiales de Veracruz a S.M. (18 de noviembre de 1596), México, legajo 351.
2. DII, 12:277.
3. François Chevalier, *Land and Society in Colonial Mexico: the Great Hacienda*. Trans. by Alvin Eustis, ed., by Lesley Byrd Simpson (Berkeley and Los Angeles: University of California Press, 1963), p. 145.
4. Fernando B. Sandoval, *La Industria del Azúcar en Nueva España* (Mexico: Universidad Nacional Autónoma de México, Instituto de História, 1951), p. 32.
5. DII, 23:532. "Somos informados de que en muchas partes de la Nueva Spaña, ay tierras muy buenas e aparejadas para poner cañas de azúcar y hacer yngenios, porque son tierras templadas y de mucha agua, ansi cerca de la Mar del Norte [Atlantic] como a la Costa de la Mar del Sur [Pacific]. Procurareis que algunas personas se encargen de hacer algunos yngenios de azúcar, e favorecerlos eys en lo que buenamente se podiese hacer dándola tierras donde hagan los yngenios y planten las cañas..."
6. Sandoval, *La Industria del Azúcar*, p. 49.
7. Chevalier, *Land and Society in Colonial Mexico*, p. 77.

8. J. Antonio de Villaseñor y Sánchez, *Theatro Americano. Descripción general de los reynos y provincias de la Nueva España y sus jurisdicciones*, 2 tomos (México: Ed. Nacional, 1952), 1:360.

9. Sandoval, *La Industria del Azúcar*, p. 51. Sandoval's estimate is rather conservative for, as we have seen above, Veracruz alone had at least forty-six mills (including small trapiches) by the end of the sixteenth century. Also by this time, there were mills in Cuernavaca and Oaxaca, and Michoacán with several mills was becoming a relatively important sugar producing province. See AGI, Carta de Monterey, a S.M. (4 de agosto de 1597), México, legajo 23, sección V, ramo 4. For more details on the development of the sugar industry in the Cuernavaca area see Ward Barrett, *The Sugar Hacienda of the Marqueses del Valle* (Minneapolis: University of Minnesota Press, 1970).

10. *Asoleadero* was an area adjacent to the purging house in which excess moisture was removed from the sugar by exposing to the sun. In the Brazilian *engenhos* this device was called *balcão para secar*. See Frédéric Mauro, *Le Portugal et L'Atlantique*, p . 209.

11. Sandoval, *La Industria del Azúcar*, p. 127.

12. *Ibid.*, p. 31.

13. *Ibid.*, p. 36.

14. AGI, Carta del Consejo de Indias a S.M. (12 de noviembre de 1595), Indiferente General, legajo 743, folio 155.

15. Chevalier, *Land and Society in Colonial Mexico*, p. 80.

16. Sandoval, *La Industria del Azúcar*, p. 127.

17. Manuel B. Trens. *História de Veracruz*, 2:168.

18. AGI, Carta de Monterey a S.M. (3 de octubre de 1599), México, legajo 24.

19. Silvio Zavala and Maria Castelo, *Fuentes para la História del Trabajo en Nueva España*, 8 vols. (México: Fondo de Cultura Economica, 1939-1940), 4:256.

20. *Ibid.*, 4:303.

21. *Ibid.*, 5:8.

22. Chevalier, *Land and Society in Colonial Mexico*, p. 79.

23. Sandoval, *La Industria del Azúcar*, p. 33.

24. Scelle, "The Slave Trade in the Spanish Colonies," p. 14.

25. Sandoval, *La Industria del Azúcar*, p. 63.

26. Gonzalo Aguirre Beltrán, "El Trabajo del Indio comparado con el del Negro en Nueva España," *México Agrario*, Vol. 4, p. 207.

27. Jean-Pierre Berthe, "Xochimancas: Les travaux et les jours dans une hacienda sucrière de Nouvelle-Espagne au XVIIe siècle," *Jahrbuch Für Geschichte von Staat, Wirtschaft und Gesellschaft Lateinamerikas*, Vol. 3 (1966), p. 100.

28. Berthe, "Xochimancas," p. 109.

29. Chevalier, *Land and Society in Colonial Mexico*, p. 294.
30. Berthe, "Xochimancas," pp. 97-98.
31. Sandoval, *La Industria del Azúcar*, pp. 156-157.
32. AGI, Carta de los procuradores de la ciudad de México al Rey (2 de marzo de 1564), México, legajo, 94.
33. AGI, Carta de los procuradores de la ciudad de México al Rey (8 de octubre de 1568), México, legajo 94.
34. Berthe, "Xochimancas," p. 99.
35. *Ibid.*, p. 203.
36. Chevalier, *Land and Society in Colonial Mexico*, p. 79.
37. For details on this problem see AGI, "Los mercaderes de Nueva España con el Fiscal de Su Magestad sobre la tasa de los esclavos" (1557), Justicia, legajo 204, ramo 1, and AGI, Testimonio de Juan de Merida en nombre de la ciudad de México (17 de mayo de 1558), Justicia, legajo 204, ramo 1.
38. Chevalier, *Land and Society in Colonial Mexico*, p. 79.
39. Palmer, "Negro Slavery in Mexico," p. 22.
40. Chevalier, *Land and Society in Colonial Mexico*, p. 79.
41. P. Alonso de Sandoval S. J. *De Instauranda Aethiopium Salute. El mundo de la Esclavitud Negra en America* (Bogotá: Biblioteca de la Presidencia de Colombia, 1956), p. 91.
42. AGI, Carta del Licenciado Juan de Ibara a El-Rey (1612), Charcas, legajo 54.
43. Gonzalo Aguirre Beltrán, "Tribal Origins of Slaves in Mexico," *Journal of Negro History*, Vol. 31 (July 1946), p. 292.
44. AGI, Carta de Martin Enríquez a El-Rey (17 de diciembre de 1574), México, legajo 19, ramo 4.
45. Sandoval, *La Industria del Azúcar*, p. 157.
46. Taunay, *Subsídios*, p. 545.
47. AGI, Carta de la Audiencia de México a El-Rey (8 de octubre de 1568) México, legajo 94; AGI, Carta de Monterey a S.M. (4 de agosto de 1597), México, legajo 23, ramo 4; Death rates, although always high, showed considerable fluctuation over the years reflecting, in most cases, the incidence of epidemics. It has been argued that in most slave systems slaves died in greater numbers during the acculturation or "seasoning" period. While it is difficult to prove that this was the case in Veracruz it is not unreasonable to assume that this general rule would apply to conditions in the Mexican province. See Stanley L. Engerman "Comments on the Study of Race and Slavery," in Stanley L. Engerman and Eugene D. Genovese, eds. *Race and Slavery in the Western Hemisphere: Quantitative Studies* (Princeton, N.J.: Princeton University Press, 1975), p. 507.
48. Sandoval, *La Industria del Azúcar*, p. 30.

Slave Labor in the Sugar Estates 39

49. Carlos Basauri, "La Población Negroide Mexicana," *Estadística*, Vol. 1 (December, 1943), p. 100.
50. Quoted in Palmer, "Negro Slavery in Mexico," p. 110.
51. Palmer, "Negro Slavery in Mexico," p. 110.
52. *Archivo General de la Nación,* Mexico City (hereafter cited as AGN), Inquisición, tomo 256, Expendiente 4, p. 129.
53. AGN, Inquisición, tomo 256, Exp. México 15, pp. 308-308v.
54. Palmer, "Negro Slavery in Mexico," p. 110.
55. AGI, Carta del Presidente de la audiencia de Charcas a El-Rey (12 de marzo de 1593), Charcas, legajo 17; AGI, Carta de Fray Alonso de Montufar, arzobispo de México, y los obispos de Tlaxcala, Oaxaca, Chiapas, Nueva Galicia y Yucatán al Rey (1575), México, legajo 336.
56. AGI, Carta de la Audiencia de México a El-Rey (febrero de 1572), México, legajo 69.
57. Davidson, "Negro Slave Control and Resistance," p. 245.
58. *Ibid.*
59. AGI, Ordenanzas sobre el buen tratamiento que se debe dar a los negros (Siglo XVI), Patronato, legajo 171, no 2, ramo 10.
60. *Ibid.*
61. Richard Konetzke, *Colección de documentos para la historia de la formación social de Hispanoamérica 1493-1810,* 3 vols. (Madrid: Consejo Superior de Investigaciones Cientificas, 1953-1962), Vol. 2, Part II, p. 754.
62. Marvin Harris, *Patterns of Race in the Americas* (New York: Walker and Co., 1964), p. 76.
63. AGI, Ordenanzas sobre el buen tratamiento que se debe dar a los negros (Siglo XVI), Patronato, legajo 171, no 2, ramo 10.
64. Konetzke, *Colección,* Vol. 12, Part I, p. 183.
65. Don Eusebio Bentura Beleña, *Recopilación Sumaria de todos los Autos acordados de la real audiencia y sala del crimen de esta Nueva España, y providencias de su superior Gobierno; de varias Reales Cedulas y Ordenes que después de publicada la Recopilación de Indias han podido recogerse asi de las dirigidas á la misma Audiencia o Gobierno, como de algunas otras que por sus notables decisiones convendrá no ignorar* (México: Don Felipe de Zuñiga y Outiveros, año 1787), Libro II, Mandamientos y Ordenanzas, Documento 83, p 73.
66. *Ibid.*, Documento 84, p. 73.
67. AGI, Carta del Cabildo Secular de Veracruz a S.M. (15 de junio de 1547), México, legajo 350.
68. Konetzke, *Colección,* Vol. 2, Part II, p. 588.
69. David Brion Davis has argued that given a choice a slave would prefer to live his captive life in a "... society that held out some hope of eventual freedom," and that "The ease and frequency of manumission

would seem to be the crucial standard in measuring the relative harshness of slave systems." If one accepts these contentions as, at least, partially valid, one would arrive at the following conclusion: that while the slave system of Veracruz offered more hope of eventual freedom than the slave systems, for example, of the states of the American south, it also failed miserably in fullfilling the dream through frequent instances of manumission. See *The Problems of Slavery in Western Culture* (Ithaca, N.Y.: Cornell University Press, 1966), p. 54. Davidson, "Negro Slave Control and Resistance in Colonial Mexico," p. 239.

70. Davidson, "Negro Slave Control and Resistance in Colonial Mexico," p. 240.

71. For an excellent study of myths concerning the Negro see Melville J. Herkovits, *The Myth of the Negro Past* (Boston: Beacon Press, 1968).

CHAPTER IV

SOCIAL AND CULTURAL LIFE AT THE PLANTATION

The sugar plantations of Veracruz were for the most part self-sufficient, self-contained economic, social, and cultural entities. Santísima Trinidad, Orizaba-Tequila, and Tuxtla produced practically everything they consumed. In addition to their refinery and cane fields, they cultivated many acres of maize to feed their slaves and other workers. A large number of cattle, sheep and mules were also raised in these plantations to provide food for the residents, power the mills, and drive the wagons. Fuel to fire the great boilers was also produced locally. In addition to burning dry sugar cane residue, most of the great plantations burned large quantities of timber from their own wooded areas set aside for this purpose.

Some plantations had shops in which tools were made and defective equipment repaired. The larger plantations even had their own *obrajes*, or textile mills, to make clothing for their slaves and other workers.

Many of these plantations had several groups of buildings resembling a small town. Orizaba-Tequila, for instance,

... formed a veritable village in 1580, with the owner's house and the stone church, four big buildings for refining the sugar—"some spanned with two arches ... and built of masonry with brick vaulting"—its little adobe houses for the Spaniards or Negro foremen, and its cabins for the other slaves and indians.[1]

Santísima Trinidad was an equally imposing sight with its eleven *caballerías* of cane fields, its refinery buildings, a chapel, and an elaborate two story plantation house.[2] According to Chevalier, these sugar plantations "constituted the first great feudal estates and, as early as the sixteenth century, anticipated the classical Mexican hacienda."[3]

The plantation constituted a separate community. Within the boundaries of his property the plantation owner ruled like a feudal lord. His whim, or that of his *mayordomo*, was law. Within the plantation the master was the sole dispenser of justice and the determiner of the social order. As we have seen above, each plantation had its own body of regulations. Penalties for those who broke these regulations were also determined locally, regardless of royal decrees, and often in direct conflict with them. The plantation owners' status or political position gave them the necessary protection and immunity from the law. Even *mayordomos* often occupied government positions, or had connections in government. The *mayordomo* of Cortés' sugar mill at Tuxtla, for instance, was also the *alcalde mayor* of the village of Tuxtla, and a close friend of the *alcalde mayor* of Cuernavaca.[4]

The social mores of the plantation were also unique. Since the plantation owner had complete control over all residents of the plantation, he determined where and how they were to live, if and who they were to marry, and even how they dressed. Under these circumstances, prestige and status at the plantation was determined by how close, or how valuable one was to the plantation owner, or his *mayordomo*.

The owner's house was the most imposing building and the heart of the plantation. It was not only the center of authority, but the very symbol of the plantation system. The lifestyle at the plantation house was ostentatious. Although, according to Mauro, they never reached the importance of the seventeenth century *senhores de engenho* in Brazil,[5] sugar mill owners in

Social and Cultural Life at the Plantation 43

Veracruz lived and enjoyed an aristocratic life. While in their plantations, where they spent part of the year, the men enjoyed many outdoor activities. Favorite among these were bullfights and horse riding. On holidays, extravagant fiestas were held at the plantation, always including tournaments, bullfights, and other outdoor activities. The greatest celebration was on August 13, St. Hippolytus day, which commemorated the fall of Tenochtitlán. On these occasions illustrious guests came and stayed at the plantation house. On one of these festive days, the region's bishop came to Santísima Trinidad. In regal fashion, the plantation owner rode out to meet his guest accompanied by a large number of horsemen and escorted him to the plantation house,[6] in a visual demonstration of his wealth and power.

Inside the house numerous slaves waited on their white masters. Male slaves followed their masters around and handled the heavier chores. The women stayed home and served their mistresses as completely as ladies-in-waiting in a medieval castle. They became attached to their mistresses and usually served them until they were too old to work, or died. If her mistress went to a convent, the slave usually went with her.[7] If a young mistress was given in marriage, her slave went along as part of the dowry.

In direct contrast with the opulence of the plantation house were the slave huts. These were round structures with conical roofs, usually made of straw. They formed a small cluster surrounded by a fence with a single entrance. This village-like arrangement was known as *el real de negros*.[8]

In the *real* slaves had little or no privacy. They often lived in a communal manner, sharing their huts with others, regardless of sex or relationship, surrounded by their pigs or chickens. Most slaves preferred common-law relationships and only a small number were married. Even those who were legally married had no real family life. Despite state and church emphasis on the inviolability of the family, slave familes were always threatened with, and often subjected to, separation. Legal provisions to the contrary notwithstanding, husbands were often sold away from their wives, children as young as eleven or twelve were taken away from their mothers and sold, and wives were often separated from their husbands through a bill of sale. It has been argued that while a slave did not have a legal right to marry in Protestant America, masters in the United States made a stronger effort to recognize and protect slave marriages than their Catholic counterparts in Latin America.[9] The master's financial advantage rather than religious or humanitarian considerations was the most important factor controlling the preservation or separation of slave families in Veracruz.

Only in rare occasions slaves had the courage to complain to the authorities about the separation of their families. When this happened, the Holy Office of the Inquisition was the appropriate agency to hear the slave's case. In 1618, Juan Matso, a slave living in Veracruz with a wife in Mexico City, petitioned the Holy Office to bring them together by forcing his wife's master to sell her to a person residing in Veracruz. Unfortunately, the disposition of this case is not known.

Despite the miserable conditions under which they lived and the little free time which they had, Negro slaves in Veracruz managed to preserve for some time at least part of their cultural heritage, their religion and traditions. Some of these traditions survived and made a small but lasting contribution to the development of the region's folklore. The strongest influences are still found in music and popular dances. Musical instruments still in use today, such as the marimba and the *artesa*, are of African origin.[10] Some of the dances still popular in Veracruz, such as the "chuchumbe" and the "sacamandú" were introduced by African slaves and were classified by the Spaniards during the colonial period as *"bailes deshonestos,"*[11]

Negro slaves were very fond of music and dancing, and whenever possible indulged in such activities. In the evenings, on Sundays and holidays, on the plantations were recreation was permitted, *el real de negros* became a kaleidoscope of sound and movement.

Slaves from certain areas were more musically inclined than others. Apparently Negroes from Angola were the most accomplished musicians. They showed great skill in playing an instrument called "banza." This was a small six-string, guitar-like instrument which sounded very much like a harp.[12] They also learned to play the European flute, horn, and bassoon. These Negro musicians were widely used by religious orders throughout Spanish America to play during their religious services.[13] Slaves from Guinea also played crude *vihuelas* (guitars), with strings made of lamb gut. They also enjoyed singing and noisemaking, for which reasons they were considered the loudest among the slaves. The "guineos" as they were called, were particularly fond of dancing. Whenever possible, they indulged in such activity for long periods of time. Their endurance through long hours of energetic dancing was always a cause of amazement to the Spaniards.[14]

To the extent that it was possible, Negro slaves continued to practice their own religions. Most of these cults centered around witchcraft, animism and fetishism. Because of their highly superstitious character these African cults found favorable ground among the Indian population who relied on similar methods of worship. Like the Indians, Negro slaves frequently resorted to exorcism, and the use of amulets and talismans to help solve their problems. Such practices and objects were widely used by Negro slaves in Veracruz and other parts of Mexico to cure diseases, to bring good luck, to obtain better treatment from their masters, and to gain another person's love and affection.[15] One sure way to win the heart of the beloved man was for the hopeful woman to serve him a small amount of her menstrual blood mixed in with his chocolate.[16] Other "ingredients" were also used for several purposes and with varying degrees of effectiveness. The heart of a crow for instance, was supposed to have the power to calm the fires of sexual desire. In 1621, Damiana Lopez, wife of Francisco Partida kept the heart of a crow for the purpose of quieting down her wandering husband.[17] Stirring a love potion with the finger of someone who had been put to death was supposed to greatly increase the effectiveness of the mixture. In 1621, a Negress named Isabel, slave of Doña Leonor Calderon was reported to be the proud owner of one of these fingers which had been cut from the hand of a person who had been hanged.[18]

Interestingly enough, no major effort was made to instruct Negro slaves in the Christian faith. Contrary to the massive conversion and indoctrination campaign directed at the Indian population throughout Spanish America, little was done to impose Catholicism upon the Negroes. Although many Negroes were supposedly converted to Christianity,[19] the great majority were not baptized and were left without religious instruction. As early as 1572, members of some religious orders deplored the fact that Negroes were the people with the most need of religious instruction and whose spiritual welfare had been the most neglected.[20] In 1595, the Archbishop of Lima wrote the Council of the Indies expressing concern with this problem and recommending that all Negroes be baptized before they left the Portuguese factories in Africa.[21] Also troubled by this situation, the Crown periodically instructed slave owners to provide priests for the spiritual guidance of their slaves. Separate parishes should be organized for Negro slaves, and the priests were to be paid by the slave owners.[22] Little attention, however, was paid to these instructions. Although there must have been exceptions, the records show little evidence of a genuine concern on the part of Mexican slave owners for the salvation of their slaves through instruction in the Catholic faith.

Even when slaves received religious instruction and formed their own *cofradías*, constant surveillance and discriminatory practices were likely to temper their interest in their masters' religion. For fear of conspiracies, Negroes were not permitted to assemble in *cofradías*, or to worship collectively without the presence of a prelate or a so-called "*persona grave*,"[23] a responsible or important person. Because they were considered a lowly race even inferior to the Indians, Negroes and mulattoes were also usually denied access to the priesthood. It is significant that the Crown while at times criticizing the slave owners for not giving their slaves religious instruction, repeatedly issued decrees prohibiting the ordination of Negroes and mulattoes.[24] Some religious orders also discriminated aganst Negroes and mulattoes. The Order of St. Augustine in Mexico for instance, as late as the eighteenth century, still flatly refused to accept Negroes and mulattoes because they were "individuals generally scorned by society, unworthy of occupying public office, and of being charged with the guidance of souls."[25]

The nature of relations between masters and slaves varied from plantation to plantation. Since most of the work-related functions were supervised by overseers and *mayordomos*, relations were closer between masters and their domestic slaves. Because of the more frequent and direct contact required by personal service, these more intimate relationships invariably developed.

Domestic slaves were taught Spanish and were soon able to communicate better with their masters. These slaves often served as interpreters between their masters and other slaves, and between Spaniards and Indians. Although the records do not abound with examples, many of these Negroes, no doubt, became the trusted companions of their masters.

Frequent contact, and the unusual beauty of some African women, often led to amorous relations between masters and their female slaves. In fact, it was most common for a female slave to become her master's concubine. Remarking on the wide usage of such customs, a slave owner stated in 1580 that "it was no sin to live in concubinage with his slave, because she was his own money."[26] In some occasions, though much less frequently, these unions were made legal when masters pressured by the Church, decided to marry their slaves.

Miscegenation was therefore widespread, accounting for the increasing population of mulattoes, or *Afro-mestizos*.[27] The children of illicit unions between masters and slaves normally followed their mothers into slavery. Those of legal intermarriages were often given their freedom, particularly in the seventeenth century when pressure from the Church was intensified.[28]

These master-slave marriages constituted one of the very few avenues for voluntary manumission. In fact, according to Davidson, the recorded instances of voluntary manumission in New Spain were few and far between.[29] Considering the high cost and short supply of Negroes during the seventeenth century, it is not difficult to imagine why plantation owners, shunning religious and humanitarian reasons, chose to cling to their slaves for as long as they could be economically productive.

In Veracruz, the slaves' world was a different and separate one. In such a milieu, few were the slaves' moments of privacy and happiness. Long, however, were the hours of strenuous work and suffering they endured. Slaves were the property of their masters and were treated as such. They were denied the most basic rights of a human being. Their time, their families, their lives, all belonged to their masters. The master's convenience, or financial gain, usually was the sole determiner of how, where, and with whom a slave was to spend his life. Few were the instances when a kind master gave one or more of his slaves their freedom. As a rule, slaves were condemned to spend their most productive years in captivity. Avenues to freedom were few and mostly unsuccessful. To revolt and escape was the last and most desperate resource. And escape the slaves did. As legislation became more restrictive, the rebellions grew in frequency, resulting in greater numbers of escapees.

NOTES
1. Chevalier, *Land and Society in Colonial Mexico*, p. 82.
2. Sandoval, *La Industria del Azúcar*, p. 127. A *caballería* was a piece of agricultural land allotted to a *caballero*; approximately 100 acres.
3. Chevalier, *Land and Society in Colonial Mexico*, p. 82.
4. Sandoval, *La Industria del Azúcar*, pp. 34-35.
5. Frédéric Mauro, "México y Brasil Dos Economías Coloniales Comparadas," *Historia Mexicana*, Vol. 10, No. 40 (April-June, 1961), p. 584.
6. Chevalier, *Land and Society in Colonial Mexico*, pp. 306-307.
7. "Un Matrimonio de Esclavos," AGN História, Legajo 1. *Boletín del Archivo General de la Nación*, Vol. 6 (July-August, 1935), p. 541.
8. Chevalier, *Land and Society in Colonial Mexico*, p. 293.
9. David Brion Davis, "The Comparative Approach to American History: Slavery," in Laura Foner and Eugene D. Genovese, eds., *Slavery in the New World* (Englewood Cliffs, N.J.: Prentice Hall, Inc., 1969) p. 64.
10. Basauri, "La Población Negroide Mexicana," p. 107.
11. *Ibid.*, p. 106.
12. Sandoval, *De Instauranda Aethiopium Salute*, p. 89.
13. AGI, Carta del Consejo de Indias al Rey (9 de noviembre de 1627), Charcas, legajo 2.
14. Sandoval, *De Instauranda Aethiopium Salute*, p. 64.
15. AGN, Inquisición (1621), tomo 339, folio 639.
16. AGN, Inquisición, tomo 356 (1626), Tepeaca, 2a.parte, fol. 115.
17. AGN, Inquisición (1621), tomo 339, fol. 671.
18. AGN, Inquisición (1621), tomo 339, fol. 673.
19. Basauri, "La Población Negroide Mexicana," p. 105. "Negroes converted to Christianity were called '*latinos*.' Through the corruption of the language, this term was changed to '*ladinos*,' and was applied to those Negroes who embraced Catholicism and Spoke Spanish."
20. AGI, Carta de Martin Enríquez al Rey (28 de abril de 1572), México, legajo 19, ramo 3.
21. AGI, Carta del Arzobispo de Lima al Consejo de Indias (13 de mayo de 1595), Lima, legajo 1.
22. Konetzke, *Colección*, Vol. II, Part I, p. 100; also *ibid.*, Vol. II, Part II, p. 754.

23. *Ibid.*, Vol. II, Part I, p. 88.

24. *Ibid.*, pp. 356-357; Manuel B. Trens in his *História de Veracruz*, 2:167, states, perhaps too generally, that Negroes or mulattoes were not admitted to any ecclesiastical position. Another author however, indicates that descendants from Negro parents could, at least on paper, be admitted to certain monasteries and religious orders, after careful scrutiny. (For details on this subject see Nicolás León, *Las Castas del México Colonial o Nueva España. Noticias Etno-Antropológicas* (México: Talleres Gráficos del Museo Nacional de Arqueologia, Historia y Etnografía, 1924), pp. 5-6. It cannot be doubted that as some mulattoes became rich and influential, these *casta* barriers were gradually removed, and they and their children began to be treated as white Spaniards and to have many of the same privileges.

25. León, *Las Castas*, p. 6.

26. Aguirre Beltrán, *La Población Negra de México*, p. 252.

27. AGI, Carta de Martin Enríquez a S.M. (9 de enero de 1574), México, legajo 19, ramo 4, Also Juan López de Velasco, *Geografía y Descripción Universal de las Indias* (Madrid: Establecimiento Tipografico de Fortanet, 1894), p. 43.

28. Davidson, "Negro Slave Control and Resistance in Colonial Mexico," p. 239.

29. *Ibid.*

CHAPTER V

SLAVE RESISTANCE AND REBELLIONS

Contrary to the humanitarian provisions of *Las Siete Partidas*, which, if applied, would have made it considerably milder, slavery in Veracruz was a cruel and inhuman institution. Excessive work, unhealthful conditions, and harsh punishments, made the slave's life intolerable. It is not surprising, therefore, that slaves did not passively resign themselves to their condition. To save themselves and their children from their deplorable fate, slaves, as we have seen, devised many forms of resistance. Abortion, infanticide, and suicide were some of the avenues used by slaves to escape their misery.

Less subtle, and more successful, forms of resistance were slave revolts. The frequent slave revolts which occurred in New Spain during the colonial period, are perhaps the best indication of the harsh nature of slavery under the Spaniards and of the slave's desire to flee from the unbearable conditions of life and work in the plantation. Because the most brutal revolts took place in the mines and in the sugar plantations,[1] this can be taken as another indication that the treatment of slaves in these two industries was considerably harsher than in other activities where slaves were employed.

Fugitive slaves, or *cimarrones*, had been a constant problem since the first Negroes were brought to New Spain. The first attempt to organize a sizeable revolt, however, was reported in 1537.[2] In December of that year, Viceroy Antonio de Mendoza wrote to the king about a plot by fugitive slaves from the slopes and lowlands of Veracruz and from central Mexico, to take over the entire colony.

> I was warned [the viceroy wrote] that the Negroes had chosen a king, and had agreed amongst themselves to kill all Spaniards and rise up to take the land and that the Indians were also with them.[3]

Whether such a conspiracy actually existed has never been satisfactorily established. Nevertheless, the viceroy launched an extensive manhunt to apprehend the suspects. The alleged "king" and his cohorts, after "confessing" to the charges were killed and quartered.[4] A large number of Negroes, some no doubt innocent, were slaughtered on this occasion. The bodies of many of them were quartered, salted, and brought to the presence of the Viceroy,[5] a gruesome evidence of their destruction.

The major effect of this incident was to create an almost paranoid fear of slave rebellions among the Spanish population. Their apprehensions reinforced by the occurrence of other revolts in the 1540s, citizens began calling for stricter measures of slave control. In response to popular pressure, a number of restrictions were imposed upon the Negro population. In 1548, Viceroy Mendoza banned the sale of arms to Negroes throughout the country and instituted a night curfew on Negroes in Mexico City. In 1552, Viceroy Luis de Velasco ordered the establishment throughout the country of the *Santa Hermandad*, a vigilante type militia[6] similar to those later found in the Southern United States, to control slave revolts. Under the rule of viceroys Mendoza and Velasco, Negroes caught with a large knife or any other weapon were castrated.[7] Later in the century, as we have seen, the legal punishment for this offense was reduced to from 100 to 200 lashes plus having one hand nailed to the whipping post in the public square for a couple of hours.[8]

These restrictive measures had little effect on the more remote areas of the country. In Veracruz, slaves continued to escape with great frequency and in ever increasing numbers. Towards the end of the century, many of these slaves had established small settlements in the area between Orizaba and Veracruz.[9] From these locations, the *cimarrones* raided neighboring estates and terrorized travelers by attacking and robbing them on the roads.[10]

Conditions worsened rapidly in Veracruz, and soon several nuclei of slave rebellions were found throughout most of the territory. As early as 1570, the viceroy was fighting slave rebellions in Alvarado, Huatusco, Misantla, Medellín, Jalapa, Rinconada, Río Blanco, Punta de Antón Lizardo, and Orizaba.[11]

The tense situation in Veracruz soon spread to other areas. That same year slave revolts were reported in Pachuca, Guanajuato, Tlacotalpan, and Cuernavaca.[12] This upsurge of slave rebellions prompted a series of royal decrees issued between 1571 and 1574 to cope with the situation. In addition to the punitive measures discussed earlier in this study, other directives were introduced by the new fugitive slave code. A system of rewards for the capture of *cimarrones* was set up. The backlands were to be patroled by a rural police and local government force; overseers in the plantations were instructed to take a head count each night to account for fugitives; incentives were given to Negroes who joined the patrols in their search for fugitives; and finally, severe penalties were imposed on those helping the escapees.[13]

In Veracruz, however, the topography of the area proved to be of great help to the *cimarrones*. Entrenched in the rugged and mountainous terrain, their strongholds were virtually inaccessible to the government troops.[14] In the late 1570s and throughout the 1580s, the *cimarrones*, realizing their advantage, became more and more aggressive.[15] In large groups they attacked plantations to plunder and to free slaves who were incorporated into their bands. Their attacks on travelers became more frequent, and they obstructed commercial traffic on the road between the port of Veracruz and Mexico City.[16] So frequent were these attacks that by the turn of the century the great *camino real* between Mexico City and Veracruz was unsafe for travelers and commerce.[17] By this time *cimarron* activities in Veracruz were also doing considerable damage to the royal coffers. Between October 14, 1609, and February 28, 1611, 20,665 pesos gold were spent to pay for troops and supplies employed in the protection of the *camino real* and surrounding areas.[18]

The danger that such activities presented to residents and to the economy of the area prompted more repressive measures in 1579 and throughout the 1580s. On November 6, 1579, Viceroy Martin Enríquez issued a decree instituting an even harsher form of punishment for fugitive slaves. The decree stated that

> ... any slave or Negro found to have escaped from the service of his master, and if found in the mountains, for the same reason, shall be arrested and castrated, with no need for further investigation of any other crime or excess, and, if he has committed other crimes he shall receive the prescribed punishment in addition to the above.[19]

Interestingly enough, none of these measures proved effective in combating slave rebellions. Concerned with the growing danger, the viceroy in the first years of the seventeenth century, sent two unsuccessful military expeditions to fight the *cimarrones* in Veracruz. The first was led by Pedro de Yebra, and the second by two Spanish captains, Alvaro de Bahena and Antón de la Parada. The first expedition proved unfit to fight in the rugged terrain, and the second got bogged down in matters of jurisdiction and competency.[20]

Despite these renewed efforts, the number of slave rebellions in Veracruz increased significantly during the seventeenth century.[21] Most of the rebellions were small in nature, and only three of them could be considered important uprisings. They occurred in 1609, 1612, and 1670.[22] Even these, however, cannot compare in size, duration or dramatic expression with the contemporary *quilombo dos Palmares,*[23] in northeast Brazil.

Of the three revolts, the one of 1609, because it involved elaborate military maneuvers and because of the concessions made to the Negroes, is considered the most important. Throughout the years a group of about 500 fugitive slaves had gathered in the mountains near Orizaba,[24] under the leadership of a "Bron"[25] Negro called Yanga.[26] In the first days of 1609, after Mexico City had been struck by a period of heavy and prolonged rain,[27] a rumor was spread about an impending slave rebellion. It was said that on *el día de Reyes* (Catholic holiday, January 6), the *cimar-*

rones of Veracruz were going to attack the city and establish Yanga as king.[28]

The news hit the capital like a bombshell. The fear-ridden population became hysterical and barricaded themselves within their houses, expecting the worse. To inspire some confidence in his authority and hoping to restore order, Viceroy Velasco rounded up several Negroes who were already in jail for other offenses, and had them whipped.[29]

In the meantime, two attacks by *cimarrones* were carried out. First they attacked a wagon train carrying goods on the road from Veracruz to Mexico City. Bishop Mota y Escobar, traveling in the area, relates the incident in the following manner. One night while he was asleep near Cacatepec, two men came and told him that they had been attacked by a band of *cimarrones* on the road to Veracruz. The Negroes took their wagons, their goods, and 100 pesos in cash, killing their twelve year old brother, and carrying off two married Indian women with them. Rushing to the scene, the bishop found the boy beheaded and disemboweled.[30]

The second attack occurred almost simultaneously. This time, a band of *cimarrones* robbed and burned down a hacienda not far from the city of Veracruz. Most of the residents escaped, but the Negroes managed to capture six Indian women and killed a Spaniard. According to Alegre, the *cimarrones*, after killing this Spaniard, opened his head and, gathering his blood with their hands, drank it with "bárbaras supersticiones y ceremonias."[31]

These attacks in the first days of the year prompted Viceroy Luís de Velasco to organize a massive military campaign to subjugate the *cimarrones*. The command of the daring expedition was given to a Spanish captain by the name of Pedro González de Herrera, and, at the request of the viceroy, two Jesuits, Juan Laurencio, and Juan Pérez, were designated to accompany the troops.

In Veracruz, Herrera gathered a company of soldiers which included 100 Spaniards, 150 Indian archers, and many adventurers from the surrounding areas.[32] Then, to prevent alerting the *cimarrones*, a proclamation was issued prohibiting any Negro or mulatto from leaving the city. On January 26, 1609, after all preparations were made, the great march to the mountains was begun.[33]

So confident was Yanga by this time that when he learned of the march against him he dispatched a Spaniard he had captured with a letter to Herrera. In this letter he boasted of his victories against the Spaniards and challenged Herrera to come after him by using the bearer of the letter as a guide.[34] Taking the messenger along, Herrera and his men left their outpost in pursuit of Yanga. On February 22, the day after the march was resumed, the Spaniards had their first encounter with the *cimarrones*. According to father Alegre, the Negroes were coming down the mountains intent on burning down the great Orizaba-Tequila plantation.[35] Surprised by the Spanish troops, the *cimarrones* fled back to the mountains, abandoning their horses, weapons, and supplies.[36]

Instead of pursuing the fugitives, Herrera decided to set up camp and spend the night. From the Spanish camp, the main Negro settlement at Cofre de Perote, near Mount Orizaba, could be seen, "... some two leagues away, securely nestled in an imposing and rugged mountain range."[37] Yanga's settlement, although in that location for less than a year, was a well organized, self-sufficient, outpost well prepared for the eventualities of war. It had a population of well over a hundred people, including "eighty adult males, twenty-four Negro and Indian women, and an undetermined number of children."[38] To provide for themselves, the *cimarrones* raised inside their palisade some cattle, and a variety of crops. These included corn, sweet potatoes, chile, squash, beans, sugar cane, and cotton.[39]

Very early the following morning, Herrera sent two scouting parties to survey the area. Then, around eight o'clock, after hearing Mass at the camp, the Spaniards began their attack. Leaving only a skeleton force behind to guard the supplies, Herrera divided his troops in three groups. One, commanded by himself, was composed of Spaniards with firearms. The other two included Indian archers, and Negroes and mulattoes with machetes who helped clear the brush for the march.[40]

The Spaniards had not gone very far when they found a waterhole and vegetable garden used by the Negroes. Herrera stopped the march, and had the area searched before going on. This precaution proved to be a wise move because a group of *cimarrones* was hiding nearby, ready to ambush their pursuers. Uncovering the enemy, the Spaniards attacked. Armed with bows and arrows, other home-made weapons, and stones, the Negroes resisted for a brief period and then fled up the mountain.[41] Despite their more sophisticated armaments, many of the Spaniards were wounded in the encounter. One of those wounded was father Laurencio, injured by an arrow in the leg.[42] Late that afternoon, after a great deal of difficulty, the Spaniards gained the mountain top. Reaching the Negro settlement, however, they found it deserted. Yanga and his followers had left shortly before the troops arrived, leaving behind some clothing, weapons, and a great many other items.[43]

For about five days, the Spaniards remained in the Negro settlement. From there, Herrera launched one or two small expeditions against the fugitives, but failed to subjugate them. Realizing the futility of pursuing a scattered band of Negroes through such rugged and unfamiliar terrain, Herrera called for negotiations with the enemy. When the talks were over, many concessions were made to the Negroes. The runaways received their freedom and were allowed to establish a new settlement not far from where they lived before. In exchange, the Negroes agreed to stop their raids and not to give aid or shelter to new fugitive slaves. Since they professed to be Christians, the *cimarrones* also agreed to have a priest for their spiritual guidance, subordinated to the parish of San Juan de la Punta.[44] In this manner, a Negro settlement was established and recognized by the authorities. The new town, named San Lorenzo de los Negros, later became known as San Lorenzo de Cerralvo.[45] How long the Negro settlement survived is unknown. It was still thriving however, in 1698, when the Italian traveler Gemelli Carreri visited that region.[46]

The settlement with Yanga and his followers did not stop the occurrence of slave revolts throughout Veracruz. In fact, as the number of *cimarrones* continued to grow, slave revolts and raids by fugitive slaves continued to plague the region. As each of these actions was reported, fear of a massive slave uprising increased in intensity, and spread throughout the country. In 1612, rumors of a major conspiracy by Negro *cimarrones* and Indians to exterminate the whites brought these fears to a climax.

In Puebla de los Angeles and Mexico City troops were gathered to guard the city. In the capital, where the Negro population had grown considerably, the rumor created an even more acute neurosis and led to drastic and unjustifiable retaliation by the authorities. During Holy Week that year, the Audiencia ordered the churches closed and canceled all religious processions.[47] One night while the city slept the noise made by a herd of hogs running and squealing through the streets led citizens to believe that the dreaded attack by runaway slaves was beginning.[48] Even after the real nature of the disturbance was established, panic continued to dominate the citizens and the authorities. In a cruel and irrational move, the judges of the Audiencia ordered the arrest of thirty-six Negroes—twenty-nine males and seven females. Charged with conspiracy, the prisoners were hanged in a public square before a large crowd of spectators. Following the execution, the Negroes were quartered and their remains tossed around the roads. Their heads were displayed on spikes until the terrible stench necessitated their removal.[49] The much feared attack never materialized. Again, as on other occasions, there was little evidence to support the existence of such a conspiracy. The apprehensive population simply overreacted.

The 1612 episode and continued *cimarron* raids on the *camino real* led to new precautions on the part of the Spaniards. On April 14 of that year a new ordinance was issued dealing with the sale of arms to Negroes. Like an earlier decree, it prohibited the sale of any kind of weapon, ammunition, and gunpowder to Negroes. In addition, however, the new law required that those guilty of such crime be sentenced to death.[50] Another step to provide great security was to establish a Spanish town near the *camino real* de Veracruz. Out of this concern the town of Córdoba was founded in the old jurisdiction of Huatusco, on April 26, 1618.[51]

The last important slave rebellion of this period occurred in 1670. This time slaves did not revolt against conditions in the plantations. Rather, rebelling against captivity itself, or perhaps against what was in store for them, they turned against those who most directly stood to profit from the trade in African souls. On that occasion, a group of slaves being taken from the port of Veracruz to Mexico City attacked their guardians and fled to the mountains. Ironically, one of those killed in this incident was Agustín Lomelín, a Genoese *asientista*, who, during this period had with two others the monopoly to bring African slaves to the Spanish Indies.[52]

While slave rebellions in Veracruz never reached the proportions of some large revolts elsewhere in the New World, they were relevant because of their great frequency. First, such high incidence of slave rebellions is a clear indication of the harsh nature of slavery in Veracruz and of the slave's determination to escape from it. In addition it can be said that it was frequency of *cimarron* activity more than the nature of the rebellions, that generated the climate of unrest and fear which plagued the colony during that period. This was so because, as the fugitive slave population generally increased after each incident, the Spaniards feared that the worst was yet to come. The much feared conspiracies however, never materialized, and, most likely, were the figment of the imagination of the apprehensive white population.

NOTES

1. Davidson, "Negro Slave Control and Resistance in Colonial Mexico," p. 243.
2. AGI, Carta de Antonio de Mendoza a El-Rey (10 de diciembre de 1537), Patronato, legajo 184, ramo 27.
3. *Ibid.*
4. Davidson, "Negro Slave Control and Resistance in Colonial Mexico," p. 243.
5. Octaviano Corro R., *Los Cimarrones en Veracruz y la Fundación de Amapá* (Veracruz: Imprenta Commercial, 1951), p. 9.
6. Davidson, "Negro Slave Control and Resistance in Colonial Mexico," p. 244.
7. AGI, Carta de Martin Enríquez a S.M. (18 de octubre de 1579), México, legajo 20, ramo 1.
8. AGI, Ordenanzas sobre el buen tratamiento que se debe dar a los negros (Siglo XVI), Patronato, legajo 171, no 2, ramo 10.
9. Davidson, "Negro Slave Control and Resistance in Colonial Mexico," p. 246.
10. AGI, Carta de Martin Enríquez a S.M. (18 de octubre de 1579), México, legajo 20, ramo 1.
11. Aguirre Beltrán, *La Población Negra de México*, p. 210.
12. *Ibid.*
13. AGI, Ordenanzas sobre el buen tratamiento que se debe dar a los negros (Siglo XVI), Patronato, legajo 171, no 2, ramo 10.
14. Davidson, "Negro Slave Control and Resistance in Colonial Mexico," p. 246.
15. AGI, Carta de Martin Enríquez a S.M. (18 de octubre de 1579), México, legajo 20, ramo 1.
16. Corro R., *Los Cimarrones en Veracruz*, p. 10.
17. Davidson, "Negro Slave Control and Resistance in Colonial Mexico," p. 246.

18. AGI, Cuentas Reales de Veracruz (1611), Contaduria, legajo 883.
19. Trens, *História de Veracruz*, 2:169. "... cualquier esclavo o negro que se averiguase haberse huido del servicio do su amo, y se hallare en los montes, por el mismo caso sea preso y capado, sin que sea necesario averiguación de otro delito ni esceso, y si otros delitos obiere hecho sea castigado por ellos demás de lo susodicho, como el caso requiere...."
20. Trens, *História de Veracruz*, 2:312.
21. *Ibid.*
22. Basauri, "La Población Negroide Mexicana," p. 102.
23. *Palmares* was a republic of fugitive slaves established in the captaincy of Pernambuco (Brazil) in the seventeenth century. It was an African state with its own laws and an elected ruler. For over fifty years this slave community held its own against massive attacks by Portuguese and Brazilian troops. It finally fell in February, 1694.
24. Trens, *História de Veracruz*, 2:313; Corro R., *Los Cimarrones en Veracruz*, p. 11.
25. Davidson, "Negro Slave Control and Resistance in Colonial Mexico." "Bron" probably refers to Brong or Abron, a subgroup of Akan culture living to the northwest of Ashanti in present-day Ghana. p. 247n.
26. Trens, *Historia de Veracruz*, 2:315. There is little agreement as to the meaning of the word "Yanga." Trens believes the personage to be legendary and the word to mean simply "king." Other authors have used the word to personify the rebel leader. According to Alegre, Yanga was a handsome Negro who had escaped 30 years earlier, and gradually acquired a large number of followers. As he grew older, Yanga passed the command of his forces to another Negro from Angola, Francisco de la Matosa, keeping to himself the political administration of the community. See Francisco Javier Alegre, S. J., *História de la Compañia de Jesus de Nueva España*, 6 vols. (Roma: Institutum Historicum, S. J., 1956), Vol. 2, libro V, p. 176.
27. Unexpected phenomena such as this were often considered in the capital city as a sign of bad things to come.
28. Padre Andrés Cavo, *Historia de México* (México D. F.: Editorial Patria S. A., 1949), p. 272.
29. Cavo, *Historia de México*, p. 272.
30. Cited in Trens, *Historia de Veracruz*, 2:311-312.
31. Alegre, *Historia de la Compañia de Jesus*, Vol. 2, libro V, pp. 175-176.
32. Trens, *Historia de Veracruz*, 2:315.
33. *Ibid.*, 2:314.
34. *Ibid.*, 2:315.
35. Alegre, *Historia de la Compañia de Jesus*, Vol. 2, libro V, p. 178.

36. Trens, *Historia de Veracruz*, 2:316.
37. Davidson, "Negro Slave Control and Resistance in Colonial Mexico," p. 248.
38. *Ibid.*, p. 247.
39. *Ibid.*
40. Trens, *Historia de Veracruz*, 2:316.
41. *Ibid.*
42. *Ibid.*, p. 317.
43. Davidson, "Negro Slave Control and Resistance in Colonial Mexico," p. 249.
44. Trens, *Historia de Veracruz*, 2:317-318.
45. *Ibid.*
46. Juan F. Gemelli Carreri, *Viaje a la Nueva España México a fines del Siglo XVII* (México D. F.: Ediciones Libro-Mex, 1955), 2 vols., 2:240.
47. Saco, *Historia de la Esclavitud*, Vol. 2, Libro V, p. 106.
48. Irving A. Leonard, *Baroque Times in Old Mexico* (Ann Arbor: The University of Michigan Press, 1971), p. 19.
49. Saco, *História de la Esclavitud*, Vol. 2, Libro V, p. 107.
50. Bentura Beleña, *Recopilación...*, pp. 73-74.
51. AGI, Testimonio de los autos que en esta Real Audiencia se an seguido con el Fiscal de S.M. por el Cabildo de Cordoba (mandamiento de 29 de octubre de 1617), México, legajo 94, fol. 29. The title for the founding of the town of Cordoba was actually issued on November 29, 1617, although the town was not founded until April 26 of the following year. See AGI, Petición de Juan Leonardo de Sevilla en nombre del cavildo de Cordoba (undated), México, legajo 94, fol. 111.
52. Aguirre Beltrán, *La Población Negra de México*, p. 26.

PART II
NEGRO SLAVERY IN PERNAMBUCO

CHAPTER I

THE INDIAN AND FORCED LABOR

The history of the discovery and early settlement of Brazil is not surrounded by the dramatic appeal and epic dimension that characterized the conquest of Mexico or Peru. On the contrary, at the time it reached Lisbon the news of the discovery of Brazil in 1500 was received with a minimum of enthusiasm. The Portuguese were too interested in the profitable trade with India to pay much attention to the new land they had found. They did not see any evidence of gold or silver to be extracted, nor were they aware of the great potential of their new discovery. As a result, no plan for the immediate settlement and colonization of Brazil was devised. Between 1500 and 1533, the activities of the Portuguese in Brazil were limited almost entirely to expeditions to trade in brazilwood, a valuable dyewood after which the new land was named, the establishment of *feitorias*, or trading posts, and the protection of the coastline against the incursions of foreign interlopers.

The limited scope of these early undertakings and the absence of a colonization plan determined to a large extent the nature of the relations the Portuguese established with the natives they encountered. The Indians found by the Portuguese in Brazil were not many. It is estimated that no more than three to four million natives inhabited the new colony at the time of discovery.[1] There were several tribal groups, the best known of which were the Tupis who lived along the coastal regions. They were of a reddish brown color, wore no clothes, and often painted their nude bodies for adornment. They were semi-nomadic people living by fishing, hunting and gathering, and limited horticulture. They lived in long, rustic, houses made of wooden planks and covered with straw. The tribes were frequently at war with each other, and prisoners taken in these wars were, after a fattening period, eaten by their captors among great festivities and celebrations.[2] In no way did the Brazilian Indian cultures resemble the splendor of Tenochtitlán or the elaborate organizational structure of the Inca empire. Neither have they left us any evidence to suggest that there ever was an advanced "pre-Cabralian" civilization. In fact, and despite his romantic defense by Montaigne,[3] the Brazilian Indian was, at best, in one of the very lowest stages of human development, roaming around the forests and coastal areas, his freedom unrestricted by the demands of sedentary life.

In their first contacts with these primitive men, the Portuguese explorers were rather successful. The Indians were friendly towards them. They came to the beach when the Portuguese arrived and displayed great curiosity about their presence and the beads and trinkets they brought with them. Equally successful were the first brazilwood traders who followed. They were aware of their dependence on the Indians for survival and were careful not to provoke their anger. Knowing of the Indians' childlike interest in the many trinkets they brought from Europe, the traders began dispensing them as gifts to persuade the natives to work for them. In exchange for these beads, small mirrors, and other glittering objects the Indians cut brazilwood trees and carried the logs on their backs from as far as fifteen to twenty leagues[4] to the seashore, where they piled them up for shipping.[5]

During this first stage, abuses were relatively few. The Portuguese were afraid of the Indians, and the latter were eager to supply the white man with their labor in exchange for the trinkets they coveted. Most importantly, as Florestan Fernandes points out, the barter economy did not demand the presence of large numbers of foreigners, and, therefore, did not threaten the Indi-

The Indian and Forced Labor

an's authority or undermine his way of life.[6] As the brazilwood trade grew and attracted more Portuguese settlers, relations with the Indians deteriorated. The need for more labor to handle the expanded trade met with a slackening interest on the part of the Indians. Their curiosity satiated by the many trinkets they accumulated, the natives became a bit too demanding, or simply refused to work for the white man. Strengthened by their growing numbers, the Portuguese now felt in a position to establish their authority and to obtain the necessary labor by whatever means they could. First they bought war prisoners from the Indians; later they made war against the natives in order to enslave them.

The institution of slavery brought great hardship to the Indians. It undermined their authority and subverted their way of life. They no longer were free to come and go as they pleased and were now forced to work under an entirely unfamiliar system. The Indian was no weakling, or incapable of heavy labor. He was well built,[7] and proved himself strong by cutting brazilwood and carrying the logs on his back for long distances. He was, however, psychologically unprepared to withstand long hours of hard work in a regimented or routine situation. Many refused to work and were punished. Others simply could not adapt to their new life and died.

Conditions worsened under the captaincy system in the 1530s and after, when the development of plantation agriculture made the white man's hunger for land and labor virtually insatiable. Attempts to enslave the Indians became more daring and more frequent. Raids were further encouraged when the Crown declared the Caetés "perpetual slaves" for having killed and eaten Bishop Pêro Fernandes Sardinha and his shipwrecked companions in 1556. The Portuguese, of course, were quick to label every Indian they seized as a Caeté Indian.[8] By 1570, Pernambuco, where these campaigns had been most successful, was running a profitable slave trade, and even exporting Indians to other parts of Brazil. The Indians retaliated with fierce attacks, but gradually those who were not captured were pushed further and further away from their habitat, and into the less hospitable interior. By the early 1580s the Indian population in the captaincy of Pernambuco was approaching extinction.[9]

In addition to the many who died in the wars, countless others died from famines, diseases and plagues made more devastating by increased contact with the Europeans and from strenuous routine work in the sugar plantations and mills. Driven away from their lands, the Indians were not always able to find an adequate supply of food; they were often threatened by starvation. In the less habitable areas of the interior they were also victims of frequent droughts. In 1583, for instance, a dry spell caused great havoc among the Indians living in the *sertão* of Pernambuco when it practically extinguished their water supply and destroyed their small garden plots. Many Indians died of thirst and hunger, while four or five thousand others in desperation came to the Portuguese settlements where they stayed voluntarily or were enslaved.[10] The increased contact with the whites required by forced labor made the Indians more susceptible to European diseases, to which they had no immunity. Syphilis was common; fevers and epidemics were frequent, often carrying away large numbers of Indians and occasionally even doing away with entire villages of natives. Equally if not more devastating was hard labor at the sugar plantations and sugar mills. Tossed from a nomadic existence into a sedentary and arduous situation, the Indians simply could not endure. Many succumbed from overwork and maltreatment, others starved or died from eating sand; still others expired of melancholy. Perhaps more damaging than war and disease, to quote Gilberto Freyre, "... it was sugar [that] killed the Indian."[12]

While sugar was quickly destroying the labor force on which its production depended, other forces were at work to prevent the further enslavement of the Indians. Soon after their arrival in 1549, the first Jesuits launched their long campaign to protect the natives from the Portuguese and to convert them to Christianity. In 1550, father Manuel da Nóbrega criticized the settlers for not being able to do anything without the work of their slaves. In 1559, he denounced the hatred which characterized the settlers' attitude towards the Indian. The Portuguese, Nóbrega said "... not only called the natives dogs, but treated them like dogs."[13] On a more practical level the Jesuits began to gather the free Indians in *reduções*, or villages, to prevent their enslavement and to facilitate their conversion. Despite fierce opposition from plantation owners and from priests who lived in concubinage with Indian girls, the Jesuits were able, in this manner, to hinder somewhat the continuing enslavement of the natives to satisfy the needs of the growing sugar industry. To the Indian, however, the Jesuit solution was far from being a blessing. In enforcing the rigid discipline of the *redução*, the Jesuit's hand was no less firm than that of the overseer. Punishment was freely dispensed and not always less severe than at the plantation. According to João Lúcio de Azevedo, at the *reduções* it was not uncommon for the priests to have their Indians whipped even for light offenses.[14] Diseases and death also took their toll among the Indians in the custody of Jesuits. In fact, the insistence of the priests in keeping the natives fully clothed in the name of Christian modesty produced serious skin and lung diseases which greatly contributed to the decimation of the Indian population during the sixteenth and seventeenth centuries.[15] Despite their good intentions, the influence of the Jesuits over the Indians was nearly as harmful as that of the colonist from whom they constantly fought to rescue their charges.

The result, at least in part, of the Jesuit efforts were the first attempts to protect the Indian through legislation. On March 20, 1570, King Sebastião prohibited the enslavement of the Indians except those captured in a "just war." A "just war," was defined as a campaign specifically authorized by the king or the governor. The settlers, however, were still free to enslave Indians who attacked them or those who took slaves from other tribes in order to eat them.[16] The ineffectiveness of this decree is reflected in the more stringent legislation that followed. On November 11, 1595, Philip II restricted the meaning of "just wars" to those authorized by him alone, and on June 5, 1605, another decree stated that under no circumstance could the natives be enslaved.[17] The weakness of the law is again apparent in the necessity to issue still another decree. The royal decree of July 30, 1609, however, went considerably further than the previous ones. It recognized the freedom of the Indian as a natural right and extended this freedom not only to those who were baptized but also to Indians who were still pagans. More importantly, as free persons the Indians could not be forced to work or do anything against their will. Those desiring Indian labor were required to pay them as they paid any free worker. The Jesuits were to be in charge of the Indians and they alone could go into the interior to tame them. This decree was not well received by the settlers and their strong protests forced the Crown to offer a more palatable compromise measure on October 13, 1611. The new decree maintained the freedom of the Indians but allowed the settlers to, once again, capture them in wars considered "just" by the governor in consultation with a junta provided that their decision was sent to the king for approval. In case of "danger," war could be conducted without waiting for the king's reply. The earlier provision allowing for the enslavement of Indians "rescued" from enemy tribes was also re-instituted. In addition, the law determined that a *Capitão de Aldeia* be placed in charge of each Indian village to supervise the natives' relations with each other and with the whites.[18] The Captain was also responsible for assigning "the Indians as workers to the colonists for set wages. He had to be present when the Indians were paid; he was to see that they were not badly treated by their employers."[19] The payment of wages to free Indians became a well established practice from that time on.[20] Nevertheless, the enslavement of the natives through "just" or not so just wars, or rescued from their enemy's "table," continued throughout the seventeenth century and beyond, until, for a number of reasons,[21] slave-hunting was no longer a profitable business.

It would be inaccurate to conclude from the evidence that the pious efforts of the Jesuits and the protective legislation of the late sixteenth and seventeenth centuries were the most important factors forcing the Pernambuco planter to replace his Indians with African labor. Neither the Jesuits nor the law effectively prevented the planter from securing an adequate supply of Indian labor. It was, rather, the combination of depopulation and the Indian's failure to adapt to sedentary labor and to withstand the routine and strenuous work required by the primitive manufacturing processes of the sugar industry that made the plantation owner ask official permission for the importation of African slaves as early as 1539.[22]

NOTES

1. A. Souto Maior, *História do Brasil* Nona edição (São Paulo: Companhia Editora Nacional, 1971), p. 58.

2. For a detailed description of this gruesome procedure and of the cannibals' cuisine, see Jean de Léry, *Le Voyage au Brésil de Jean de Léry 1556-1558*, avec une introduction par Charly Clerc (Paris: Payot, 1927), pp. 192-203. The fattening period could last as long as one year according to Pêro de Magalhães Gandavo, "História da Provincia Santa Cruz

a que vulgarmente chamamos Brasil," in *The Histories of Brazil*, translated and annotated by John B. Stetson, Jr. (Boston: Milford House, 1972), p. 40v. (hereafter cited as *História*).

3. Michel de Montaigne, "Essais," Livre I, Chap. XXXI, in Albert Thibaudet et Maurice Rat, ed., *Montaigne Œuvres Complètes* (Burges: Bibliothèque de la Pléiade, Editions Gallimard, 1967), pp. 200-213.

4. Souto Maior, *História do Brasil*, p. 52. A Portuguese league was equivalent to 3755 1/15 geometrical paces. See C. R. Boxer, *The Golden Age of Brazil 1695-1750 Growing Pains of a Colonial Society* (Berkeley and Los Angeles: University of California Press, 1969), Appendix VII, p. 357.

5. The best study in English of the economic relations of Portuguese and Indians during this period is Alexander Marchant, *From Barter to Slavery The Economic Relations of Portuguese and Indians in the Settlement of Brazil, 1500-1580* (Baltimore: The Johns Hopkins Press, 1942).

6. Florestan Fernandes, "Antecedentes Indígenas: Organização Social das Tribos Tupis" in Sergio Buarque de Holanda, *História Geral da Civilização Brasileira* 3rd ed., 7 vols. (São Paulo: Difusão Europeia do Livro, 1968), Tomo I, vol. I, p. 72.

7. Pêro Vaz de Caminha described the Brazilian Indians he met as being "... of a finer, sturdier, and sleeker condition than we ... [the Portuguese]." "The Letter of Pêro Vaz de Caminha" in E. Bradford Burns, ed. *A Documentary History of Brazil* (New York: Alfred A. Knopf, 1966), p. 25. Gandavo said they were "For the most part well disposed, vigorous and of good stature." *História*, p. 33.

8. F. A. Pereira da Costa, *Anais Pernambucanos*, 10 vols. (Recife: Arquivo Público Estadual, 1958-1965), 1:359.

9. Fernão Cardim, *Tratados da Terra e Gente do Brasil*. Introduções e notas de Baptista Caetano, Capistrano de Abreu e Rodolpho Garcia (Rio de Janeiro: Editores J. Leite & Cia, 1925), p. 8; also Marchant, *From Barter to Slavery*, p. 130.

10. Cardim, *Tratados*, p. 331.

11. Pereira da Costa, *Anais*, 3:167.

12. Gilberto Freyre, *Casa Grande & Senzala Formação da Família Brasileira sob o Regime de Economia Patriarcal*, 14ª edição brasileira, 2 vols. (Recife: Imprensa Oficial 1966-1970), I:172-74.

13. From "Cartas Jesuiticas," cited in Mauricio Goulart, *Escravidão Africana no Brasil (Das Origenas à Extinção do Tráfico)* (São Paulo: Livraria Martins Editora, 1949), p. 34. For use of Indian slaves also see Gandavo, *História*, p. 15v.

14. João Lúcio de Azevedo, *Os Jesuítas no Grão-Pará, suas Missões e a Colonização*, 2a ed. (Coimbra, 1930), cited in Freyre, *Casa Grande & Senzala*, 1:201.

15. Freyre, *Casa Grande & Senzala*, 1:123.
16. Mathias C. Kiemen, *The Indian Policy of Portugal in the Amazon Region, 1614-1693* (Washington, D.C.: Catholic University of America Press, 1954), pp. 4-5.
17. "... por nhũ caso se podessẽ os dd. gentios catiuar..." "Registo da ley de Sua Mg.^{de} sobre os Indios em q̃ ha p̃ bem q̃ naõ sejaõ catiuos," in *Livro Primeiro do Govêrno do Brasil 1607-1633* (Rio de Janeiro: Ministerio das Relações Exteriores, 1958), pp. 71-72.
18. *Ibid.*, pp. 72-74.
19. Kiemen, *The Indian Policy*, p. 7.
20. An unidentified Dutch source writing in 1637, stated that the Indians in Pernambuco, would not work unless their wages were deposited with their 'Captain' beforehand, in Pereira da Costa, *Anais*, 1:329.
21. See Myriam Ellis, "The Bandeiras in the Geographical Expansion of Brasil" in Richard M. Morse, ed., *The Bandeirantes The Historical Role of the Brazilian Pathfinders* (New York: Alfred A. Knopf, 1965), p. 55.
22. Mauricio Goulart, "O Problema da Mão-de-Obra: O Escravo Africano" in Holanda, *História Geral*, Tomo 1, Vol. II, p. 185.

CHAPTER II

THE NEGRO POPULATION OF PERNAMBUCO

The decimation of the Amerindian, and above all, his inability to perform satisfactorily in most occupations at the sugar mill soon made clear to the planter the necessity of resorting to the more reliable and supposedly stronger African slave. Negro slaves were no strangers to the Portuguese. A perennial dark cloud hanging over the otherwise brilliant accomplishments of Prince Henry the Navigator is the very fact that his great voyages of discovery were also the initiators of the African slave trade. In 1441, Antão Conçalves took the first captives in African territory and brought them to Portugal. Three years later (1444), Lançarote, the Prince's squire and the first to obtain a license to import slaves, arrived in Lagos with a load of 235 captives.[1]

Since that time, the slave trade became a growing and profitable business. Fortifications were built at Arguim (1448), and São Jorge da Mina (1481)[2] to protect the trade, and the famous *Companhia de Lagos* was created. To supervise the trade, government controls were instituted. The *Casa de Guiné* was established in the town of Lagos. From there it was later moved to Lisbon where it operated under the name of *Casa da Mina* and later as

Casa da India. In conjunction with this organ there was the *Casa de Escravos*, which was in charge of the slave trade and collected the revenue. The apparatus of the traffic thus organized, slaves began to come to Portugal in large numbers. Between 1486 and 1493, 3, 589 were imported from Guinea by the Crown. In the years 1511-13, 1,265 slaves, also owned by the Crown, passed through the *Casa de Escravos*. For each slave brought into the country a 5 percent tax was levied in favor of the Order of Christ, as determined by Prince Henry, while the Crown received one tenth of the revenue.[3]

As early as 1551 there were 9,950 slaves in Lisbon out of a total population of over 100,000 inhabitants. By 1620, the slave population had reached 10,470 and consisted almost entirely of Negroes.[4] Although most of them were domestic servants, others, particularly women, were seen throughout the city engaged in practically every menial occupation. Many Negro women washed clothes in rivers and streams. Another large group served as sanitation workers, collecting garbage and other refuse from the streets. Women known as *negras do pote* brought water from the fountains and rivers and delivered it to the homes. A smaller but equally colorful group exhibited their culinary talents by selling seafood, rice, and other delicacies on the street.

During the fifteenth century, Lisbon became a major distribution center exporting slaves to Seville and other European cities. With the discovery of the New World, the Portuguese, who controlled the major trading centers in Africa, began supplying Negroes to the Spanish-American colonies. The profits from this trade together with the opportunity to smuggle goods in and precious metals out of the Spanish colonies were so great that Portuguese traders were reluctant for a long time to shift directions and supply the comparatively small demands of the settlers of Brazil.[5] Nevertheless, it was from Lisbon that the first Negroes were brought to Brazil. The date of their first arrival has never been, and perhaps can never be, accurately established. There is general agreement, however, that the first Negroes came with the early expeditions, as domestic servants to the first settlers. It is highly probable that Negro slaves accompanied Pedro Álvares Cabral in his voyage of discovery in 1500,[6] since in those days it was common for slaves to travel with their masters or to work as crew members aboard ships. As early as 1511, the ship *Bretoa* came to Brazil with two young Negroes as part of her crew, one of them being a slave of the ship's owner.[7] Although these Negroes might have returned with the ship, others no doubt remained when their owners stayed. Some *feitores*, or managers of the trading posts, almost certainly owned slaves. Pêro Capico, a Portuguese captain who lived in Brazil between 1516 and 1526, apparently owned slaves who helped him make the first sugar in the new land.[8] Cristovão Jaques, who established a *feitoria* in Pernambuco during this period, also must have owned slaves. Nevertheless, the number of Negro slaves brought to Brazil during this period was relatively small. The first Africans came only sporadically and in small numbers, and they worked mainly, though not exclusively, as domestic servants. Brazilwood was still the mainstay of the economy and the Indians still comprised the great bulk of the labor force. It is not until the establishment of the captaincy system that specific requests for Negroes become frequent, reflecting the growing demand for African labor brought about by the development of plantation agriculture and the establishment of the first sugar mills. To protect the Brazilian coast from foreign intruders, King João III made large grants of land to persons of rank or of the lesser nobility who were capable of settling and colonizing them. According to this plan and beginning in 1534, the territory was divided into fourteen *capitanias* assigned to twelve *donatários*.

While the other captaincies failed, São Vicente and Pernambuco grew and became important sugar-producing centers.[9] Pernambuco, granted to Duarte Coelho,[10] soon became the most prosperous, and in a few years the colonists who came with its *donatário*, became wealthy and were able to enjoy an almost luxurious if not extravagant life style.[11] By the first half of the seventeenth century, Pernambuco was already the leading sugar producer in the world being often referred to as *"suikerland,"* by the great sugar merchants of Amsterdam.[12]

Although sugar cane was planted in Pernambuco before the arrival of Duarte Coelho, it was the *donatário* who encouraged the growth of plantations and who ordered the construction of the first *engenhos*, or sugar mills. It is therefore not surprising to find Duarte Coelho, as early as 1539, asking the king for a license to import Negro slaves to work in the plantations of Pernambuco. As the captaincy flourished and the infant sugar industry began to grow, more intense became the need for slave labor. A clear picture of this development is conveyed in Duarte Coelho's letter of April 27, 1542. On that date the *donatário* informed the king that he was building more sugar mills to handle the large quantities of sugar cane then available in Pernambuco, and, his earlier request not granted, pleaded with the monarch for Negro slaves, emphasizing their importance for the success of the captaincy.[13] The relation of Negro slaves to the progress and survival of Pernambuco is again stressed in 1555. In that year, the *Capitão Mor*[14] Jerônimo de Albuquerque wrote to the king asking for a supply of slaves to rebuild two sugar mills in Olinda and Igarassú which had been burned by the Indians. In his plea Albuquerque stresses that the introduction of large numbers of Negroes would contribute greatly to the development of agriculture, the safety of the community and the economic welfare of the captaincy.[15]

The need for African slaves was not limited to Pernambuco. As plantations multiplied throughout the colony the problem of labor became acute. Some planters feared economic ruin if they could not secure an adequate supply of slaves. Pêro de Goes, the *donatário* of the captaincy of São Tomé, wrote to his partner in Lisbon begging him to send no less than sixty Negroes, otherwise his sugar industry would be faced with bankruptcy.[16] As perhaps a first step to help the economy of the colony, a shipment of Negroes arrived in the new city of Salvador in 1550, the first slaves to come directly from Africa to Brazil.[17] They were imported by the Crown to be divided among the first settlers,[18] the purchase price to be deducted from their wages and salaries. According to Mauricio Goulart, this was the first time that the Negro was exported to Brazil as merchandise for the use of the community.[19] This shipment, of course, could hardly be expected to satisfy the needs of colonists elsewhere. The demand for Negroes continued and more effective action from the Crown was needed if the Brazilian economy was to be saved from stagnation. In order to prevent economic disaster, and as an indication of its desire to encourage the sugar industry, the Crown finally answered the planters' requests. The *Alvará*, or royal decree of March 9, 1559, gave permission to persons owning sugar mills in operation, or building them thereafter, to import at their own expense from the Congo, up to 120 *peças de escravos* for each of the said mills, paying only one-third of the duties required. To avoid abuses the interested person had to produce a certificate of ownership of a sugar mill in Brazil issued by the *Casa da Índia*.[20]

While slaves had actually come directly from Africa to Brazil prior to its proclamation, the *Alvará* of 1559 marks the official opening of the slave traffic between the two regions. According to its provisions and under other individual licenses granted by the Crown, Negroes began arriving with greater frequency, being shipped to practically every corner of the colony. The writings of the contemporary chroniclers, sometimes inaccurate, serve in this case as an illustration of this increase in the Negro slave population. Mauricio Goulart, based on the number of *engenhos* listed by Gandavo, gives a total of two to three thousand for the year 1570.[21] Father Fernão Cardim (1583) gives a rather low figure of 2,000 Negroes for Pernambuco, and three to four thousand in Bahia.[22] The Jesuit José de Anchieta (1584) compensates for Cardim's small numbers by placing the Negro slave population of Pernambuco at 10,000.[23] A more accurate estimate for Pernambuco should be somewhere between the estimates of the two priests. Considering that Pernambuco had, by 1584, sixty-six[24] *engenhos*, and giving each a high average of eighty slaves, we have a total of 5,280 Negroes. Adding, perhaps too generously, another 100 to account for those working as domestic servants and in other occupations in the towns, I would put the Negro slave population of Pernambuco at this time right around 5,380. It cannot be doubted, however, that by this time Pernambuco planters were receiving large numbers of slaves. In 1574, Francisco Mendes and Garcez Mendes, residents of the city of Porto (Portugal), received a refund of duties unlawfully collected from them by the customs officials of Olinda for the introduction of forty-eight *peças de escravos* brought from the island of São Tomé.[25] In 1577 the Crown ordered the customs of Pernambuco to refund 284 thousand reis to Pedro de Noronha. Again this sum had been erroneously or illegally collected at Pernambuco when Noronha introduced 142 *peças* from São Tomé in 1575.[26]

It is during the seventeenth century, however, that the importation of African slaves into Pernambuco first assumed striking proportions. Following the extraordinary growth in the sugar industry between 1576-1600, a stream of Negroes began to flow into the port of Recife. According to a statement made by the council of Olinda to Count Maurits of Nassau, the Dutch governor of Pernambuco (1637-1644), slaves were entering the captaincy at the rate of 4,000 per year during the early part of the seventeenth century.[27] This figure, given by the chamber of Olinda, does not seem too far off the mark when compared to the findings of contemporary historians. Joannes de Laet, for instance, writes that between 1620 and 1623, 15,430 Negroes were shipped to Pernambuco from Angola alone,[28] an average of approximately 3,858 for each of the four years. By 1630, the year in which the Dutch occupation of Pernambuco (1630-54) began, there were approximately 40,000 Negro slaves, some from Africa, others born in Brazil, working in sugar mills located in the area between the Rio Grande and the São Francisco rivers which included the captaincies of Pernambuco, Itamaracá, Paraíba and Rio Grande.[29] At this time there were 166 sugar mills in this region. Since 131 of them were located in Pernambuco alone, it follows that the great majority of the slaves mentioned above lived in that captaincy.[30]

The Dutch invasion of Pernambuco in February of 1630, and the six years of war that followed, greatly affected the size and status of the Negro population of that captaincy. Fearing the Calvinist invaders and the wave of death and destruction they were inflicting upon the colony, many Portuguese planters fled south to Bahia, taking along as much of their property as they possibly could and setting afire the vast cane fields which once were the very symbol of their wealth and power. Following their masters, thousands of Negro slaves also went into exile. João Pais Barreto, one of the wealthiest planters in the captaincy, was able to escape the enemy fury and managed to take with him 350 slaves even though he lost his house and two sugar mills.[31] Others like Agostinho Cezar de Andrade, were less successful. In addition to losing his sugar mill and all its equipment, he lost all his slaves. A few of these were seized and sold, while the great majority escaped into the forest.[32]

Many slaves participated in the struggle by fighting in both the Portuguese and Dutch armies. Those who sided with the Portuguese were, for the most part, volunteered by their owners for the defense of the colony. This was the case of one Gonçalo Rebello, owned by Balthazar Gonçalves, who with many other slaves fought in the Negro regiment of Henrique Dias.[33] Those who marched with the Dutch were seized by the invaders, or joined them voluntarily to escape from their Portuguese and Brazilian owners.[34]

The great majority of slaves, however, took advantage of the confusion that reigned in the captaincy during the war to escape into the forests. From their hideouts they emerged periodically to sack the villages and plantations, successfully fending off the few troops that could be spared to pursue them. By 1637, after the war had ended, the victorious Dutch were confronted with a sad picture of the captaincy. Many of the plantations had been burned to the ground, countless *engenhos* were *de fôgo morto*, or inoperative, damaged or destroyed by the war. Most important, the shortage of Negro slaves had become crucial. The massive migration to Bahia, the large number of fugitives, and the minimum arrival of new Negroes between 1630-36,[35] left Pernambuco without an effective labor force. The Dutch authorities soon realized, as did Father Antonio Vieira somewhat later (1648), that "without Negroes there is no Pernambuco"—in other words, without slave labor there is no sugar.

The Negroes brought to Pernambuco since the beginning of the traffic came from Portuguese-controlled entrepots along the west coast of Africa, around the Cape of Good Hope, and the coast of Mozambique, as well as from the interior of the "Dark Continent." It would be erroneous therefore, as Nina Rodrigues points out, to suggest that the Bantus were the Negroes "that colonized Brazil."[37] Although the Bantus were among the best known, practically every nation, or group, in large or small numbers, was represented in the *engenhos* of Pernambuco. The Berbers, Wolofs, Ardras, Minas, Angolas, Congos, as well as Negroes from São Tomé, Calabar, Sierra Leone, Cape Verde, the Sudan, and other areas were transported to Recife during the years of the slave trade.[38]

In the early years of the traffic, the great majority of the captives came from Guinea and São Tomé. Gradually, the center of the trade moved south, and by the early seventeenth century most of the Africans were coming from the areas then known as the Congo and Angola. According to Charles R. Boxer, during this period approximately 15,000 slaves were being exported from these two regions to Brazil and Spanish America, "in an average good year." Over half of this total went to Brazil, 4,000 going to Bahia and Rio de Janeiro, and 4,400 going to Pernambuco.[39] With the Dutch occupation in 1630, the shipment of Negro slaves from the Portuguese factories in Africa to Pernambuco came to a halt.[40] By 1637, it was obvious to Nassau that to rebuild the captaincy's economy from the ashes of war it was imperative to secure a plentiful source of slave labor.

The most logical course of action in the eyes of the Directors of the Dutch West India Company was to capture some Portuguese entrepots on the West coast of Africa. Accordingly, an expedition left Recife for Guinea on June 25, 1637, with the objective of taking Elmina, an important Portuguese stronghold on the Gold Coast. About two months later the fleet arrived, and on August 28, Elmina fell to the Dutch. Soon after the taking of Elmina, slaves from Guinea were being sent to Pernambuco, but the faster the captaincy recovered the larger the number of slaves it needed. On December 5, 1637, the *Escabinos*, or assemblymen of Olinda wrote to the Heeren XIX (the Directors of the W. I. C.), stating that a minimum of 2,000 Negroes should be imported each year if the sugar industry in Dutch Brazil was to be maintained.[41] With little hesitation the Dutch moved to attack the Portuguese colony of Angola, and on August 26, 1641, São Paulo de Luanda surrendered to the forces of Captain Jol. Angola was known at this time for its vast reservoir of Negroes. According to a Portuguese official writing in 1591, the supply was so great that it "would not be exhausted until the end of the world."[42] And indeed, after seizing Elmina, Angola, and later São Tomé, the W. I. C., according to Hermann Wätjen, no longer needed to worry about supplying its Brazilian possessions with Negro slaves. From the end of 1636 until the summer of 1645 no less than 23,163 Africans were brought to Pernambuco.[43] The African trade in itself became one of the most profitable activities of the Company. The slaves mentioned above, exchanged in Africa for objects worth 38 to 55 florins, sold in the Recife auctions for 200 or 300 each on the average, and sometimes, if they were in good physical condition, for as much as 600 to 800 florins. Selling at such high prices, these Negroes brought the Company, which kept the monopoly over the trade, a gross profit of 6,714,423.12 florins.[44]

A breakdown of the number of slaves sold by the year is of considerable value in illustrating the flow of Negroes into the

Years	Number of Slaves Sold	Years	Number of Slaves Sold
1636	1,031	1641	1,437
1637	1,580	1642	2,312
1638	1,711	1643	3,948
1639	1,802	1644	5,565
1640	1,188	1645	2,589

Adapted from: Hermann Wätjen, *O Dominio Colonial Hollandez no Brasil. Um Capítulo da História Colonial do Século XVII.* Recife, 1938, p. 487.

captaincy from 1636 to 1644, and a sharp drop in that influx as the result of renewed war. It must be pointed out that the Negroes who arrived in Recife were by no means all those shipped there from Africa. The slaves traded in the Recife market were only those who survived the voyage across the Atlantic. Thousands of others simply did not endure the incredible hardships of the crossing and never lived to see the palm-lined beaches of Pernambuco.

At the African entrepôts, Negroes were packed in the ships' holds, the tweendecks, the poop deck, in fact wherever any little space happened to be available. As many as 500 Negroes were packed by the Portuguese in a small *caravela*.[45] Conditions were said to be worse in Dutch ships. Eager to meet the great demand of the planters of Pernambuco, the Dutch crowded incredible numbers of Negroes into their small ships and yachts. Ships ranging from 100 to 400 tons in size carried 300, 400, 500, and even 600 slaves besides a crew of from 30 to 35 persons.[46] In addition to overcrowding their charges the Dutch frequently did not provide them with an adequate supply of victuals or fresh water. Overcrowding, lack of an adequate diet, lack of fresh air and water, and lack of sanitary facilities claimed the lives of thousands of Negroes aboard slavers. It is not without reason that the Portuguese called the slave ships *tumbeiros*, or "undertakers."[47] During the years from 1637 to 1646, it is estimated that from 20 to 30 percent of the Negroes shipped out perished during the course of an average voyage.[48] So great were the losses that the Dutch finally took steps to reduce them. By 1645 the number of deaths had been greatly reduced in the voyages from Angola although severe losses continued to plague the longer crossings from Guinea.

By the time improvements in the conditions aboard the slavers made it possible for more Negroes to survive, war, once again, interfered with the traffic. After the departure of Nassau in 1644, dissatisfaction with the Dutch occupation increased and, with the instigation of the Portuguese government in Bahia, a rebellion broke out in Pernambuco in 1645. Once again the sugar industry was victimized by the struggle between Brazilian and Dutch troops. Plantations were burned and sugar mills laid waste. With the sugar industry so crippled, the market for Negro slaves fell sharply. In 1645, the number of slaves brought to Pernambuco dropped to less than half the figure in 1644. During 1646, the arrival of a slaver in the port of Recife was a rare sight. Because of the low demand for Negroes caused by the war, the Dutch authorities diverted their shipments to the Spanish colonies, Barbados and other places where the Negroes could be exchanged for indigo, cotton, or tobacco. Between 1648, the year Angola was retaken by the Portuguese, and 1652, the introduction of new Negroes in Pernambuco was negligible—an average of 500 for each of the four years.[49].

The importance of the Negro population of Pernambuco during the first half of the seventeenth century becomes even more apparent when compared with the total number of Africans brought to Brazil during the same period. Approximately 108,000 Negroes came to Pernambuco between 1601 and 1652, while it is estimated that 200,000 entered Brazil during the first half of the seventeenth century.[50] During the third quarter of the century, the importation of Africans to Brazil rose considerably reaching a total of over 7,000 per year.[51] Accounting for a good part of the increase was of course the resumption of the traffic to Recife after the expulsion of the Dutch in 1654.

There was no question that without Negroes there would be no sugar. So, while sugar was king, Pernambuco received veritable armies of African slaves to work its sugar mills. It is estimated that from three to five million Negroes were brought to Brazil over the whole period of the trade.[52] Since during the last quarter of the sixteenth and practically all of the seventeenth centuries Pernambuco received over half of the total number brought to

Brazil, it would be no exaggeration to say that during the period we are studying at least 250,000 Africans came to that captaincy to be "the hands and the feet of the sugar mill owners."[53]

NOTES

1. For a description of these expeditions see Prince Henry's great Chronicler Gomes Eanes da Zurara, *Crónica de Guiné*, Segundo o ms, de Paris. Introdução, notas, novas considerações e glossário de José de Bragança (Lisboa: Livraria Civilização Editora, 1973), pp. 71-120.

2. J. Lúcio de Azevedo, *Épocas de Portugal Económico Esboços de História*, 3a edição (Lisboa: Livraria Classica Editora, 1973), p. 169.

3. Azevedo, *Épocas*, pp. 69-71.

4. Mauro, *Le Portugal et L'Atlantique*, p. 147.

5. Goulart, *Escravidão*, p. 57; Azevedo, *Épocas*, p. 76.

6. Taunay, *Subsídios*, p. 532.

7. Marchant, *From Barter to Slavery*, p. 37.

8. Goulart, *Escravidão*, p. 97.

9. Bahia, whose *donatário* Francisco Pereira Coutinho was killed by the Tupinambá Indians, recovered under the Central Government, and also became a major sugar-producing region.

10. A capitania, or captaincy, was a grant of land made by the king to a *donatário*, or donee, which consisted of a number of leagues along the coastline, extending as far inland as the imaginary line of Tordesillas. The extension along the coast varied with the captaincies. Pernambuco, given to Duarte Coelho had sixty leagues of coastline. The grants were hereditary but did not imply actual ownership of the land. The instruments of the Royal grant were the *carta de doação* which described the area or the lands granted, and the *foral* which listed the obligations of the donee. The granting of Pernambuco to Duarte Coelho (made actually on March 10, 1534), is seen as the starting point of the captaincy period of Brazilian history. For a copy of the letter of donation see Carta de Doação *de Duarte Coelho* (Évora, Janeiro (hereafter cited as BNRJ) códice I-5-2-4-no 1. For a copy of the foral, or charter, see *Traslado do foral da Capitania de Pernambuco* (Évora, 23 de setembro de 1534), BNRJ códice I-5-2-4-no 2.

11. Pedro Calmon, *História da Civilização Brasileira* 5a edição (São Paulo: Companhia Editora Nacional, 1945), p. 24.

12. Basilio de Magalhães, *O açúcar nos primórdios do Brasil colonial* (Rio de Janeiro: Edição do Instituto do Açúcar e do Alcool, 1953), p. 24.

13. *Carta de Duarte Coelho a D. João III* (Olinda, 27 de abril de 1542), BNRJ, códice I-31-20-4.

14. Title given to a *donatário*, in this case of the captaincy of Pernambuco.

15. In the years 1540-70, there was frequent strife in Pernambuco between hostile Indians and the colonists. For this reason, Negroes were armed and used as small private militias for the protection of the sugar mills against Indian attacks. See F. A. Pereira da Costa, "Origens Históricas da Industria Assucareira em Pernambuco," *Arquivos* (Recife: Prefeitura Municipal), nos 7-20, 1945-51, p. 276. In fact, to safeguard the inhabitants against these attacks, D. João III in the "Regimento," or Royal ordinance given to Tomé de Sousa in 1548, ordered that sugar mills should not be built in isolated areas but instead should be located as close to the settlements as possible. They should also be equipped with towers or fortress-like buildings where the inhabitants could find shelter in case of attack. See Duarte Coelho, *Cartas de Duarte Coelho a El Rey, Reprodução fascsimilar, leitura paleográfica e versão moderna anotada por José Antonio Gonsalves de Mello e Cleonir Xavier de Albuquerque* (Recife: Universidade Federal de Pernambuco, Imprensa Universitária, 1967), note 14, p. 107. For more details on this Regimento, see A. da Silva Rêgo, *Portuguese Colonization in the Sixteenth Century: A Study of the Royal Ordinances (Regimentos)* (Johannesburg: Witwatersrand University Press, 1965), pp. 85-92.

16. Taunay, *Subsídios*, p. 533.

17. A shipment of Negroes from Africa to Bahia is believed to have been made by a Jorge Lopes Bixorda in 1538. See Taunay, *Subsídios*, p. 533; Arthur Ramos, *The Negro in Brazil*. Trans. by Richard Pattee (Washington, D. C.: The Associated Publishers, Inc., 1951), p. 17.

18. In 1549, after buying the Captaincy of Bahia from the heirs of Francisco Pereira Coutinho, the king sent Tomé de Sousa to establish a Central Government in Brazil and to become its first Governor General. From the time of his arrival on March 29, through August 6, the new Governor laid the the foundations of his capital, the new city of Salvador. Accompanying Tomé de Sousa came an army of 320 soldiers, who soon turned to agriculture, 400 convicts, and six Jesuits (see Calmon, *História*, p. 25). These people comprised most of the population of Salvador in 1550, and it was to them that most of the slaves were sold.

19. Goulart, *Escravidão*, p. 99.

20. *Arquivo Histórico Ultramarino* (Lisbon) (hereafter cited as AHU) Alvará de 9 de março de 1559, documentos referentes a Pernambuco, Livro 1º de Oficios, códice 112, fls. 196v. A *peça de escravo*, or *peça de Indias* "... was a prime young male slave; all other slaves of both sexes counted less than a *peça*. This term might, therefore, include two or even three individuals depending on their age, sex, and physical fitness, children at breast not counting separately from their mothers." C. R. Boxer, *The Portuguese Seaborne Empire 1415-1825* (New York:

Alfred P. Knopf, 1969), p. 100. Perdigão Malheiros, *A Escravidão*, Tomo II, part 3, pp. 19-20, without mentioning his source, makes reference to an *Alvará* dated March 29, 1549. According to this decree, sugar mill owners were authorized to import 120 slaves from Guinea and the Island of São Tomé for each of their mills. I could not find any documentary evidence for this *Alvará* of 1549, and believe it to be the same as the one I cited above. Apparently a mistake must have been made regarding the date of the decree. Assuming that the two decrees are the same, the original document at AHU reads "up to 120 *peças de escravos"* not 120 slaves as suggested by Perdigão Malheiros. Taunay, *Subsídios*, p. 533, and Raymundo Nina Rodrigues, *Os Africanos no Brasil* (São Paulo: Companhia Editora Nacional, 1932), p. 26n. repeat the same information from *A Escravidão* taking no notice of the apparent errors.

21. These slaves were mostly found in the sugar mills of Pernambuco and Bahia. See Goulart, *Escravidão*, p. 99.

22. Cardim, *Tratados*, pp. 334 and 288.

23. Pereira da Costa, "Origens Históricas," p. 267.

24. J. H. Rodrigues, *Brasil: Periodo Colonial* (Mexico: Instituto Panamericano de Geografia e História, 1953), p. 56. The large *engenhos* had about 100 Negroes, the medium sized about 50 and the small ones about 20. See C. R. Boxer, *The Dutch in Brazil, 1624-1654* (New York and Oxford: Clarendon Press, 1957) p. 32.

25. Pereira da Costa, *Anais*, 1:349.

26. AHU, Documentos referentes a Pernambuco, códice 112, 1º Livro de Oficios, fls. 146v.

27. Mauro, *Le Portugal et L'Atlantique*, p. 179.

28. Joannes de Laet, *História ou Annaes dos Feitos da Companhia Privilegiada das Indias Occidentais desde o seu começo até o fim do anno de 1636*. Tradução dos Drs. José Hygino Duarte Pereira e Pedro Souto Maior, 2 vols. (Rio de Janeiro: Officinas Gráficas da Bibliotheca Nacional, 1916 and 1925), 1:239.

29. Pereira da Costa, *Anais*, 2:419. The Rio Grande is located in the present state of Rio Grande do Norte. The São Francisco river formed the southern boundary of the Captaincy of Pernambuco. The four captaincies named above were occupied by the Dutch in the first half of the seventeenth century.

30. Hermann Wätjen, *O Dominio Colonial Hollandez no Brazil. Um Capitulo da História Colonial do Século XVII*, Tradução de Pedro Celso Uchoa Cavalcanti (Recife: Edição Especial da Companhia Editora Nacional para o Govêrno do Estado de Pernambuco, 1938), p. 418; João Baers, "Olinda Conquistada," tradução de Alfredo Carvalho

(Recife, 1898), p. 43, cited in, Luís da Câmara Cascudo, *Geografia do Brasil Holandês* (Rio de Janeiro: Livraria José Olympio Editora, 1956), pp. 181-182.

31. Pereira da Costa, *Anais*, 2:377. For a detailed and vivid account of the planters' exodus, see Frei Manoel Calado, *O Valeroso Lucideno e Triumfo da Liberdade*, 2 vols, (Recife: Edição da Cooperativa Editora de Cultura Intelectual de Pernambuco, 1942), 1:84-85.

32. AHU, Petição de Agostinho Cezar de Andrade (10 de março de 1676), Documentos referentes a Pernambuco, caixa 35.

33. AHU, Consulta do Conselho Ultramarino (9 de julho de 1659), Documentos referentes a Pernambuco, caixa 7.

34. Some slaves went as far as denouncing their owners to the Dutch for trying to hide property from the authorities. See AHU, Consulta do Conselho Ultramarino, Petição de Manoel da Cunha Andrade (14 de novembro de 1648), Documentos referentes a Pernambuco, caixa 1.

35. Goulart, *Escravidão*, p. 109; Mauro, *Le Portugal et L'Atlantique*, pp. 179-180.

36. Antonio Vieira ao Marquês de Nisa (12 de agosto de 1648), cited in José Antônio Gonsalves de Mello, *Tempo dos Flamengos: Influencia da Ocupação Holandesa na Vida e na Cultura do Norte do Brasil* (Rio de Janeiro: Livraria José Olympio Editora, 1947), p. 204. This relationship between Negroes and sugar permeates the entire history of Pernambuco during the period we are studying. in the "Rezão do Estado do Brasil" written in 1612, it is stated that without slaves it is impossible to operate the plantations, and that the most serious problem the colony could face would be a shortage of slaves (see Engel Sluiter, "Report on the State of Brazil, 1612," HAHR, v. 29, November 1949, p. 523). In 1638, Dutch officials reported that without slaves "it is impossible to do anything in Brazil: without them the engenhos will not function, nor can the land be cultivated..." (See "Breve Discurso Sôbre o Estado das Quatro Capitanias Conquistadas de Pernambuco, Itamaracá, Parahyba e Rio Grande Situadas na Parte Septentrional do Brasil" tradução de J. Hygino Duarte Pereira, *Revista do Instituto Archeologico e Geographico Pernambucano*, dezembro de 1888, no 34, p. 172, hereafter cited as RIAGP). And, as late as 1677, João Fernandes Vieira asked the king to allow the introduction of more Negroes because "without them there cannot be sugar mills." See AHU, Carta de João Fernandes Vieira ao Rei (26 de julho de 1677), Documentos referentes a Pernambuco, caixa 35.

37. Nina Rodrigues, *Os Africanos no Brasil*, p. 32.

38. José Antônio Gonsalves de Mello, "A Situação do Negro sob o Dominio Hollandez," *Novos Estudos Afro-Brasileiros* (Rio de Janeiro:

Civilização Brasileira Editôra, 1937), p. 215; Nina Rodrigues, *Os Africanos*, p. 35.

39. Charles R. Boxer, *Salvador de Sá and the Struggle for Brazil and Angola 1602-1686* (London: The Athlone Press, 1952), p. 224.

40. Most of the slaves that entered Pernambuco between 1630-36 were going elsewhere on ships captured by the Dutch navy. In 1631, a ship coming from Angola with 450 Negroes was captured by the Dutch fleet under Commander Boom-eter off the coast of Pernambuco. (See Laet, *História*, 2:629); On November 6, 1636, the *"Pijn-appel"* brought in a ship carrying about 400 slaves. The vessel was travelling between Angola and the West Indies. (See Laet, *História*, 2:597).

41. Carta dos Escabinos de Olinda ao Conselho dos XIX (Recife, 5 de dezembro de 1637) cited in Mello, *Tempo dos Flamengos*, p. 210.

42. Boxer, *Salvador de Sá*, p. 229.

43. Wätjen, *O Dominio Colonial*, p. 486.

44. *Ibid.*, p. 487.

45. Mello, "A Situação do Negro," p. 213.

46. Mello, *Tempo dos Flamengos*, p. 209.

47. C. R. Boxer, *The Golden Age of Brazil*, p. 5.

48. Mello, *Tempo dos Flamengos*, p. 209.

49. Goulart, *Escravidão*, p. 112.

50. *Ibid.*, p. 113.

51. Curtin, *The Atlantic Slave Trade*, p. 116.

52. Estimates for the importation of slaves into Brazil vary greatly. Some are obviously exaggerated and therefore have not been cited here. The more conservative and also more reliable estimates run between 3 and 5 million. I personally believe that a figure around 3 million is probably the closest to the truth. Roberto Simonsen estimates that 3 million and 300 thousand slaves were brought into Brazil (cited in Goulart, *Escravidão*, p. 97); Pierre Chaunu states that the figure for Brazil is "the most definite," and puts it at 3 million Negroes, or 40 percent of the total imported to the Americas (see Pierre Chaunu, "Pour une 'Geopolitique' de L'espace Americain" in Richard Konetzke and Hermann Kellenbenz, eds. *Jahrbuch für Geschichte von Staat, Wirtschaft und Gesellschaft Lateinamericas*. Cologne 1964, vol. I, p. 16); Nöel Deerr puts the Portuguese trade to Brazil at 3,325,000 (see Noel Deerr, *The History of Sugar*, 2 vols. (London: Chapman and Hall, 1949-50), 2:284); Oliveira Martins estimates the total importation into Brazil at 5 million (cited in Curtin, *The Atlantic Slave Trade*, p. 11); Arthur Ramos arrives at about the same total as Martins: "[not-]...more than five million Negroes [were] actually brought to Brazil." See Arthur Ramos, *The Negro in Brazil*, p. 20. All of the above figures

are the result of calculations by the respective authors, each using his own method and therefore are no more than approximations. It is impossible to ascertain the true volume of the Brazilian traffic because of the almost complete absence of official records. Following the proclamation of the Republic (1889) the Brazilian government ordered the destruction of all records pertaining to slavery. Ostensibly this was done to make the nation forget that shameful period in its history. More likely, this measure was taken to prevent former slave owners from later seeking compensation based on those documents.

53. Antonil used these words to describe the importance of Negro slaves in the 17th century. See André João Antonil, *Cultura e opulencia do Brasil por suas drogas, e minas, com varias noticias curiosas do modo de fazer o assucar; plantar, & beneficiar o Tabaco; tirar ouro da minas; & descubrir as da Prata; E dos grandes emolumentos, que esta conquista da America Meridional dá ao Reyno de Portugal com estes, & outros generos, & Contractos Reaes* (Lisboa: Officina Real Deslandesiana, 1711), Livro I, Cap. 9, p. 22.

CHAPTER III

SLAVE LABOR IN THE SUGAR ESTATES

After 1550 and throughout the entire seventeenth century sugar and Penambuco were synonymous. But when was the precious sweetener brought to Brazil? As with the arrival of the first Negroes, there is great controversy over when and where sugar cane was first planted in the Portuguese colony. It has been said that sugar cane grew wild in Brazil when the Portuguese arrived, but that is rather unlikely, argues Luís da Câmara Cuscudo, who categorically dates the introduction of the *sacharum officinarum* in Pernambuco from 1503.[1] More conservative historians shy away from a specific date and simply state that sugar cane was introduced in Brazil with the first expeditions.[2] In any case, certainly by 1516, sugar cane was already planted in Brazil. An accepted testimony to this fact is the royal instruction of that year charging the *Casa da Índia* with the job of recruiting an expert in the manufacturing of sugar for the purpose of building an *engenho* in Brazil.[3] In order to justify such a project, an adequate supply of sugar cane must have been available in the colony at that time.

As to the site where sugar cane was first planted in Brazil, opinions are more or less divided according to regional lines:

89

Paulista historians say São Vicente, the captaincy of Martim Afonso de Sousa had the privilege; historians from the Northeast affirm that sugar cane was first planted in the fertile *várzeas*[4] of Pernambuco. The latter version is probably more accurate. It is known that sugar was already being made in Brazil by Pêro Capico between 1516 and 1526[5] and that the first sugar from Pernambuco and Itamaracá paid duties at the *Casa da Índia* in Lisbon in 1526.[6]

There is more agreement, however, regarding the origins of sugar cane and the place from where it was brought to Brazil. During the Middle Ages, sugar came "from the Orient and from the eastern Mediterranean through Venice, from Morocco, and after the sixteenth century from Sicily, even the Spanish region of Valencia."[7] When the Portuguese reached India they brought sugar cane to Portugal, and by the sixteenth century they had established plantations in the Azores, Cape Verde, Principe, Madeira and São Tomé islands. It was probably from the last two islands that the plant was brought to Brazil.

In Brazil, sugar cane was planted in all captaincies but was most successful in Pernambuco. In Duarte Coelho's captaincy, the *massapê*, a type of soil characterized by compact, viscous, reddish and black spots, rich in humus and clay, proved to be unsurpassed for growing the new plant.[8] With the encouragement of the *donatário*, the fertile lands of Pernambuco were soon covered with sugar cane, marking the development of plantation agriculture and carrying with it the evils of a destructive monoculture.

Of vital importance to the cultivation of sugar cane was an abundant supply of water. Accordingly, the *sesmarias*[9] granted by Duarte Coelho and his successors[10] for the planting of sugar cane were located in the *várzeas* or lowlands along the rivers and streams. Thus, Igarassú, Olinda, Beberibe, Casa-Forte, and Várzea were among the fist centers of cultivation. It was in these areas, and more particularly along the Várzea do Capibaribe, that the cultivation of sugar cane established itself and "the first Brazilian aristocracy [that of the] *senhores de engenho* planted its roots."[11]

It was in these lowlands along the rivers that the first sugar mills were established in Pernambuco.[12] The first *engenho* belonged to Jerônimo de Albuquerque and was built in 1542 in the proximity of the city of Olinda. It was powered by water and was named "Engenho Nossa Senhora da Ajuda."[13] From this time on, the sugar industry received great encouragement from Duarte Coelho and the Crown. the *donatário* often contracted with people in Portugal to come or send someone to build sugar mills in Pernambuco,[14] while the Crown initiated a number of measures to promote the industry. In the *Regimento* given to Tomé de Sousa in 1548, the king ordered the new governor to "take particular interest in the establishment of sugar factories along any rivers or water courses."[15] Persons who built sugar mills were exempted from paying taxes on them for a period of ten years. Among those who profited from the exemption were "the brothers Fernão, and Diogo Soares on behalf of the *engenho* Suassuna in Jaboatão, built in 1587."[16] As a result sugar mills multiplied rapidly. By the end of 1542 at least two mills were in operation.[17] By 1550, five *engenhos* were functioning in Pernambuco.[18] Twenty years later Pernambuco boasted twenty-three sugar mills.[19] Beginning in the last quarter of the sixteenth and through most of the seventeenth centuries, the exportation of sugar from Pernambuco experienced an unprecedented growth which coincided with the great expansion in the sugar industry itself. By 1618, the sugar produced in Pernambuco and the two captaincies of Itamaracá and Paraíba was enough to load each year "one-hundred and thirty or one-hundred and forty [ships] many of which [were] of very large size."[20] On the eve of the Dutch invasion, the tithes levied on the sugar exported from Pernambuco alone "were valued at between 70,000 and 80,000 cruzados by the Portuguese and at 1,050,000 florins by the Dutch."[21] During this period, the number of mills jumped from fifty in 1587,[22] to ninety in 1612,[23] to 150 in 1629 and to 246 by 1710.

The sugar mills of Pernambuco were of three general types. In the early days of the industry, sugar was made in small, hand operated mills known as *alçapremas*. More advanced than the *alçaprema* was the *trapiche*. These mills, like the "São João Salgado" In Ipojuca, "Santa Lúcia" in Santo Antônio do Cabo, and "São Paulo" in Muribeca[25] were limited production operations, usually located in small tracts of land and powered by oxen. More numerous and more productive were the water-driven mills. These were large factories capable of producing from nine to thirteen thousand *arrobas* of sugar a year,[26] located in sizeable tracts of land surrounded by numerous buildings and vast fields of cane, and known individually as *engenho*, or *engenho real*. This type of mill was of necessity located near a river, stream or other source of water. Because of their dependence on that source of energy for their operation, many *engenhos* were named after the river, stream, or simply the water from which they derived their power. Thus, *engenhos* such as "Lagoa-dos-Ramos-de-Baixo," "Pôço Comprido," "Vertente Grande," Cachoeira-de-Cima," "Riacho-do-Padre," "Alagoa-do-Meio," "Ribeiro-da-Pedra," "Cacimbas," "Pôço Sagrado," "Dois Rios," "Três Lagoas," "Várzea-do-Una," "Água Azul," "Água Comprida," "Água Fria," "Água Clara, "Águas Belas," and "Pedra d'Água," paid tribute to the source of their sustenance and, as Gilberto Freyre suggests, added an almost poetic flavor to the rural scenery of the Brazilian northeast.[27]

The establishment of a sugar plantation was a major undertaking requiring a large investment of capital.[28] Land was necessary for the cane fields[29] and to provide the firewood for the furnaces in the mill. The manufacturing end of the operation usually consisted of three buildings: the mill house, where the wheel and the mill with two or three presses was located, a boiler house, and a purging house. A considerable amount of heavy and costly equipment was required. The *engenho* "Apipucos," a medium size mill, had, in 1577, three boilers in its boiler house, 4,000 moulds and 600 cones in its purging house, and a large number of smaller copper utensils.[30] An adequate number of oxen and carts had to be kept for plowing, the transportation of cane from the fields to the mill, and of sugar to the market, or to the river for embarkation.

The most important part of any operation, however, was its labor force. Like other types of plantation agriculture during this time, sugar was entirely dependent upon the availability of an adequate supply of slave labor. The first slaves were, as we have seen, the Indians, but as they proved inept for the task they were gradually replaced by African slaves. At least twenty of these Negroes were needed for the operation of a small mill, or *engenhoca*.[31] A medium size factory required some sixty slaves,[32] and large mills, such as the "Suassuna" in Jaboatão, had one hundred or more slaves.[33]

The life of these Negro slaves in the sugar plantations of Pernambuco was a miserable one. So miserable in fact, as to

Slave Labor in the Sugar Estates

make André João Antonil's remark that Brazil was "hell for Negroes"[34] not so far fetched as it might seem. Those who worked in the fields or toiled in the manufacturing of sugar worked long hours and rarely had some free time for themselves. Even though slaves were, in theory, supposed to have the day off on Sundays and holidays to work their *roças* or small vegetable gardens, attend religious services and rest, repeated urging by contemporary chroniclers that this be observed is a good indication that such generosity was far from widely practiced.[35] One of those masters who made his slaves work their own *roças* was João Fernandes Vieira. In the instructions he wrote for the *feitor-mor*, or head-overseer of each of his plantations, Vieira directed them to make the Negroes work in their *roças* on holidays and also on Saturdays during the winter or off-season.[36] It can be accurately stated that few masters actually allowed their slaves any day off during the grinding season except, of course, for those not connected with production, such as domestic slaves and a few others. Among these exceptions we might find a so-called "*negro de banda forra.*" This was a slave who managed to pay the *senhor* as much as one half of the price of his freedom. He was allowed to have Sundays off to work for himself and usually had a small vegetable garden or planted some corn. Presumably this slave, if he worked hard enough, could somehow earn the rest of the money necessary to buy his freedom. There is no evidence indicating how frequently this was accomplished, but given existing conditions at the plantations it could only be rarely. During the Dutch occupation, slaves were also denied the free day on Sundays by their Dutch masters. Although the Dutch Political Council in Pernambuco prohibited work on Sunday since 1635, this law was scarcely obeyed in the plantations. In the cities, however, where the law could be more effectively enforced, slaves employed in urban occupations benefitted from this provision to a much greater extent.[37]

Work was especially arduous during the grinding season, which could last from six to nine months beginning usually in August or early September. During the season the mills operated continuously, twenty-four hours a day, seven days a week, grinding from twenty-five to thirty cartloads of cane each day.

The typical work day for those laboring in the fields lasted from dawn until all light had vanished on the horizon. During the summer months this meant as many as seventeen hours a day.

When the days were shorter slaves were sometimes given additional chores which they "could perform with artificial light"[38] in order not to remain idle. Adult males cut the cane while women tied the cane in bunches of twelve. Each adult slave was required to cut 350 bunches a day. In addition to their work in the field, women performed a number of domestic chores around the *senzala* or slave quarters.

For most slaves the day began with a routine head-count by the *feitor-mor*. After taking notice of any slave that might be sick or missing, the head overseer sent the others out to their daily tasks, not infrequently with the encouragement of the *bacalhau*, a strong whip made of twisted rawhide. By 5 a.m. the slaves were already at work either in the fields or at the mill. In most cases no meal was given the Negroes before they went to work,[40] but some carried secretly with them a piece of fish or some manioc flour. Besides these furtive snacks no food was consumed until the midday meal was distributed at 11 a.m.

The slave diet was both inadequate and lacking in variety. It consisted mainly of manioc flour usually eaten dry or mixed with water like a gruel. The richer and more benevolent masters gave their slaves manioc flour with a small piece of dried meat or salted fish for lunch. In the smaller plantations a ration of manioc flour alone was the usual. Whenever he could, the Negro tried to make up for the inadequacy of his diet by eating practically anything he could lay his hands on. Snakes, such as the *Guacú* and *Gibóia*, lizards of several kinds, and particularly a large winged ant were "much appreciated by the Negroes."[41] Also very much in demand were the different varieties of river crabs. Because of their abundance and because they were easy to catch, these crabs, especially a variety named *siri*, were a common item in the slave diet.[42] Fortunately for the slave, Pernambuco offered an assortment of fruits, such as papaya, mangoes, *cajú, pitanga*, guava, and others, which helped supply some, though far from all essential vitamins. Severe mineral deficiencies resulting from the poor diet were made apparent by the common practice of eating earth among the slaves. The consumption of substantial quantities over a period of time, and such was not infrequent, often led to the death of the slave. Eating earth was actually a disease, or a deficiency of mineral salts, particularly calcium. To prevent a slave from eating earth, masters and overseers made him wear a metal mask which prevented access to the mouth. Fugitive slaves were often found wearing the bizarre device. It is also believed that slaves afflicted with *banzo* or melancholy did sometimes resort to eating earth as a way to end their miseries.

There were masters who did not recognize any obligation to feed their slaves. Some of these masters gave their Negroes a free day (Sunday) each week to work in their *roças* and gather their food. Others made no such provision and simply left their slaves to fend for themselves. Masters who did not provide their slaves with a ration, miserable as it was, were, I believe, in the minority. There is little doubt, however, that the great majority of masters were more concerned with the diet and general welfare of their horses and oxen than with that of their slaves. João Fernandes Vieira, for instance, ordered his *feitores* to "take great care that the oxen that work one day do not work the next" in order that the work will be easier for them to bear.[43] When slaves were not provided with their sustenance they either starved or secured their food by stealing it from wherever they could. Horses were particularly vulnerable to this practice, being often stolen and killed to satisfy the slaves' appetite.[44]

Because most cane fields were far from the *senzala*, or slave quarters, lunch was usually prepared and eaten in the field in order to save time. After lunch, work was resumed by the slave gangs. Each gang worked under the watchful eyes of a *feitor*, or overseer. These, as well as the *feitor-da-moenda* (overseer of the mill), reported to the *feitor-mor*, or head-overseer, who was responsible for the entire operation. Male overseers supervised both male and female gangs. For the most part the *feitores* were white Portuguese and occasionally foreigners,[45] but Negroes and mulattoes, slaves and free, were also used. In many cases, Negro overseers were considerably harsher than their white counterparts.[46] Overseers' salaries varied from plantation to plantation. In an *engenho real*, overseers working in the fields could make as much as forty or forty-five thousand reis; a *feitor-de-moenda* received forty, or fifty thousand reis, and the *feitor-mor* was paid a salary of from 60,000[47] to 100,000 reis.[48]

As in other plantations, the overseers in the plantations of Pernambuco were instructed to force as much work out of the slaves as they possibly could. For this reason, the overseers gave the slaves no peace, and not infrequently worked them to exhaustion.⁴⁹ Little or no consideration was given to reducing the workload of those slaves who could not handle it such as those of advanced age, the sick, and even women in advanced stages of pregnancy.

At seven or eight in the evening, or whenever it got too dark to work in the fields, the slaves returned to the *senzala*. There they ate their evening meal which, like lunch, consisted of manioc flour gruel and a small piece of dried meat or salted fish.

For those toiling in the mill, work continued through the night, the slaves working in rotation twenty-four hours a day. The manufacturing process consisted of three basic stages. First, the grinding of the cane in the *casa-do-engenho*, or *moenda*, where the mill itself was located;⁵⁰ second, the skimming and the transformation of the cane juice into sugar crystals by heating in the *casa-das-caldeiras*, or boiler house, and the purging or further refining of the sugar in the *casa-de-purgar*, or purging house.

In the larger Brazilian mills at least seven or eight slaves, both men and women, were needed in the *casa-do-engenho*:

> three to bring in the cane; one to pass it [through the rollers of the mill]; another to pass the residue [or *bagaço*]; another to care for and light the *candeas*,⁵¹ of which there were five in the mill, and to clean the *côcho do caldo*⁵² ... and to clean and cool the gears of the mill with water to prevent overheating...; and finally another to throw away the residue [or straw] into the river or the *bagaceira*⁵³ where it was later burned. And if it was necessary to take the residue any farther one slave was not enough but another was required to help her, otherwise the removal of the residue was not done fast enough and the mill would be obstructed.⁵⁴

To supervise the work of the slaves and to make sure that the mill was maintained in proper operating condition a *feitor-de-moenda* and or a guard or watchman-of-the-mill were always on duty twenty-four hours a day.

The *casa-do-engenho*, or *moenda*, was the most dangerous place to work. After long hours of toil, an exhausted and sleepy slave feeding the cane into the rollers of the mill was prone to have his hand caught and his entire body dragged and crushed between the cylinders. So frequent were these accidents that practically

Slave Labor in the Sugar Estates

every *engenho* kept next to the mill a sharp machete with which to sever promptly the slave's hand or arm if necessary in order to save a life.

While the *casa-do-engenho* had the worst accident record, work in the *casa-das-caldeiras*, or boiler house, was the most strenuous. Here the cane juice brought from the mill was deposited in large cooper vessels placed atop furnaces or boilers and heated until it reached the desired thickness, the impurities being skimmed as they rose to the foamy head. The *melaço* (molasses) was moved successively to vessels of diminishing sizes until it changed into sugar crystals and was placed in a cold vessel and allowed to cool off.[55] In the seventeenth century, a large mill such as the "Engenho Tapicura" [sic] owned by Manuel Fernando Cruz, had eight[56] or more of these furnaces, each tended by a Negro called "*metedor de lenha*" who constantly nourished its fire with huge quantities of firewood.[57]

Near the furnaces the heat was so intense and the smoke so overpowering as to evoke the following image to the mind of a contemporary observer: "Prison of fire and perpetual smoke, and vivid image of the volcanoes, Vesuviuses, and Etnas, and [I] almost said, of Purgatory, or of Hell."[58] So arduous was the work of tending the furnace that it was reserved for the most miserable lot of slaves. Those afflicted with severe infectious diseases and advanced cases of syphilis were always preferred for the purpose. Ostensibly this was done so that the copious perspiration would purge their bodies from the ("*humores Gallicos*") disease. Closer examination, however, makes it clear that in reality, it suited the master better to condemn a sick slave to the unhealthful task of tending the furnaces than to expose a strong and healthy Negro to the debilitating rigors of the job. The undesirability of working the furnaces rather than its curative properties is further suggested by the fact that the job of *metedor de lenha*, or furnace tender, was also used as punishment for recalcitrant slaves. It was customary in Brazil to fasten these Negroes with long iron chains to a position in front of the furnace where they were expected to work a twelve-hour shift, feeding the fire or skimming the *melaço*, their disposition being stimulated by the frequent visitations of the whip.[59]

In addition to the furnace tenders, slaves such as the *tacheiros* and others, handled the *melaço* in the vessels and performed other minor chores around the so called "boiler house." But by far the most important job in the boiler house, and indeed in the entire *engenho*, was that of *mestre de açúcar*. The master was a person who, through many years of experience, could examine the melaço in the boiler house and determine the exact point when it had reached the desired thickness and quality. The quality, and to some extent the quantity, of sugar to be obtained from a certain amount of cane juice depended almost entirely on the master's experience and know-how. The *mestres de açúcar* were indispensable for the operation of the sugar mills; they were described by Cardim as the true *senhores de engenho*. They commanded considerable respect and received a salary of up to 100,000 reis in addition to other benefits.[60] The master worked during the day inspecting the heating and cleaning of the juice and supervising the moving of the *melaço* from vessel to vessel. In the evening he was relieved by the *banqueiro*, or *contramestre*, who served as his assistant and had the same duties as the master during the night shift. Both the master and the *banqueiro* were usually white men,[61] but a number of experienced slaves also served as *mestres de açúcar*.[62]

From the boiler house the sugar was taken to the *casa-de-purgar* for further refining. Here the sugar, placed in cone shaped vessels (with a hole in the bottom or narrow end) called *fôrmas*, was deposited on special shelves and allowed to rest for six to eight days. Then the sugar was further compressed into the fôrma and a layer of thin clay was spread over it through the top opening of the fôrma. The clay was then sprayed with water and allowed to sit for six days. After that, the first layer of clay was removed and the operation repeated a second, and sometimes a third, time. The moisture from the wet clay passing through the sugar gradually lightened its color until it became completely white.[63] Interestingly enough, this process was discovered by accident when one day a chicken with wet clay on its feet jumped onto a *fôrma* filled with sugar, leaving white footprints on the otherwise brownish sugar.[64] When the sugar was completely white it was removed from the *fôrma* and placed in the *balcão de secar*, or sun deck, where it was let to dry under the sun. The final stage was the packaging of the sugar in wooden boxes for shipment.

At least four slaves, either men and women, were required for the purging operation while several others were needed for the preparation of the clay and emptying of the vessels. In the *balcão de secar*, two experienced women known as "mothers of the *balcão*" were helped by as many as ten Negresses in handling the drying of the sugar. Packaging required an additional supply of slaves, the number varying according to the production of the mill. A *purgador*, usually a white man, supervised the entire purging operation; in his absence, this was done by the *mestre de açúcar*.

In addition to slaves doing manual labor and serving as overseers, and skilled workers such as the *purgador, banqueiro,* and *mestre de açúcar* the plantations of Pernambuco employed several other workers in many different capacities. These included brick-makers (usually Negro slaves), herdsmen, ironsmiths, and carpenters. These workers were usually whites,[65] mulattoes, *mestiços*, and Indians, but sometimes they were Negro slaves who had learned the trade.

Besides the field hands and those engaged in the production of sugar the *engenhos* of Pernambuco employed a large number of Negroes as domestic servants.[66] The women usually worked in the kitchen, cooking and baking or cleaning the Casa Grande, or plantation house. Others served as nannies and wet nurses to their masters' children while the younger ones served as playmates and companions to their young mistresses or *sinházinhas*. Male slaves took care of the heavier chores around the house, worked as waiters, butlers, and valets, served as footmen, and drove their masters' carriages. Young Negroes were the playmates and constant companions of their young white masters.[67] Because of the nature of their work, their direct contact with their owners, and, most important, because they had acquired habits and manners more acceptable to their white masters, these Negroes had a much easier life than their brothers and sisters in the refinery or in the fields.

In the Brazilian markets prices varied considerably according to supply and demand, which in turn was affected by variations in sugar prices, famines, smallpox epidemics, and the incidence of deaths among the slaves. Except for short periods of crisis,[68] however, African slaves were a very expensive commodity during the second half of the sixteenth century and even more so throughout the seventeenth.[69] In the last decade of the sixteenth century, Negro slaves "were valued [at] up to 40$ and none was appraised at less than 13$.[70] By comparison, Indian slaves could be bought at this time for as little as 1$ each and only if they had some special skill were they sold for higher prices.[71] By 1630, the going price of a slave in Pernambuco was from 1,400 to 1,500 escudos.[72] In 1642, slaves from Angola were sold for 300 patacas (96$000) "each peça" while the "little ones and the sick" sold for 280 patacas (89$600) each. Later that year some slaves were sold for as much as 100$000 each.[73] During the Dutch occupation of Pernambuco, particularly between 1637 and 1645, an average Negro sold for 200 to 300 florins. "When the Negroes were healthy, well built and strong the prices increased much more sometimes even to 600 and 800 florins."[74] In 1686, the price of a Negro slave dropped considerably, reaching a low of slightly over 64$000.[75] Downward fluctuations, however, were short lived. In 1703, African slaves were selling for 160$000 a head, and by 1718, their price was set at 300$000 each.[76]

In addition to supply and demand, other factors influenced the price of slaves. Among these were age, sex, physical condition, tribal origin, and special skills. A healthy, well built, strong male slave between the ages of eighteen and twenty-five, with most of his work life[77] ahead of him, obtained the highest prices in the Recife market.[78] Older slaves and single women were less desirable and therefore commanded a lower price. Youngsters aged from eight to fifteen (*molecão* (male), and *molecona* (female)) were sold for less, but with little difference in price between the sexes. Children aged eight or less as well as adults between 35 and 45, were valued as 1/2 *peça*. Infants would go with their mothers and did not count.[79] There is no indication if a mother with a new-born baby was worth more than a single woman.

As the characteristics, real or imaginary, attributed to particular tribal groups or slaves from certain African regions[80] became known, preferences for one type or another also affected the market price. Negroes from certain areas were preferred for their physique, their adaptability to hard work, or for their docility. Thus, during the seventeenth century the Bantu Angolas were the most in demand because they were hard working. The Ardras were less desirable because, with few exceptions, they were lazy, stubborn, dull, and rebellious.[81] Those from Calabar were even less esteemed than the Ardras because they were lazy, stupid, and negligent.[82] Slaves from Guinea, Sierra Leone, and Cape Verde were not nearly as suitable for hard work as the Angolas. But because of their attractive features, especially among the women,

Slave Labor in the Sugar Estates

cleanliness, and somewhat more "polished" manners, they were sought after by the Portuguese who employed them as domestic servants.

Special skills were also very much in demand and were, of course, eagerly promoted by the slave-traders. Negroes who had learned a trade such as carpenters, ironsmiths, or artisans, usually commanded a higher price. Slaves who had learned Portuguese (*ladinos*) and were more accustomed to the colonists' ways were in most cases preferred to those just arrived from Africa (*boçaes*). Needles to say, if a Negro who had learned the job of *mestre de açúcar* were put up for sale he would obtain the highest price the market could bear.

Even though he was considered an expensive and indispensable piece of equipment, the Negro slave did not receive the care and attention usually accorded an expensive animal or a costly piece of machinery. In fact, it must be asserted here that during most of the colonial period Negro slaves in the *engenhos* of Pernambuco, as well as other parts of Brazil, were treated with as much comtempt and cruelty as their counterparts in most other colonies of the New World. If they survived the crossing from Africa, the Negroes were taken to warehouses on the Rua dos Judeus or elsewhere, where they waited for auction day. On auction day,

> these poor people, half dead from hunger and thirst, were forced to crawl out of there as hogs or lambs exiting from the corral... [and taken] one by one to the market where Portuguese and Dutch traders examine them right and left, to determine if they are young or old, or afflicted with scurvy, syphilis or other serious illness.[83]

After a slave was bought he received as a welcoming gift to his new life at the *engenho*—the planter's initials or other identifying mark, affixed to his forehead, chest, shoulder, or other part of his body with a red-hot branding iron. Branding was used regardless of sex and age to mark the slave as property, as it was done with cattle, and for easier identification in the case of fugitive or stolen Negroes.[84]

With the exception of domestic servants, slaves worked under the supervision of an overseer. Because they were expected to make the slaves produce as much as possible, most overseers treated the Negroes with great cruelty. They forced them to work long hours in the fields, and in the strenuous tasks of the mill and boiler house, often driving them beyond the limits of their physical or emotional strength. When the Negroes faltered or collapsed from exhaustion they were whipped, or they were tied and beaten with a rod until they bled. The overseer made no concessions to age or sex and in his rage would strike man or woman, young and old with the same fury. Antonil, obviously having witnessed similar abuses, called on the masters never to allow the overseer to kick pregnant women in their stomachs.[85] Suffering from malnutrition, forced to toil long hours under miserable working conditions, susceptible to epidemics, and being frequently and severely punished, slaves soon became ill, and died in large numbers. In most cases, though by no means always, deaths were more frequent in the larger plantations or in those where the owner was absent.[86] Although there were a number of kind masters who treated their slaves well, these were clearly the exception.[87] Punishment as a rule was severe and dispensed with great frequency. Practically every known method, device or instrument used to punish and torture slaves was found in the sugar plantations of Pernambuco. In addition, some Portuguese and Brazilian masters devised techniques of their own, which on account of their cruelty would rival with the worst to be found in any plantation in any of the New World colonies.

The whip was used to keep the slaves working and also as an instrument of punishment. In the latter instance, the Negro was tied or chained to a post, or tied face down to the platform of an ox-cart, and whipped. In many cases, however, this was not enough to satisfy the masters. João Fernandes Vieira, certainly not to be counted among the worst masters, did not permit his overseers to beat his slaves with a rod, or to throw bricks at them (as others did). Instead, he instructed the overseers to punish the slave with a whip and

> after [the slave] is well whipped, have him pricked with a razor or a sharp knife. And [then rub the wounds] with salt, lemon juice, and urine and put him in chains for a few days.[88]

Vieira's female slaves were whipped indoors, being spared the humiliation of a public spectacle. When the number of lashes to

Slave Labor in the Sugar Estates

be given was so great as to threaten the life of the slave, the penalty was sometimes divided in *novenas* or *trezenas*. According to this system the Negro was given a certain number of lashes every day at the same time for the next nine or thirteen days.[89] To prevent the slave from screaming or uttering some curse against them while they were being whipped, some masters had a large piece of wood placed across the Negro's open mouth.

The *tronco* was also widely used in Pernambuco. This device, of which there were several varieties, was known in Cuba as *cêpo* (stock or pillory) and consisted of a rectangular wooden frame opened in half with four small openings for the slave's hands and feet, and sometimes a larger opening for the head. The halves were separated, the slave's limbs passed through the holes, and then the halves were again united and secured in place with a chain and lock. In this most uncomfortable position (sitting or lying down) the slave was forced to stay for days without food or water. In some cases, the Negro's misery was made worse by placing some food and water in front of him but not within his reach.

The metal mask, used primarily to prevent slaves from eating earth, was also used as punishment. Slaves who were inclined to drink to excess or to steal food were oftentimes forced to wear the mask so as to keep them from eating and drinking. This was a very handy device because it served its (actual though not corrective) purpose without interfering directly with the slave's work.

The hot branding iron used for identification was also used as punishment. As late as 1741, the king actually condoned this practice by ordering that fugitive slaves found in a *quilombo* voluntarily and for the first time be branded with the letter "F" on one of the shoulders. According to the same order, each slave captured in a *quilombo* a second time would have one of his ears cut off.[90]

Another instrument of torture was the *anginho*. This was the equivalent of the *vis-à-pression* used to punish slaves in the French and English colonies. In using this instrument, the victim's thumbs were placed in two rings which were gradually tightened until the thumbs were completely crushed. In Brazil, it was still being used by the authorities in the nineteenth century to extract information and confessions from fugitive slaves.

Rebellious slaves received the most severe punishment. By law, leaders of slave revolts received the death penalty. As early as

1573, seven Negroes were hanged by the authorities in Pernambuco for mutiny and for assaulting and robbing the residents.[91] Also by law, a slave who murdered his master, or the master's son or wife, or either his overseer or the overseer's wife was put to death. Needless to say, in the confines of the *engenhos* neither masters nor overseers waited for the encouragement or support of the law to avenge themselves. On one occasion, a Negro having confessed the murder of his master was summarily crushed alive in the mill.[92] Many Negroes were simply assassinated by their masters. A certification issued in Olinda in 1671 shows a number of Negro slaves killed by shotgun, sword, and stabbing with a knife.[93]

In addition to the whip, long chains and heavy iron collars were the most common instruments of punishment. Even though they were the lesser of many evils, chains and collars often caused open wounds around the slave's wrists, ankles, or neck and were a source of constant humiliation when they were worn.

Although a variety of cruel devices and methods were available to punish the slaves, some masters searched in the confines of their warped imaginations for even more inhuman ways of castigating their Negroes. There were masters who cut their slaves' ears or noses, broke their teeth, disfigured their faces, cut off their hands or feet, or even a Negress' breast. Castration, though not provided for by legislation as in the Spanish colonies, was by no means an uncommon form of punishment in the *engenhos* of Brazil. There were even cases of masters who went as far as destroying slaves by throwing them into the furnaces.[94] Other heartless masters punished their Negroes by burning them with drops of hot sealing wax and by touching their lips and their mouths with live coals.[95]

Domestic slaves, though by no means exempt from any of the above sufferings, were usually exposed to different kinds of punishment. The most common device used to discipline them was the *palmatória*. This was a heavy wooden disk, 1/2 an inch thick, with a diameter of about 4 1/2 inches, and attached to a long handle. Holding the *palmatória* by the handle the master, mistress, or in some cases an overseer, would strike the palm of the slave's hands. The strikes were called *bôlos* and were usually counted in dozens. This type of punishment was not only painful but among the most humiliating.

Degrading and humiliating the slaves was a way of life in many plantation houses. Whenever masters or mistresses were displeased with one of their servants, they called them names, made other injurious remarks, and cursed them. This, according to Jorge Benci, was so frequent in Brazil that from "dawn to dusk" it was difficult to hear anything other than insulting names and terrible curses around the Casa Grande.[96]

In one aspect, however, the domestic slaves, especially the women, were more vulnerable to their owner's fury than those working elsewhere. This occurred when an attractive young Negress became, as it was often the case, the object of her master's attentions. Once this was known, the usually innocent victim incurred the hatred of her jealous mistress and was oftentimes subjected to incredible atrocities. One well known story tells of a jealous wife who, enraged at her husband's praise of a young slave's beautiful eyes, ordered them gouged out with a knife and served them to her husband at dinner the next evening.

A detailed description of all the instruments of torture and methods of punishment could, and has filled the pages of at least one sizeable volume.[97] It will suffice to say here that during the seventeenth century abuses in the *engenhos* were so frequent that in 1688 the Crown, as a matter of conscience, made some effort to curb them. In two royal letters (March 20 and 23), the king ordered his royal governor to investigate reports of excessive cruelty on the part of the masters. Masters found guilty of cruelty were to be forced to sell their slaves and were to be prosecuted by the authorities. Unfortunately, the following year the king cancelled these instructions because of the problems that, according to the Governor, their enforcement would create.[98]

The slave's appearance often was another source of debasement and frequent humiliation. Few masters recognized any obligation to provide adequate clothing for their slaves. As a result most slaves, both male and female, were dressed in rags, and more frequently went around in nothing more than a loin cloth or short skirt wrapped around the waist. Young Negroes and sometimes adults walked about completely naked. Masters who denied their slaves clothing usually argued that they could not afford to clothe so many Negroes and Negresses. Although they gave them nothing to wear, some of these masters and mistresses expected their domestic slaves, especially the women, to be appropriately dressed. The Negresses were expected and even, in some cases, encouraged to obtain their clothing elsewhere. This they did by resorting to prostitution. So it was not uncommon to see a proud mistress followed by a number of young and attractive Negresses decked with jewelry and wearing dresses "so various in silks, and in colors, as were various the hands from [which they] were received."[99] Attractive female slaves were also in many cases showered with dresses and gifts by their own masters and even became their concubines. It could be argued that slaves in their wretched condition did not really resent their nudity. This is not true. Having to appear naked in front of other slaves or in front of the master or mistress, and not infrequently having to listen to remarks about their private parts was greatly resented by the Negroes. Sometimes male slaves, not having the success of the females, were driven to extremes in order to obtain the clothing with which to cover their nudity. On one occasion in Pernambuco, a Negro kidnapped an Indian from inside a monastery and took him to a cane field where he killed him for the sole purpose of stealing his clothes.[100]

The coming of the Dutch in 1630 did not significantly change the way the Portuguese masters treated their slaves. In the confines of the plantation, sugar was king, and so was the *senhor de engenho*. But how were the slaves treated by the Dutch invaders? In general it can be said that Dutch treatment of both the Indian and the Negro was better than that accorded them by the Portuguese colonists. From the very beginning of their Brazilian adventure, the Dutch made it a matter of policy that all peoples— Portuguese, Indians and others—found in Brazil should be respected and allowed to retain ownership of their land, houses, and sugar mills.[101] Although this was not always carried out to the letter, it set a pattern of racial tolerance which continued throughout the Dutch period.

This tolerance first manifested itself in relation to the Indians. From the outset, the West India Company prohibited in the "most categorical terms" the enslavement or forced labor of the natives. And, except for some abuses in the more remote areas such as Maranhão, this rule was generally followed. In addition the Dutch tried to deal with the Indians in an honest and humane way. Better treatment of the natives soon gave the Dutch a privileged position among them. Some Indians from Ceará for instance, begged Governor Maurits of Nassau to come and take the Portuguese fort in that area, and free them from the oppression in which they lived. Again, when the rebellion broke out in 1645, many Indians refused to fight against the Dutch. In a reply to Antonio Felipe Camarão, an Indian who commanded the natives siding with the Portuguese, Chief Pero Potí refused to join him and stated that: "we live [among the Dutch] more freely than any of you who remain under a nation that never concerned itself with anything but enslaving us."[102] Then Chief Potí emphasized his support of the Dutch by adding that "no one ever heard say that they have enslaved any Indian or kept him as such or that they have, at any time, assassinated or mistreated any of us."[103] In 1654, Father Antonio Vieira gave further testimony of this preference. Speaking of the Indians of the Amazon estuary he said that,

> they have conceived such hatred and aversion for the Portuguese nation that they wish to have neither peace nor trade with us whereas they usually have both with the nations of the North who frequent this region because they say that they find them more truthful and that their freedom is safe with them.[104]

Dutch attitudes towards the Negro were also more tolerant and more humane than those of the Portuguese.[105] Officially, one of the first acts of Nassau after he arrived in Recife was to curb the power of the masters over their slaves. The Count refused to return to their masters those slaves who left them to side with the Dutch during the war. Only those fugitives who escaped after their masters had sworn fidelity to the Dutch would be returned.[106] Although he allowed masters to continue punishing their slaves with the whip, the *tronco*, and the rod, penalties of branding, mutilation, or death could only be imposed after appropriate proceedings conducted by Dutch authorities. Work on Sundays was also prohibited.

As individuals, few Dutchmen became *senhores de engenho*. Those who bought *engenhos* lacked the inclination and the ability to run them well and had to rely on the Portuguese to manage their operations.[107] Some of them, after a brief trial period, sold their property and became merchants. Most of the Dutchmen who owned slaves, therefore, were city people who employed them as carriers, or in their stores, and as domestic servants, where work was not as demanding as in the plantation, and treatment was usually better.

As an economic system, slavery in the sugar plantations of Pernambuco was grossly inefficient. Despite all the prodding by the overseers, productivity was very low. Slaves in Pernambuco were reluctant workers and their labor, like that of slaves elsewhere, was characterized by carelesssness and wastefulness, as well as deliberate and calculated sabotage.

The average plantation required about fifty slaves.[108] Since slaves were very expensive, most of them had to be bought on credit. Because of the miserable working conditions, excessive punishment, and susceptibility to disease[109] many of these Negroes escaped or died within a short time. Deaths were so frequent during the "seasoning" period that many of the slaves perished before they were paid for.[110] The frequent depletion of the labor force necessitated that slaves be replaced immediately if the plantation was to continue in operation. In order to save the harvest or the capital already invested, sugar mill owners were forced to borrow money or to buy more slaves on credit paying as much as 2 1/2 to 4 percent interest per month.[111]

This created a vicious circle that placed even the apparently more prosperous planters further and further into debt. Gradually the income from the *engenhos* dwindled, compelling their owners to borrow more money to pay debts and taxes or else secure postponement of their collection from the king or royal governor. The documents of this period deplore the economic situation of the planters and abound with petitions from the *senhores de engenho* asking the authorities to postpone collection of the taxes because they could not afford to pay them. Thus in 1613, 1617, 1667, and again in 1677, the *senhores de engeho* of Pernambuco, following the example of those of Bahia (1610), asked the Governor for a moratorium on the collection of taxes, the second and third times (1617 and 1667) being on account of the great loss caused by smallpox epidemics.[112]

During the Dutch period the situation gradually worsened. After hostilities subsided, and in order to rebuild the sugar industry, the W.I.C. and local merchants began lending money, advancing supplies, and selling slaves on credit (the latter to be paid for in three years) to the sugar mill owners.[113] Due to the high price of Negroes, the low productivity of slave labor, and the high incidence of deaths among the slaves, history repeated itself. By 1640-41, as the Company's deficit was already up in the millions of florins, it became clear to the Dutch authorities that the planters were unable to pay their debts or even their taxes.

Even the more powerful planters, owners of several *engenhos*, were in financial difficulties. By 1642, the Company as well as other creditors were confiscating sugar, Negroes, and copper utensils from the mills in order to recover some of their money. To save their property from confiscation and to meet their creditors' demands, the planters were again forced to borrow money at very high interest rates. As this caused them to go deeper and deeper into debt and threatened the very survival of the sugar industry, a system of "contracts" was put into effect. The contract consisted of the Company's assuming each planter's debts to other creditors while debiting that amount from what those creditors owed the Company. In this manner, the planter consolidated all his debts into a larger one owed to the W.I.C. The Company, in turn, allowed each planter a rather extended period in which to pay his debt with the revenue from the *engenho* and charged him only 1 percent per month interest.[114] Owing to the problems mentioned above and those inherent in a slave economy, even these generous terms could not be met. Thus, through bribes and widespread corruption among Company officials the deadlines were extended, the loans refinanced, and even rebates given.[115]

Many benefitted from these arrangements. Jorge Homem Pinto, for instance, the owner of several mills had two contracts with the Company. The first, for 340,403 florins and nineteen stuyvers, was paid (or refinanced) in 1645. Then a second contract was made for a period of six years for the amount of 937,997 florins and nineteen stuyvers. Pinto's debt to the Company at this time exceeded his assets by 50 percent. The arrangement was said to have been secured with the help of a valuable gift to the Company's officials.[116] Jerônimo Cadena had a debt of 215,724 florins to be paid in three years, the first payment to be made in August, 1645.[117] Manuel Fernandes Cruz owed the Company 60,795 florins to be paid in three years, the first payment to be made on January 1645. João Lourenço Francês had a debt of 84.509 florins to be paid in the same manner. Of the four persons mentioned above the last three were considered bad risks because of their financial insolvency.[118] Among those receiving rebates on their taxes in 1641 we find Moysés Navarro (36,000 florins), and João Fernandes Vieira (38,000 florins), one of the leading figures in the revolt against the Dutch.[119]

It must be emphasized here that credit, originally intended as operational loans to be paid when sugar was made and sold, almost from the beginning had turned into a form of subsidy. Dependent as it was on slave labor and plagued by all the evils of a slave economy (low productivity, wastefulness, and a high incidence of deaths among the Negroes), the sugar industry of Pernambuco could not survive without continued subsidies. Despite the apparent prosperity of some of the planters, the sugar industry of Pernambuco was, during this period, largely insolvent.

The realization by the *senhores de engenho* that they could not do without the subsidy and that they could never pay off their debt to the W.I.C., was the single most important motive behind the revolt to expel the Dutch from northeast Brazil. It is no coincidence that the rebellion was planned in the *engenhos* of Pernambuco, began in the year when many planters were to start repaying their loans to the W.I.C. (1645), was quickly joined by most of those who owed the Company money, and had as its secret password, the word "sugar."

NOTES

1. Luís da Câmara Cascudo, "Universalidade do Sabor da Sacarose da Cana de Açúcar," *Sociologia do Açúcar* (Recife: Instituto do Açúcar e do Alcool, Museu do Açúcar, 1971), p. 27.
2. Magalhães, *O Açúcar*, p. 19.
3. Azevedo, *Épocas*, pp. 238-39; J. H. Rodrigues, *Brasil: Periodo Colonial*, p. 47; Câmara Cascudo, "Universalidade do Sabor da Sacarose...," p. 25.
4. Várzea - fertile low grassy land bordering rivers and streams.
5. Goulart, *Escravidão*, p. 97.
6. J. H. Rodrigues, *Brasil: Periodo Colonial*, p. 47; Magalhães, *O Açúcar*, p. 60; Goulart, *Escravidão*, p. 95; Câmara Cascudo, "Universalidade do Sabor da Sacarose," p. 25. There is no record of the existence of an *engenho* in Pernambuco at this time. This early sugar must have been made either by the primitive process of slashing the sugar cane with a machete and allowing the juice which ran out to crystalize by exposing it to the sun (see Pereira da Costa, "Origens Históricas," p. 257; Frei Vicente do Salvador, *História do Brasil 1500-1627*, 5th edition (São

Paulo: Edições Malhoramentos, 1965), p. 365), or by *alçapremas*, small mills operated by hand, and in use at the island of Madeira at this time (see Azevedo, *Epocas*, p. 220). The *alçapremas* were probably the equivalent of the *trapichillos a mano* used in Mexico and other Spanish colonies in the early days of the sugar industry.

7. Mauro, *Le Portugal et L'Atlantique*, p. 183.

8. For a very interesting, almost poetic description of the virtues of the massapê, see Gilberto Freyre, *Nordeste, aspectos da influência da cana sôbre a vida e a paisagem do Nordeste do Brasil*, 4a. Edição (Rio de Janeiro: Livraria José Olympio Editôra, 1967), pp. 7-10; Gaspar Barléu writing in the seventeenth century stated that the soil of Pernambuco was "second to none in the world in fertility." See *História*, p. 333; Otto Schmieder, "The Brazilian Culture Hearth," *University of California Publications in Geography*, Vol. 3, No. 3, August 1929, cited in Freyre, *Nordeste*, note 2 of chapter II, p. 37, testifies to the superiority of the Pernambuco soil over those of Cape Verde, Canaria, Valencia and India for the cultivation of sugar cane.

9. A *sesmaria* was a piece of land given by the king or his representative to a settler for cultivation.

10. According to the *Carta de Doação*, the *donatário* had the right to give *sesmarias* for the cultivation of sugar cane and to collect tribute, usually a percentage of the sugar produced. See *Carta de Doação*, BNRJ, códice I-5-2-4-no. 1.

11. Freyre, Nordeste, p. 24; *Senhor de engenho* was the title given to a sugar mill owner, the head of the family in the patriarchal sugar aristocracy. This title was even used by the king when referring to the sugar mill owners in his letters and decrees. See *Diálogos das Grandezas do Brasil*, 2ª edição integral segundo o apógrafo de Leiden, por José Antônio Gonsalves de Mello (Recife: Universidade Federal de Pernambuco, Imprensa Universitária, 1966), p. 10

12. Even though the first sugar made in Brazil came from Itamaracá and Pernambuco, the first actual sugar mill was built in the captaincy of São Vicente. In 1532, Martim Afonso, the *donatário* of that captaincy, formed a partnership with a Dutchman Erasmus Schetz to build the "Engenho dos Erasmos." See Calmon, *História*, pp. 25-26. In 1533, there was a sugar mill in São Vicente named "Engenho do Governador" (probably the same mill), the first in Brazil according to Azevedo. See *Épocas*, p. 243. According to Mauro, the first mill was one belonging to Martim Afonso built in 1533 in São Vicente, not far from the present city of Santos. See *Le Portugal et L'Atlantique*, p. 192.

13. This *engenho* is probably the one referred to by Duarte Coelho in his letter of 1542 as being under construction and nearing completion. See Carta de *Duarte Coelho a D. João III* (Olinda, 27 de Abril de 1542),

BNRJ, códice I-31-20-4; also J. H. Rodrigues, *Brasil: Periodo Colonial*, p. 47; Mauro, *Le Portugal et L'Atlantique*, p. 192; Freyre, *Nordeste*, p. 20; J. A. Gonsalves de Mello, also makes reference to this engenho in the introduction to Adriaen van der Dussen, *Relatório sôbre as capitanias conquistadas no Brasil pelos holandeses (1639) Suas condições econômicas e sociais*, Tradução, introdução e notas de José Antonio Gonsalves de Mello, neto (Rio de Janeiro: Instituto do Açúcar e do Álcool, 1947), p. 18.

14. "Carta de Duarte Coelho a El-Rey" (Olinda, 15 de abril de 1549) in Duarte Coelho, *Cartas*, pp. 67 and 71.

15. Silva Rêgo, *Portuguese Colonization*, p. 87.

16. Pereira da Costa, "Origens Históricas," p. 267; also *Diálogos das Grandezas do Brasil*, p. 78. After the expulsion of the Dutch from Pernambuco, and in order to rebuild the sugar industry from the ashes of war, the same exemption privilege (10 years) was granted to those who rebuilt their mills or constructed new ones. Captain André de Barros Rego, having rebuilt his *engenho* "São João" located in São Lourenço, Pernambuco, was one of the many who applied for this benefit. See AHU Consulta do Conselho Ultramarino (27 de janeiro de 1679), Documentos referentes a Pernambuco, caixa 35. The Crown was also interested in seeing to it that Brazilian sugar was of the finest quality. The king's High Treasurer was to make sure that quality control was enforced in each of the captaincies. See "Traslado do Regimento do Provedor-mor da Fazenda d'El-Rey Nosso Senhor destas partes do Brasil," *Documentos Históricos, Biblioteca Nacional do Rio de Janeiro*, Vol. 13, p. 191; also "Traslado do Regimento dos Provedores das Capitanias de todo o Estado do Brasil de como hão de servir," *Ibid.*, p. 55.

17. Carta de *Duarte Coelho a D. João III* (Olinda, 27 de abril de 1542), BNRJ, códice I-31-20-4.

18. "Carta de Duarte Coelho a El-Rey" (Olinda, 24 de novembro de 1550), in Duarte Coelho, *Cartas*, p. 83.

19. Gandavo, *História (Treatise on the Land of Brazil)*, p. 132.

20. *Diálogos das Grandezas do Brasil*, p. 77.

21. Boxer, *The Dutch in Brazil*, p. 32.

22. Soares de Sousa, *Tratado Descritivo do Brasil*, p. 29; Father José de Anchieta estimated the number of mills in Pernambuco at 66 in 1585. See Mauro, *Le Portugal et L'Atlantique*, p. 193.

23. Sluiter, "Report on the State of Brazil 1612," p. 548. Wätjen estimates the number of mills in Pernambuco at 120 in 1600. See *O Dominio Colonial*, p. 417.

24. Mauro, *Le Portugal et L'Atlantique*, p. 193.

Slave Labor in the Sugar Estates 113

25. van der Dussen, *Relatório sôbre as capitanias* conquistadas, pp. 33, 34, 45.

26. *Diálogos das Grandezas do Brasil*, p. 86. One arroba was equal to from 25 to 32 pounds depending on the region.

27. Freyre, *Nordeste*, p. 26. Testifying to the deep religious feelings of their owners, or simply for good luck, many engenhos were named after favorite saints, or had their chapels "dedicated" (invocação) to a patron saint. Thus we have in Ipojuca: "Sibiró de Baixo invocação de São Paulo," "Bom Jesus," "Nossa Senhora do Rosário," "Nossa Senhora da Conceição;" in Cabo: "São Braz Coimbero," and "Nossa Senhora das Candeias;" in Jaboatão: "Nossa Senhora da Apresentação," "Nossa Senhora da Conceição," "Sant' Ana," and "Nossa Senhora da Guia;" in Muribeca: "Santo André," "São José," and "São Bartolomeu;" in Várzea: "São Sebastião," "São Timóteo," "Santa Madalena," "São Jerônimo," "Santo Antônio," "São Tomé;" in São Lourenço: "São Bento," "Nossa Senhora de Monserrate;" in Serinhaém: "Todos os Santos," "Nossa Senhora da Palma" and "Nossa Senhora do Rosário;" in Pôrto Calvo: "Santo Antônio" and "São Francisco;" in Alagoas (during this period the present state of Alagoas was part of the captaincy of Pernambuco): "Nossa Senhora da Ajuda" and "Nossa Senhora da Encarnação;" in Alagoas do Sul: "Engenho Novo-Nossa Senhora do Rosário" and "São Miguel," to name only a few. See van der Dussen, *Relatório das capitanias conquistadas*, pp. 31-62; Freyre, *Nordeste*, p. 25.

28. The author of the *Diálogos das Grandezas do Brasil*, estimated in 1618, that an investment of "around ten thousand cruzados" was necessary for the establishment of a sugar mill. See p. 84. *Cruzado* was a Portuguese coin worth 400 *reis* in 1517. "During the seventeenth century the *cruzado* was roughly valued at four shillings (English). See Boxer, *The Portuguese Seaborne Empire*, p. 389.

29. Many plantations rented out some of their land to *lavradores* who agreed to plant cane and, at harvest time, deliver a certain number of *tarefas* to the mill. "Each *tarefa* represents [the amount of cane] that a mill can grind in one day and one night, that is, in an ox-driven mill between 25 and 35 carts of cane and in a water-driven mill between 40 and 50 carts." The sugar produced was divided between the *senhor do engenho* and the *lavrador*, according to contract provisions. Usually 1/3 to the *lavrador* and 2/3 to the *senhor* or 2/5 for the *lavrador*, and 2/3 for the *senhor*. Independent *lavradores* who owned their own land also planted cane for the sugar mills. In this case the division of the sugar produced was normally on a fifty-fifty basis. See van der Dussen, *Relatório sôbre as capitanias conquistadas*, p. 93.

30. "Certidão de 7 de Dezembro de 1847 da escritura de compra e venda do engenho Apipucos lavrada em 5 de Dezembro de 1577," *Revista do Museu do Açúcar*, Vol. I, No 7 (Recife: 1972), p. 86.
31. Boxer, *The Dutch in Brazil*, p. 32.
32. "Apipucos" had (in 1577) sixty slaves, "fifteen from Guinea and forty-five da Terra." See "Certidão," p. 86.
33. Pereira da Costa, *Anais*, 1:583; Large numbers of slaves were required in part because productivity under most slave systems was low. As Genovese pointed out, slaves were reluctant workers and could only be made to work efficiently under close supervision. For most planters the cost of such supervision was prohibitive. See Eugene D. Genovese, *The Political Economy of Slavery*. Studies in the Economy and Society of the Slave South (New York: Pantheon Books, 1965) p. 26.
34. Antonil, *Cultura e Opulência do Brasil*, Livro I, p. 24.
35. Jorge Benci, S. J., *Economia Cristã dos Senhores no Governo dos Escravos (Livro Brasileiro de 1700)*, 2a. ediçao, preparada e prefaciada por Serafim Leite, S. J. (Pôrto: Livraria Apostolado da Imprensa, 1954), pp. 38 and 135; Antonil, *Cultura e Opulência do Brasil*, Livro I, pp. 24-25; also Perdigão Malheiros, *A Escravidão*, Tomo II, Part 3, pp. 29-30.
36. José Antônio Gonsalves de Mello, "Un Regimento de Feitor-Mor de Engenho, de 1663," *Boletim do Instituto Joaquim Nabuco de Pesquisas Sociais*, Vol. 2 (Recife: 1953), p. 83.
37. Mello, *Tempo dos Flamengos*, pp. 221-222.
38. Waldemar Valente, "Tratamento do escravo africano no Brasil," *Antropologia do Açúcar* (Recife: Museu do Açúcar, 1972), p. 82.
39. The slave system, as Engerman points out, increased the role of women and children in the work force. See "Comments on the Study of Race and Slavery," p. 523.
40. During the off season some masters gave their slaves a "breakfast" ration consisting of the foam, or head of the fermented cane juice, or molasses.
41. Joan Nieuhof, *Memorável Viagem Marítima e Terrestre ao Brasil*. Tradução do Inglês por Moacir N. Vasconcellos, confronto com a edição holandesa de 1682, introdução, notas, critica bibliográfica e bibliografia por José Honório Rodrigues (São Paulo: Livraria Martins, 1942), pp. 32, 34, 35.
42. When they had time, slaves could fish in the rivers nearby. Few masters, however, even the more benevolent, permitted their slaves to fish in the plantation's pond. See Rodrigues de Carvalho, "Aspectos da influência africana na formacão social do Brasil," *Novos Estudos Afro-Brasileiros* (Rio de Janeiro: Civilização Brasileira Editôra, 1937), p. 29.

43. Mello, "Um Regimento de Feitor-Mor," p. 84; Benci, *Economia Cristã*, pp. 35-36; Freyre, *Nordeste*, pp. 66-67; Antonil, *Cultura e Opulência do Brasil*, Livro I, p. 26.

44. *Diálogos das Grandezas do Brasil*, p. 170.

45. A Florentine, André de Veneza, worked at one time as *feitor* in the *engenho* owned by Francisco Lopes Brandão. See "Memorial de todos os estrangeiros que vivem nas capitanias do Rio Grande, Paraíba, Itamaracá, Pernambuco e Bahia, dos quais se não pode ter suspeita. Enviado pelo governador D. Luís de Sousa a Sua Magestade (1618)," in *Livro Primeiro do Govêrno do Brasil*, p. 185.

46. Robert Southey, *History of Brazil*, 3 vols. (London: Longman, Hurst, Rees, Orme, and Brown, 1817-1822), 3:782-83; J. A. Goulart, *Da Palmatória ao Patíbulo (Castigos de Escravos no Brasil)* (Rio de Janeiro: Coleção Temas Brasileiros, Conquista, 1971) p. 90.

47. Antonil, *Cultura e Opulência do Brasil*, Livro I, p. 17. Reis (plural of *real*) was "a small Portuguese copper coin of low value which was abolished in the sixteenth century, but its multiples were retained to use as money of account." See Boxer, *The Portuguese Seaborne Empire*, p. 393; 4,000 reis were worth 27s. 6d., in 1720, *Ibid.*, p. 391.

48. In some cases the *feitor-mor* also received payment in kind in addition to his salary, such as a certain amount of wine and meat each week. See Mauro, *Le Portugal et L'Atlantique*, p. 214. There is no indication as to whether slaves serving as *feitores* in the fields received the stipulated salary or some kind of a bonus.

49. See Mello, "Un Regimento de Feitor-Mor," p. 83.

50. For a description of a typical mill mechanism used throughout Brazil, see Antonil, *Cultura e Opulência do Brasil*, Livro II, pp. 47-52. For a detailed description of the manufacturing of sugar in Brazil and other parts of the Western Hemisphere see Edmund O. von Lippmann, *História do Açúcar*, Trans. by Rodolfo Coutinho, 2 vols. (Rio de Janeiro, n. p., 1941), Vol. 2, Part XI, pp. 101-146.

51. A *candea* was a small oil lamp.

52. A receptacle, usually made of a dug out log, used to catch the cane juice as it came out of the mill.

53. *Bagaceira* was the ground near the mill where the *bagaço* (or cane residue) was deposited after the grinding. Often associated in literature with the sugar plantation "culture."

54. Antonil, *Cultura e Opulência do Brasil*, Livro II, pp. 54-55.

55. van der Dussen, *Relatório sôbre as capitanias conquistadas*, p. 94.

56. José Honório Rodrigues suggests that this mill, which was located in the district of Serinhaém, was either the "Itapicurú de Cima," or "Itapicurú de Baixo." See Nieuhof, *Memorável Viagem*, pp. 86-87.

57. The amount of wood burned in fires like these, caused the admiration of contemporary chroniclers. Antonil, commented that only Brazil with its vast wooded lands could have possibly satiated the appetite of the many furnaces of the *engenhos* of Pernambuco, Bahia, and Rio de Janeiro. See *Cultura e Opulência do Brasil*, Livro II, pp. 59-60. Such enormous consumption of wood unfortunately led to the devastation of many valuable forests located in the proximity of these sugar mills.

58. *Ibid.*, p. 59. The Vesuvius is an active volcano in Western Italy, near Naples. In A.D. 79, an eruption of the Vesuvius destroyed the ancient city of Pompeii, located 14 miles southeast of Naples. The Etna, the highest active volcano in Europe, is located in Eastern Sicily.

59. During the grinding season, the mill operated twenty-four hours a day, and slaves working in the manufacturing process worked in two twelve-hour shifts.

60. Cardim, *Tratado*, p. 321.

61. Boxer, *The Dutch in Brazil*, p. 143.

62. Manuel Diégues Júnior, *O Banguê nas Alagoas traços da influência do sistema econômico do engenho de açúcar na vida e na cultura regional* (Rio de Janeiro: Edição do Instituto do Açúcar e do Alcool, 1949), pp. 147, 151.

63. van der Dussen, *Relatório sôbre as capitanias conquistadas*, p. 95.

64. Fray Vicente do Salvador, *História do Brasil*, p. 366; *Diálogos das Grandezas do Brasil*, p. 86.

65. In addition to the Portuguese and Dutch, other Europeans worked in some of these occupations. An Italian from Naples worked as a cowboy at the "Engenho Velho da Conceição" towards the end of the sixteenth century (See José Antônio Gonsalves de Mello, ed. *Confissões de Pernambuco, 1594-1595; primeira visitação do Santo Ofício às partes do Brasil* (Recife: Universidade Federal de Pernambuco, 1970), p. 12), while a Florentine worked as a carpenter in another *engenho* during the first decade of the seventeenth century. See "Memorial de tôdos os estrangeiros," p. 185.

66. As late as in the last decade of the sixteenth century, Indians also worked as domestic slaves. (See Mello, *Confissões de Pernambuco*, pp. 11-12.) Gradually however, they were replaced by African slaves, in and outside the Casa Grande.

67. For the best treatment of the role of the domestic slave in the Casa Grande, and his or her contribution to the formation of Brazilian society, see Freyre, *Casa Grande & Senzala*, Vol. II.

68. A problem arose in 1644 when the Dutch W.I.C. ordered that Negroes brought from Angola be sold for ready cash or sugar only.

Because the *senhores de engenho* could only afford to buy their Negroes on credit there were no sales, and the price of slaves came crashing down to between thirty and fifty patacas a head. Finding itself with a surplus of Negroes the Company was ordered by the Heeren XIX, to sell in installments. See Nieuhof, *Memorável Viagem*, p. 329; also Boxer, *The Dutch in Brazil*, p. 139.

69. Concern with the high prices of Negroes lasted throughout the entire colonial period and led to calls for the formation of Portuguese Companies which would have a monopoly over the trade and hopefully sell the slaves at lower prices. The Companies were created but the lower prices did not materialize. See *Arquivo Nacional da Tôrre do Tombo* (Lisboa), "Projecto para formação de uma Companhia para fazer com monopolio o commercio em Africa principalmente o contrato dos negros" (undated), Manuscritos do Brasil, Livro 1096, fls, 38-40.

70. Mello, *Confissões de Pernambuco*, p. 11; 40$ is equal to 40,000 reis, or 40$000.

71. *Ibid.*

72. Pereira da Costa, *Anais*, 2:419.

73. Calado, *O Valeroso Lucideno*, 1:265. *"Peça"* here can be taken to mean one adult slave. The figures in thousands of reis are from Pereira da Costa, *Anais*, 2:421.

74. Wätjen, *O Dominio Colonial*, p. 487.

75. Pereira da Costa, *Anais*, 2:421.

76. Perdigão Malheiros, *A Escravidão*, Vol. 2, Part 3, p. 36.

77. It has been estimated that the "effective life of each slave was limited to 7 years." See Goulart, *Escravidão*, p. 97.

78. This was a slave at his prime, or a *"peça," "boa peça,"* or *"peça das Índias."* See Mauro, *Le Portugal et L'Atlantique*, p. 173. During the seventeenth century and as late as 1821, the Rua dos Judeus (Jews' street) later called Rua da Cruz (Cross street), today Rua do Bom Jesus (Good Jesus street) was the center of the slave trade in Recife. During the Dutch rule, the Jews, thanks to the leniency of Nassau, were engaged in a variety of commercial activities and above all, in the buying and selling of African slaves. See Joaquim Cardozo, "Observações em tôrno da história da cidade do Recife, no período holandês," *Revista do Serviço do Patrimonio Histórico e Artístico Nacional*, No. 4 (Rio de Janeiro: Ministério da Educação e Saude, 1940), pp. 390-396.

79. Mauro, *Le Portugal et L'Atlantique*, p. 173.

80. "Neither the Dutch nor Portuguese slave-traders could distinguish between the numerous tribes from which the West African slaves were drawn, but they grouped them into four main divisions named after the respective coastal districts where they were secured. These were the Ardras, Minas, and Calabares from Upper Guinea,

and the Angolas from the Congo and Angola." Boxer, *The Dutch in Brazil*, pp. 137-38.

81. "Breve Discurso Sôbre o Estado das Quatro Capitanias Conquistadas," pp. 171-172; Barleu, *História*, p. 133.

82. "Negligence," or deliberate carelessness was sometimes used by slaves as a form of resistance or sabotage. See Chapter V.

83. The description is by Zacharias Wagner, cited in Mello, *Tempo dos Flamengos*, p. 212.

84. Young slaves aged 10 to 12 were already acquainted with the branding iron. See J. A. Goulart, *Da Palmatória ao Patíbulo*, p. 68.

85. Antonil, *Cultura e Opulência do Brasil*, Livro I, p. 15.

86. Some absent masters required their overseers to account for all deaths by reporting on how and why each slave died. The same was to be done for each ox that died. See Mello, "Um Regimento de Feitor-Mor," p. 86.

87. Slaves owned by religious orders were usually treated with considerably more humanity. The Benedictines for instance, who owned sugar mills and had a large number of slaves, were kind.

88. Mello, "Um Regimento de Feitor-Mor," p. 83.

89. J. A. Goulart, *Da Palmatória ao Patíbulo*, p. 94. Benci was not entirely against flogging, but recommended moderation: "thirty or forty [lashes] today" and the same dosage every other day until the total desired was reached. See, *Economia Cristã*, p. 145. According to Vilhena, in the sugar mills of Bahia, a slave found guilty of stealing would receive at least 200 lashes on the buttocks. Luis dos Santos Vilhena, *Cartas Soteropolitanas e Brasílicas*, cited in J. A. Goulart, *op. cit.*, p. 99. When all lashes were given on a single occasion, it was not uncommon for the slave to die. See AHU, Certificação de Antônio Soares, tabelião público de Olinda (10 de Agôsto de 1671), Documentos Referentes a Pernambuco, caixa 6;

90. On November, 1813, the Prince Regent D. João, prohibited the use of the iron for identification purposes and ordered that in its stead slaves should wear a collar bearing the necessary identification. As it was often the case, the order was apparently not complied with in Brazil because newspaper ads published 13 years later described fugitive youngsters as being marked by the branding iron. Luis, a youngster aged 10 to 12, had the initials FMP on his chest. Another youngster aged 11 to 12 was marked with the letters N and B. See J. A. Goulart, *Da Palmatória ao Patíbulo*, pp. 67-68, 161.

91. "Historia de la fundacíon del colegio de la capitania de Pernambuco," *Anais da Biblioteca Nacional do Rio de Janeiro*, Vol. 49 (1927), p. 23. (Hereafter cited as ABNRJ.)

92. Nieuhof, *Memorável Viagem*, p. 309.

93. AHU, Certificação de Antônio Soares, tabelião público de Olinda (10 de Agôsto de 1671), Documentos Referentes a Pernambuco, caixa 6.
94. Benci, *Conômia Cristã*, p 139.
95. *Ibid.*, p. 136.
96. Benci, *Econômia Cristã*, pp. 125-27; also see Boxer, "Negro Slavery in Brazil," p. 43.
97. For the most complete study on this topic see J. A. Goulart, *Da Palmatória ao Patíbulo*.
98. See Royal Letters of March 20 and 23, 1688, and Royal Letter dated February 23, 1689, in J. A. Goulart, *Da Palmatória ao Patíbulo*, pp. 186-87.
99. Benci, *Econômia Cristã*, pp. 48-51; Antonil also makes reference to prostitution of slaves. See *Cultura e Opulência do Brasil*, Livro I, p. 24.
100. AHU Carta do Governador Fernão de Souza Coutinho ao Rei (1° de junho de 1671), Documentos Referentes a Pernambuco, caixa 6.
101. Algemeen Rijksarchief (The Hague), Acte van de Staten-Generaal in Zake Brasilië (16 mei 1625) West Indische Compagnie, Oude Compagnie.
102. Pereira da Costa, *Anais*, 3:243.
103. *Ibid.*
104. Cited in Boxer, *The Dutch in Brazil*, p. 136.
105. According to Boxer, this was also true in Angola "where the Portuguese admitted that the Dutch treated the Negroes (other than slaves) far more kindly than they did themselves." Letter of Bento Teixeira de Saldanha, Luanda, 10 April, 1653, cited in Boxer, *The Dutch in Brazil*, p. 137, and *Salvador de Sá*, p. 270.
106. Barleu, *História*, p. 52. Among the Negroes and mulattoes who fought with the Dutch and served as their spies and guides, the most famous was the mulatto Domingos Fernandes Calabar. Calabar deserted from the Portuguese forces and guided the Dutch to the enemy's most vulnerable points becoming one of the most valuable collaborators of the Dutch. He was later captured and killed by the Portuguese. At the request of Calabar's wife, and in gratitude for the "great services rendered the Company" the Dutch Political Council granted a pension of 8 florins a month for each of Calabar's three sons. Dagelijkche Notule, April 13, 1636, cited in Mello, *Tempo dos Flamengos*, p. 206.
107. The superior ability of the Portuguese in caring for the cane fields, and particularly in getting the Negroes to work was recognized by van der Dussen. See *Relatório sôbre as capitanias conquistadas*, p. 86.

108. Dom Diogo de Menezes to the King (Olinda, August 23, 1608), ABNRJ, Vol. 57 (1935), p. 39.

109. Smallpox epidemics did, from time to time, wipe out large numbers of slaves accounting for considerable fluctuation in death rates over the years.

110. Dom Diogo de Menezes to the King (Bahia, May 8, 1610), ABNRJ, Vol. 57 (1935), p. 67; ANTT Discurso dos generos para o comercio que há no Maranhao e Pará. Composto por Duarte Ribeiro de Macedo (1633), Manuscritos do Brazil, No. 39.

111. Nieuhof, *Memorável Viagem*, p. 80; Barleu, *História*, p. 336.

112. "Requerimento da Câmara de Olinda em nome dos moradores da Capitania de Pernambuco, lavradores e senhores de engenho ao Governador D. Luís de Sousa..." *Livro Primeiro do Govêrno do Brasil*, p. 147. The *senhores de engenho* in Bahia had asked the Crown for a three years moratorium. See Dom Diogo de Menezes to the King (Bahia, May 8, 1610), ABNRJ, Vol. 57 (1935), p. 67; AHU, Consulta do Conselho Ultramarino (Lisboa, 10 de janeiro de 1667), códice 16, fols. 219-219v. In 1664, the residents of Pernambuco sent more than two hundred and twelve boxes of sugar and some tobacco as their contribution to the dowry of the Queen of England, and the Peace with Holland. This however represented only a little over one-fifth of the amount required of them. In a letter concerning the shipment, the Assembly of Pernambuco stated that it was impossible to obtain the total required (the equivalent of 25 *contos*; one conto was worth 1 million reis) because of the miserable condition of the people at that time. See AHU, Carta da Câmara de Pernambuco ao Rei (20 de agôsto de 1664), Documentos Referentes a Pernambuco, caixa 5. This coincided with a serious smallpox epidemic which began in 1664 and lingered on until 1666, killing a large number of Negroes. See AHU, Consulta do Conselho Ultramarino (Lisboa 28 de junho de 1677), Documentos Referentes a Pernambuco, caixa 35.

113. Nieuhof, *Memorável Viagem*, p. 82. This sale of Negroes was labelled "true slave loans" by the author of "O Machadão do Brazil," trans. by A. Souto Maior in RIAGP Vol. 13, No. 71 (Recife, March 1908), p. 163.

114. Nieuhof, *Memorável Viagem*, p. 89

115. For a detailed description of the economic problems afflicting Dutch Brazil and the corruption of W.I.C. officials, see "O Machadão do Brasil," pp. 125-70, and "A Bolsa do Brasil," Trans. by José Higyno Duarte Pereira, in RIAGP, Vol. 4, No. 28 (Recife, January-March, 1883), pp. 127-167.

116. "A Bolsa do Brasil," p. 141.

117. *Ibid.*, p. 143. Cadena was one of the leaders in the rebellion against the Dutch in Paraíba.
118. *Ibid.*
119. *Ibid.*, p. 149.

CHAPTER IV

SOCIAL AND CULTURAL LIFE AT THE PLANTATION

The *engenhos* of Pernambuco were largely self-sufficient and independent entities with an economic, social, and cultural structure of their own. "Apipucos," "Mussurepe," "Tapicura," and "Suassuna," for example,, produced practically everything they needed for their operation. In addition to their cane fields, large mills had an area of about eight square miles or more, divided into pasture and woodland. On this pasture, cattle were raised to power the mills when necessary and to pull the carts. The thicket or woodland furnished the vast supply of wood to feed the demanding furnaces at the boiler house. Many mills had small shops where equipment was repaired and carpentry and ironsmithing were done. Some *engenhos* also had an *olaria*, or shop where bricks, tiles and *fôrmas* (cones) were made out of clay.

Food, though it could be obtained locally was, according to Freyre, usually of low quality and nutritional value. Manioc, which replaced wheat—since the climate was not favorable for the cultivation of the latter—and vegetables, were cultivated erratically by Indians and Negroes. Fruits, though many grew wild in the lands of the plantation, were usually hit by the birds, or eaten by worms before they made it to the planters' tables. Cattle were too expensive and too important for the work of the mill to be eaten regularly. So meat, as well as milk and poultry, was not common in most planters' diets. Fishing in the rivers nearby and sometimes in the ocean provided a little variety to both the master's and the slave's diets.

Some of the larger *engenhos* had several buildings and housed within their boundaries populations of from 150 to 250 people. At the turn of the seventeenth century the "Engenho Santiago de Camaragibe" and the "Casa Forte," for instance, must have looked like small villages with their mill houses, purging houses, olarias, the houses of the *lavradores*, the *senzalas* or slave quarters, their small churches and their owners' houses or casas grandes built in the form of a tower or fortress.

Each *engenho* was a small separate world, in which life rotated around the triangle formed by the mill, casa grande, and the chapel. The mill provided a livelihood for the master and his family and a miserable existence and early death for the slaves. The casa grande was the center of the plantation system where the master sat as the supreme arbiter and unchallenged dispenser of all justice; the chapel, found in practically every *engenho*, provided a spiritual outlet for the master's family and represented the presence of God, though most frequently God and the master were one and the same, riding proudly on a horse and carrying a whip.

In the plantation the master's will was supreme and, except for the payment of taxes (*dízimos*) on the sugar produced, his authority bowed to no law or royal decree. In fact, it was often the Crown or its representatives who backed down fearing the reaction of the powerful planters.[1] The master determined the economic and social order of the plantation. In his all-powerful capacity he had complete control over the lives of all those who resided within the boundaries of his property. In the case of slaves he determined not only where and how they were to live, but also how they dressed, who they married, if they married at all, and in some cases even when and how they were to die. The master also set the standards of conduct in the plantation, and of course decided what was right or wrong, what was moral or immoral.

The master's residence, or casa grande, was the very heart of the plantation. It was not only the center of power but it represented the foundation of the sugar aristocracy. The casa grande, as Freyre suggests, together with the *senzala*, stood as the symbol of a complex and self-contained economic, social and political system.[2]

During the sixteenth and early seventeenth centuries, as we can see from the paintings of Franz Post,[3] these imposing structures were characterized by a tall and solid tower or a fortress-like appearance such as in the casas grandes of the *engenho* "Camaragibe" or the "engenho da Torre," and "Megaípe-de-Baixo."[4] The fortification of the casa grande was necessary during this period to safeguard the inhabitants of the *engenho* against frequent attacks by the Indians. Actually, in the *Regimento* given to the first Governor-General Tomé de Sousa in 1548, the Crown made fortification of the casa grande mandatory. Towards the end of the seventeenth century and during the eighteenth century, the Indian menace removed, these houses acquired a more hospitable and pleasant appearance. With their many rooms, large kitchens, inviting verandas, and sometimes a chapel attached to the main building, these later casas grandes were likened by Freyre to a Portuguese convent.[5]

The lifestyle at the casa grande varied according to the size and importance of the *engenho*, the economic situation of the owner, and also according to the occasion. In the smaller mills the master's family lived rather frugally and their diet was far from adequate. While Father Cardim left us an account of how some planters were given to holding lavish banquets accompanied by large quantities of imported Portuguese wine,[6] this extravagant way of life was not the general rule among all planters, but rather, "circumscribed to privileged families of Pernambuco and Bahia."[7] In the larger plantations, however, these "privileged families," although most of them were constantly in debt, lived in an ostentatious and extravagant manner. They were the families of the powerful *senhores de engenho* whose title gave them as much prestige as that of *fidalgos* in Portugal. Their individual incomes could reach (in 1587) as much as ten thousand cruzados,[8] but their expenses were that much or more.[9] They were men who, according to Father Anchieta, had their olives, oil, vinegar, cheese, wheat flour, and other footstuffs imported from Portugal,[10] and who often shared their table with numerous visitors, relatives, and hangers on.

In the larger *engenhos*, the masters and their families enjoyed many luxuries. The women dressed very elegantly in the finest taffetas, silks and velvets imported from Portugal, and, during the Dutch period, from Holland. And according to Fray Manoel Calado, "so many were the jewels which adorned them, that it seemed as if the pearls, rubies, emeralds and diamonds, had rained upon their heads and necks." As for the men, "there were no expensive accessories for swords and daggers nor clothes of the latest fashion with which they did not adorn themselves."[11] During the Dutch period these *senhores de engenho* displayed great pride in wearing the finest linen from Holland and in decorating their hats with the most beautiful feathers that could be obtained. Fine leather saddles were a status symbol, and during this time those made of Russian leather were very much in demand. Even items of lesser importance such as candles were imported from Holland by the sugar mill owners. Such elegance was displayed by the large planters and their families that another seventeenth century chronicler wrote that he heard that not even at the court in Madrid did people dress better than the Brazilian sugar mill owners, their wives and daughters.[12]

In the larger, more prestigious mills, banquets, parties and celebrations were rather frequent. On special occasions, such as the wedding of a daughter, festivities were even more elaborate.

> Relatives and friends dressed, some in crimson velvet, some in green, and others in damask and other silks of several colors [while] the bridles and saddles of the horses were of the same silks [their riders] were wearing.[13]

There were bullfights, tournaments and other games, all very ornate and costly. Music flowed in great profusion, provided by hired bands or sometimes by Negro slaves. Many Negroes in Brazil were very skilled at playing musical instruments. François Pyrard de Laval, a seventeenth century French traveller, was amazed to hear in the *engenho* of Baltazar de Aragão in Bahia, an orchestra composed of thirty Negroes under the direction of a French conductor.[14] In fact, Negro musicians from Brazil particularly those of Angola stock, were very much in demand in some parts of Spanish America. In 1627, Gaspar Sobrino, a

Social and Cultural Life at the Plantation 127

representative of the Society of Jesus in Paraguay, petitioned the Crown for a license to import duty free eight or ten Negro musicians from Brazil. The slaves were needed to provide the music during the religious services the Jesuits held for the benefit of the Indians.[15]

Inside the casa grande a complement of several slaves, usually more than the number necessary to take care of the household chores, waited on their white masters and mistresses. Male slaves served their masters in practically every capacity. They helped them dress, tie their shoes, or even wash themselves. "According to tradition," Freyre writes, "a sugar mill owner from Pernambuco could not forego the Negro's hand even for the most intimate details of the toilette."[16] Some slaves followed their masters around the plantation or carried them, their mistress, or their guests, on hammocks or sedan chairs to visit friends and relatives or to town. The sedan chair (*liteira* or *palanquin*, as the Portuguese variety was called) was one of the most popular means of transportation used by the sugar mill owners and other important figures in the captaincy. Adult Negroes also handled the heavier chores around the house, such as bringing wood for the stove, or moving heavy furniture. The unpleasant task of carrying barrels of human waste out of the house to unload them also fell to the male slaves. In Recife, up until the nineteenth century, the slave who carried these barrels to unload them on the beaches was called *tigre* (tiger).[17] Young Negroes were the playmates of their young masters or *sinhôzinhos*. They were almost inseparable. The young Negro or *moleque* was always in a submissive position, being not only the playmate but also serving as punching-bag (*leva-pancadas*) and always acquiescing to the white boy's every whim. Not infrequently, the young master's sadistic tendencies made the moleque become his first outlet for sexual intercourse.[18]

As for the women, some worked in the kitchen and became expert cooks. Others cleaned the house or waited at the table. Some followed their mistresses around helping them dress, combing their hair, serving at their companions, in short, catering to their every wish. Many grew up with their mistresses, often becoming part of their dowry when they married or going with them to a convent. If the mistress moved or went abroad, she usually took her Negress with her. In several instances Dutch mistresses upon returning to Holland took their female slaves with them. A certain Mrs. Otto Etthmeyer who had a W.I.C.-owned Negress employed as a nannie to her son, would not hear of making the trip back to Holland with her child, but without the trusted nannie. The Company finally acquiesced on condition that the Negress be returned to Recife at the first opportunity.[19]

A shocking contrast to the casa grande was the *senzala*, or slave hut. The *senzala* was a small, one room, rectangular hut built of lath and plaster and covered with straw or palm leaves. Each hut had one door and a small opening high up in the wall close to the roof, which served as a window. Some were windowless. Several *senzalas* were grouped within a small area forming a small community within the *engenho*. The community of huts was also referred to as the *senzala*.

Four or five slaves, regardless of family ties, sex, or age, lived in each of these huts. Inside they slept on straw mats or in hammocks and shared their food with each other. There was no comfort or privacy. Few slaves were married. Even though the masters permitted cohabitation and promiscuity, many of them prevented their slaves from getting married. In the early days this was done for fear that the slave would become free if he married.[20] Later, masters argued that if the Negro married he would tire of the relationship, fall into a state of melancholy, and would eventually kill himself. The few who did marry were rarely assured of a lasting family relationship. When slaves were sold, no consideration was given to their marital status or to their dependents. Children were taken away from their parents, brothers, and sisters and sold, and married couples were frequently separated by the sale of one of the spouses.[21] An exception to this practice was found in the *engenhos* owned by the Benedictine friars. In "Mussurepe," "Goitacá" and "São Bernardo," the good friars arranged marriages between their slaves, did not permit the separation of the couples, and allowed their children to play most of the day. The same was not true regarding slaves owned by all religious orders. The Jesuits, with few exceptions were never as active in defense of the Negroes as they were in defense of the Indians, while the Carmelites were perhaps the harshest in the treatment of their slaves.[22]

The adversities of slavery notwithstanding, the Negroes in the plantations of Pernambuco managed not only to retain a great part of their African heritage, religion and traditions, but also to make a significant contribution to the culture and folklore of northeastern Brazil. The African slave was very fond of music. Domestic slaves with more time to themselves were the best musicians but, other Negroes, during celebrations or whenever they could, also enjoyed music and dancing. With unusual skill, the Negro was able to reproduce in the *engenho* a number of the musical instruments he had known in Africa, and also to learn how to play the white man's flute, clarinet and later the piano.[23]

Among the instruments of African origin used by the Negroes in Pernambuco we find: drums of practically all sizes and shapes, including the *Atabaque*, a type of loud drum; the *marimba* which consisted of several gourd cups with wooden keys spanning their mouths arranged in sequence and secured to a wooden base. Like its modern counterpart this primitive instrument was played by hitting the keys with a stick; the *marimbau*, probably a variation of the marimba; castanets, the *matungo*, a primitive version of the African *mbira*; the *buzina*, a horn or coronet made of the horns of animals or a conch shell (*buzio*). Ironically, the Negro used the very object of his enslavement—the sugar cane—to help him make music and make his sorrow the lighter. Out of the cane stick the African slave made the *cangá*. This was an instrument made of a cane stick with both extremities closed by the joints of the plant and with holes on it resembling a flute.[24] He also learned to play the European flute, the tambourine and the *berimbau*, an instrument consisting of a wooden bow mounted on a gourd, and a gut string connecting the two extremes of the bow. Since most of his instruments were percussion instruments, the Negro added another dimension to his music by singing a number of songs and laments often characterized by the repetitive nature of the lyrics.

Some Negroes became accomplished musicians and not infrequently played for the enjoyment of their masters at the casa grande. Some slaves who joined their masters in the revolt against the Dutch carried their instruments with them to the battlefield. According to Calado, the Negroes who fought the battle of Tabocas in August 3, 1645, went into combat playing their flutes, *atabaques* and horns.[25]

The musical inclination of the Africans also found expression in their singing. They not only sang their chants and laments to help forget their sorrows but they often attached a song to many of their daily occupations. So, sometimes they sang on their way to the fields, kept rhythm with their machetes while cutting the cane by singing a tune and either sang or whistled on their way back to the *senzala*. Those who worked in the convents and *engenhos* of the religious orders often learned to sing religious hymns. On the occasion of the coming of D. João VI and Da. Maria I, to Brasil in the nineteenth century, Negroes trained by the Jesuits were able to perform by themselves "not only Te Deums and European masses but even complete operas of the Italian school."[26] Even in death the Negro found a way to express his emotions by singing at the funerals of his fellow Africans. This of course occurred only when the deceased Negro was baptized and was allowed some kind of funeral.

> When a Negro died, men, women, and children gathered and danced to the sound of drums and other instruments. From time to time they sang [a few lines] asking:—Aye, aye, aye, why did he die?; —Aye, aye, aye, does he lack the bread?; —Aye, aye, aye, does he lack the fish?, and thus they would [go on asking] for all kinds of food and beverage.[27]

African slaves were also fond of dancing. On festive occasions, when and where such was permitted, the Negroes gathered to dance to the sound of their primitive instruments. Among these African dances the best known was the *batuque* and the *maracatu*. There were two types of batuque, the *congolês* (or congolese), and *de Luanda* (from Luanda). In the *batuque congolês*, the dancers, musicians and spectators formed a circle while two or three couples danced on the inside of it. The dance started with the slow, sensual swaying of body and limbs picking up speed as the music increased its tempo until the dancers reached a state of near frenzy. In the *batuque de Luanda*, the dancers also assembled in a circle, but instead of couples only one Negro or Negress danced in the center. After the dancer in the middle performed for a while, he or she would choose a substitute by pushing his or her belly against that of the person they selected. This act was called *embigada*, or *samba*.

The *maracatu* is the better known of the two dances because, unlike the *batuque*, it has become an important part of the folklore of Pernambuco. Although somewhat modified, the *maracatu* is still danced by several groups every year during the festivities of *carnaval*. The *maracatu* is intended to represent a royal procession with all the pomp and luxury of the court.

> Leading the procession, a standard bearer is escorted by archers, following and forming an aisle come two lines of beautifully dressed women, with turbans adorned with ribbons of different colors, little mirrors and other adornments, appearing between these lines various personages, among them those who carry the religious fetishes—a wooden cock, a stuffed alligator, and a doll dressed in white with a blue cloak—and following in line, come the dignitaries of the court, and closing the procession, the king and the queen.
>
> These two personages displaying the signs of royalty such as crowns, sceptres and long robes sustained by attendants march under a large umbrella... protected by archers.
>
> In back come the instruments: drums, horns and other of African characteristics, which accompany the marching songs and different dances with a terrible noise.
>
> The marching song, sung by all the retinue with the loud accompaniment of the instruments consists of [singing repetitive lyrics such as the following]:
> Aruenda qui tenda, tenda,
> Aruenda qui tenda, tenda,
> Aruenda de totororó.[28]

These dances as well as others the Negroes enjoyed were considered to be immoral because of their sensuous movements. In the second half of the eighteenth century they were even denounced to the Holy Office of the Inquisition. Upon investigation by the authorities it was agreed that the *maracatu* and *batuque* were harmless and could be tolerated. The dances which should be condemned were

> those that the blacks from the Coast of Mina [Elmina] do secretly or inside houses... with altar of idols, wor-

shipping live goats, and others made of clay; anointing their bodies with several oils or blood of a cock, giving to eat corn bread after several superstitious blessings, making the naive believe that [with] that bread they give fortune, [and] make women love men... [29]

The ritual described above was one of the early versions of a voodoo cult known as *xangô*, which with some modifications is still practiced in Pernambuco today.

Although the avowed reason for enslaving the Africans was to save their souls by instructing them in the Catholic faith, little was done in the plantations of Pernambuco to accomplish that objective. Slaves coming from Angola, Mozambique, and other places where there were Portuguese authorities were baptized as a group as they boarded the slave-ships. Those coming from elsewhere were to be baptized in Pernambuco. In neither case were the slaves adequately prepared to understand the meaning of the ritual and much less the basics of Catholic religion.

At the plantation, responsibility for the spiritual guidance of the Negroes rested with the masters. Although most *engenhos* had a chapel and a priest paid by the planters,[30] few slaves received religious instruction. While in theory slaves should have Sundays off to attend church, few masters were willing to make this concession. Many masters did not have their slaves baptized and neglected to give them the last sacraments of the Church at the time of their deaths. When this happened the Negro died as a heathen and was denied a Christian funeral. The "*negro pagão*" as the heathen African was called, was not buried in the slave cemetery where black crosses marked the graves. Instead he was tied to a heavy piece of wood and thrown into the river or the sea, or buried in a shallow grave on the beach. Maria Graham, a nineteenth century English traveller, witnessed, much to her horror, a stray dog unearth the arm of a Negro buried in a stretch of beach between Recife and Olinda.[31]

If the masters as a rule did not care, the Church was equally guilty of negligence. At no time during the colonial period did the Church embark on a major campaign to give religious instruction to the Africans. Never was the Church concerned with the salvation of the Negroes to the extent that it was with the conversion of the Indians. So large was the number of slaves who were not

Social and Cultural Life at the Plantation 133

baptized, and so many died without the last sacraments of the Church that the Crown became concerned. In at least two occasions (1663 and 1719) the Crown reproached the planters, priests and even bishops for their neglect and ordered that planters not be allowed to let their slaves expire without being ministered the last sacraments.

Under Dutch rule Sunday work was prohibited to allow the slaves to attend church. This prohibition, however, had little effect, and in 1638 the Ecclesiastical Council decried the fact that the Negroes were still not going to church because they had to work.[32] The Dutch also talked about establishing a school for Negroes where the Africans would receive, among other things, religious instruction. Due to the lack of qualified teachers who could communicate with the Negroes, the idea ran into difficulties and the school was never established.[33]

There were of course some slaves who received religious instruction and became practicing Catholics. For the most part these were domestic slaves, Negroes owned by religious orders, and sometimes those working in the small *engenhos* where contact with the master and his family was closer and more frequent. These Negroes were baptized, taught the catechism, and often attended Mass on Sundays. Some Negroes claimed a particular Catholic saint or the Virgin Mary as the object of their devotion. As a rule Negro slaves claimed São Benedito (San Benito de San Filadelfo-Sicily) as their patron and protector. São Benedito's parents were African slaves[34] and that saint's statue is characterized by a dark face, sometimes with African features. Another saint commonly invoked by the Negroes in their prayers was Saint Efigenia. Translated below is "the Saint Efigenia prayer" often said by Negroes in Pernambuco during religious services in the Catholic churches:

Illustrious Efigenia
Princess of Ethiopia
of the Highest Monarch
worthy spouse.

Thou art black in the colors
so fair in [thou] works
of the law exhorter
of the Faith defender.[35]

Slaves who received religious instruction, also formed their own *confrarias*, or *irmandades*.[36] In 1627, the *confraria* or brotherhood of Our Lady of Guadalupe and a church of the same name were established in Olinda. Both were established so that the *pardos*, or mulattoes, free or slave, could worship and serve the Virgin with "great devotion."[37] In the second half of the seventeenth century another brotherhood was organized. This was the brotherhood of Our Lady of the Rosary of the black men with a membership composed of Negroes, free and slaves. The slaves who actively participated were for the most part domestic servants residing in the city. The Negroes served with great devotion and contributed their labor as well as money for the building and maintenance of their church. The brotherhood had an elaborate hierarchy of kings, judges, and other officers who were elected by the Negroes for a period of one year. In 1674, Antonio Carvalho, a slave of Agostinho Carvalho, was elected king of the Angolas; Antonio Ramiry [sic] was elected king of the creoles; Pascoal de Abreu, slave of the Sargento-mór (Head Sergeant) Thomás de Abreu was elected judge of the Angolas; Domingos Correa, a slave of Captain Manoel Gonçalves Correa, was elected judge of the Creoles; Angela Ribeiro, a slave of Antonio Ribeiro Barreiros, became the queen of the Angolas; Luzia Dias, a slave of Francisco Barros, was chosen queen of the Creoles, while Brivida Roiz, a slave of João Esteves da Costa, and Joana Leytoa were respectively chosen judge of the (female) Angolas, and judge of the (female) Creoles. Each of these elected officials was expected to make a contribution of about 4$000 or more.[38] In the case of the slaves, the money was, of course, supplied by their masters. To have a slave who was an officer in the brotherhood certainly added to the status of his owner. The church itself was well maintained and beautifully decorated. In 1699, the brotherhood spent "229$750 in the gilding of the retable of the main chapel."[39]

The brotherhoods offered some services to their members and, whenever possible, intervened on their behalf before the authorities. The Brotherhood of the Rosary provided for the funeral of each of its members, free or slave. The entire complement of brothers accompanied the deceased to the grave site and the rites were officiated by the brotherhood's chaplain. In 1703 the Brotherhood of the Rosary complained to the Crown that a resident of Pernambuco did not allow his slaves to get married and refused to release them when they were ready to purchase their freedom.[40]

Because no significant effort was made to bring him into the Church's fold, the Negro retained many of his own religious beliefs and traditions. "Of all African institutions entertained in America by the Negro colonists or transmitted to their descendants, full-blooded or half-breed," says Nina Rodrigues, "the religious practices of their fetishism were the ones that were best preserved in Brazil."[41] Not only were the African rites practiced secretly at the *senzalas* but the superstitions, witchcraft, and fetishism of African religions gradually permeated Catholic beliefs creating a rather unique syncretism.

Whenever they could, Negro slaves practiced their own cults. Whenever they worshiped in the open, they disguised their own deities by associating them with a Catholic saint. So that for almost every Catholic saint there was an African equivalent, and while he seemed to be praying to the white man's saint, the Negro was really invoking the protection of *orichá*,[42] or some other African deity.

The African cults practiced in the *engenhos* of Pernambuco were mostly founded upon witchcraft, animism and fetishism. In the open, the Africans practiced their religion by dancing the *batuque* and *maracatu*. Privately, they engaged in the superstitious practices of voodoo or *xangô*. The beating of drums, sacrifices of goats, chickens and other small animals, as well as frenetic dancing characterized this ritual. There were also healers and sorcerers, known as *macumbeiros* and *mandingueiros* who professed to accomplish practically anything through the use of their magic powers. They could cure diseases, their love potions were sure to make men love women, and women love men, and they could cast a spell upon anyone or rid a person of his or her enemies.

Some of these Negroes became well known and were often sought by sugar mill owners and their families to cure their infirmities or to solve their amorous problems. While in Pernambuco Joan Nieuhof witnessed one of these sorcerers at work:

> One time I was at a friend's house when I saw enter through the kitchen, a Negro who came to cure a sick slave who, so he told us, had been a victim of witchcraft. The healer made the patient rise from the chair, and, taking a live coal from the fire, ordered the slave to lick it three times at the very point where the embers

were brightest. Then he put out the coal in a tureen of water and rubbed the coal on it until [the water] became black as ink. Following, he ordered the patient to drink the water in one gulp. The beverage [so] taken, the slave immediately felt a slight pain in the abdomen. This done the healer rubbed both sides of the patient and holding a little of meat and fat above the hip, made there, with a knife he carried in the pocket, an incision two inches deep from which [he] extracted a bundle of hair and rags. He washed the wound with what was left of the black water, and soon after the wound was closed and the patient cured.[43]

Even more in demand was the amorous or sexual oriented witchcraft. Slaves used it to make themselves loved by the man or woman they desired, to make their masters like them, and even attract the sexual desires of their owners. Not infrequently, young mistresses or their mothers resorted to this type of witchcraft to attract the love of a certain young man, or to regain the love of an estranged husband. Older and worn-out masters sought the services of the *macumbeiro* hoping to restore their sexual appetite.

Practically everything was used in these attempts to promote amorous relations or increase the sexual drive of the patient. "Under-arm and pubic hair, sweat, tears. Saliva..."[44] and fingernail shavings or powder,[45] all were used as indispensable ingredients in a number of magic recipes. A common, and supposedly most effective, way to gain a man's heart was to serve him a small amount of the hopeful woman's menstrual blood mixed in with his chocolate or coffee.[46] In Brazil, coffee was more commonly used and the love potion became known as "*café mandingueiro*." "Even the crab," Freyre writes, "is [a] tool of sexual witchcraft: prepared with three or seven peppers-of-the-Coast and thrown on the ground [it] creates disarrangements in the home."[47]

Relations between masters and slaves varied from *engenho* to *engenho*. In the small plantations, since the number of Negroes was small, the master usually had contact with a higher percentage of his slaves. In the large *engenhos* the master's contacts with his Negroes were limited in most cases to domestic slaves. Owing to this closer contact and the very nature of their chores, some of these domestic slaves won the confidence and affection of their masters and mistresses. Some were actually loved by their owners and when they died were mourned by them as if they were members of their family. This trust, affection and even physical love which sometimes developed between masters and slaves, however, was less due to the flexibility and racial tolerance of the Portuguese than to the ability of the domestic slaves to imitate their white masters, to acquire the white man's ways, in short, to become more like whites than Africans both in manner and appearance.

First of all, the Africans chosen by the Portuguese as domestic slaves were not the brutes they sent to the boiler house. They were mostly slaves from Guinea, Sierra Leone, and Cape Verde, selected because they were more attractive, cleaner, and had more delicate features. All, of course, determined according to the white man's preference and standards. Brought into the casa grande, these slaves usually dressed very much like their masters and mistresses, and unlike their brothers and sisters outside, who went around naked or in rags. The young often grew up with their masters in the casa grande. Usually they did not speak any African idioms. Their language was that of their master; their customs and manners had little that could betray their heritage, and were usually those of the master. Not infrequently the moleque and the white boy shared the same father. In short, tolerance and affection, as well as sex appeal, grew as the Negro became less and less African and more and more like the white man. It was not the pitch-black African woman whom the Portuguese sought for a continued affair or to keep as his mistress; it was the mulatto, and the lighter in color the better. It was not the coarse and ill-mannered African whom the Portuguese came to esteem, but the more gentle Negroes from Guinea, Sierra Leone, and Cape Verde, or better stil their second or third generation—the farther from Africa the better—who had gradually become more and more like him, in short, the "black with a white man's soul."

Sexual relations between the Portuguese master and a first generation African woman were likely to be, as a general rule, of an impulsive nature and of short duration. However, frequent contact, and the unusual beauty of the mulatto offsprings of other such unions, led to more lasting amorous relations between white masters and mulatto slaves. In fact, concubinage was widely practiced in Pernambuco not only by the planters but even by Catholic priests. In 1551, Father Nóbrega wrote to the fathers and brothers of the Jesuit College in Lisbon deploring the fact that the priests in that captaincy not only lived in concubinage with their slaves but "stated publicly to the men that it is licit for them to be in sin with their Negresses since they are their slaves and that they can have sexual relations because [the slaves] are dogs, and other similar things..."[48]

Some masters actually developed great passions for their mulatto mistresses and catered to their every wish. They dressed them in the finest silks and showered them with precious jewels. So scandalous was this practice that the Crown, in 1696, prohibited slaves from wearing fine silks and jewels most of which were obtained in the above manner or through prostitution. Others went as far as publicly showing their preference for their mulatto mistresses over their legal wives. In 1637, according to Calado, planters leaving Pôrto Calvo with the Portuguese troops to escape the oncoming Dutch army, carried their mulatto mistresses on horses while their legal wives walked behind them.[49] It was, no doubt, after witnessing similar displays of affection that Antonil concluded that Brazil was the "paradise of the mulattoes."[50]

While miscegenation was widespread and greatly increased the slave population, intermarriages were rare.[51] In reality, miscegenation rather than being as it has been argued,[52] the crowning example of the flexibility of the Portuguese character, contributed, in many cases, to the further debasement of the Negro slave. Although some female slaves no doubt enjoyed being the object of the master's attentions or even used them to improve their condition, it is also true that at least an equal number did not share the enjoyment of their masters when they submitted to their sexual desires. Yet, whether they liked it or not they had to submit. In fact, "the really black woman is seen as ordained for the sexual initiation of adolescents, still shy and needing the easy conquest; the mulatto is seen as the companion of adult frolics, or those of husbands anxious to escape the constraints of the marital bed."[53] And it is in this very assumption that the Negro woman must submit to the sadistic tendencies of her master that "the insinuation of racialism in its most savage, most withering form"[54] is to be found. These mixed unions were only rarely accorded the respectability of matrimony. The Negro woman could serve as a sexual outlet for the white male but was not good enough to be his wife, "so that underlying sexual relationships between different colours is the most terrifying of prejudices, which sentences a whole race to immorality in order to preserve the virginity of the women of the other race."[55]

There was no end to the slave's term of service except through death, escape, or manumission. The outlets for manumission were, at least in theory, of two general types: In the first instance the slave could buy his freedom or *alforria* by paying his master a pre-established amount usually equal to the slave's purchase price or his present market value. The second instance was when the master freed his slave voluntarily.

To earn the price of his freedom the Negro needed to have some free time in which he could work for wages. The first avenue therefore was closed to most of those slaves who worked in the fields and in the manufacturing of sugar. The majority who earned their freedom in this fashion were domestic slaves who often had some free time of their own and in some cases were even superfluous. Among them, attractive female slaves were the most successful. According to Antonil, to give the *alforria* to "coquettish Mulattoes is sheer perdition; because the money they give to free themselves, rarely comes from other mines than their own bodies [through] repeated sins..."[56] Second came the *"negro de ganho."* This was a slave whose owner sent him out to work for wages. In the majority of cases the slave had to bring home a certain amount but was allowed to keep whatever he earned in excess of the stipulated income. Considering that in the first half of the seventeenth century these Negroes usually earned "four vinteins a day,"[57] it is doubtful that many were able to save enough money to buy their freedom. An exception to this rule were the women who worked as *"negras de ganho."* Some of these women were expected to provide "flour or the bread for the [master's] table;... the meat or the fish for the plate;... pay the rents of the houses, [and]... give the oil for the light..." All this and more, they obtained in most cases through prostitution,[58] and with their larger income were more frequently able to buy their freedom. Under the best of circumstances it still took a very long time for a slave to earn enough money to purchase his or her freedom. Probably this period was longer than the average "useful life" (seven years) of the slave. In this case, it is doubtful if the transaction always benefitted the buyer. The master nearly always gained from the sale of a slave past his prime. But, given the employment opportunities of the period, it is not certain if an aging Negro did have the necessary mobility to live better as a freedman.[59]

For the purpose of buying the freedom of captives, there existed in Portugal during the sixteenth century the institution of the *mamposteiro,*

> The *mamposteiros* were responsible for the collection of alms and the product of penances which were given, destined to the redemption of captives in the hands of the infidels, [acting] as auxiliary agents of the fathers of the Holy Trinity, which Order had as its object the ransom of Christians who fell into the hands of the said infidels.[60]

In 1560, the office of *mamposteiro* was introduced in Brazil, and Francisco Fragoso was appointed for that position in the captaincy of Pernambuco. Later the office of chief *mamposteiro* was created and by 1603 there was in Pernambuco a chief-treasurer of the captives. The institution lasted until 1775, but there is no indication as to whether, and to what extent, it helped obtain the freedom of Negro slaves.

Raising the necessary sum of money, difficult as it might have been, was no assurance that the slave would receive his freedom. Although in theory the master was required to release the slave who raised the money to purchase his freedom, some masters refused to do so. Even when a previous agreement had been made to set the Negro free at a particular time some masters went back on their words. Since slaves were considered "infamous persons," these masters did not feel compelled to honor their promise and thought nothing of breaking the agreement.[61]

Voluntary manumission was more common than the *alforria* or ransom. Masters who had illicit relations with their slaves sometimes freed the children they sired even though few acknowledged their paternity. Others chose happy events such as the wedding of a daughter or the birth of a first son to free one or more slaves as an act of thanksgiving.[62] A smart slave mother could ask her master or mistress to be godparents of her child. In accepting the protectorship of the child, and in a show of generosity, the master in many cases would free the Negro baby at the baptismal font. Some masters freed their slaves out of gratitude. Hendrick Haecx, a member of the Dutch Supreme Council, showed his appreciation when he bought his longtime servant Juliana and her daughter from the W.I.C. and freed them.[63] Others freed their slaves through a will or last testament. In her will (1689) made shortly before her death, Dona Maria de Albuquerque, owner of the "Engenho da Moribeca Invocação de Santo Antonio" freed her mulatto slave Maria, "because I raised her as a daughter and always received loyal submission and good service."[64] She also freed a mulatto named Bernardo who was learning to be a cobbler in order that he would have a profession when he grew up.[65] Head-Captain Cristovão de Barros who died in 1694, also used his testament to free all of his slaves and give them the usufruct of his property in São Lourenço.[66]

The many instances of voluntary manumission have often been pointed out as evidence of the milder nature of slavery in Brazil.[67] In Brazil there were no legal restrictions to manumission, as in some parts of the United States. Instead, voluntary manumission was hailed as a pious and generous act on the part of the master. Closer examination however reveals a less than favorable picture. For the sake of objectivity, manumission in Pernambuco must be examined in two separate categories: manumission of domestic slaves, and manumission of Negroes engaged in production (i.e., field hands and those laboring in the actual making of sugar). In the *engenhos* of Pernambuco as in other plantations in the New World, domestic slaves were more commonly freed by their masters. The reasons for this preference were many: domestic slaves had closer relations with their masters who sometimes freed them in gratitude for their services; and domestic slaves in many cases did not engage in any work on a full-time basis. Many were mere hangers-on kept by their owners as a status symbol; but, above all, in the large plantations domestic slaves were not connected with the production of sugar.

Those who labored in the fields and in the mill were usually the best suited for hard work and therefore indispensable. So, in most instances when they were manumitted, it was not for humanitarian reasons but in the owner's self interest. This happened most frequently when these slaves were too sick or too old to work and became merely a burden to the master.[68] In many cases this amounted to sentencing the Negro to death since he was in no condition to earn his livelihood in the outside world. According to Boxer, such practice had been frequently denounced "officially and unofficially from the time of the Fifth Provincial Council celebrated at Goa in 1606 to Santos Vilhena's account of Bahia at the end of the eighteenth century."[69] Some masters disposed of their sick or old slaves by provoking a fatal "accident." A certain Lalao, *senhor de engenho* in Paraiba, became widely known for his cruelty. One time he ordered that a field planted with manioc be set afire. Then he told an old and weak Negro to go put down the blaze. "The fire spread, the poor old man was surrounded by flames"[70] and was burned alive.

It should be noted that during this period manumission in Brazil was seldom effected as a repudiation of the institution of slavery. By contract, during an eight year period beginning in 1782—when the Virginia legislature lifted the legal ban on manumission—"ten thousand slaves [in that state alone] received their freedom by the voluntary action of owners who took the principle of equality literally."[71] So, if anything is striking in the Brazilian experience it is the fact that, in the very absence of legal restrictions or penalties the incidence of manumission for humanitarian purposes falls far short of making an impressive record.

NOTES

1. In several instances, the Crown voided or modified its own laws, fearing strong opposition from the planters. The royal decree of July 30, 1609, prohibiting the enslavement of Indians and giving them certain rights was changed in October 13, 1611, after strong protests from the colonists, to allow them to enslave Indians rescued from enemy tribes. See "Registo da Lei de Sua M*de*. sôbre os Indios," *Livro Primeiro do Governo do Brasil*, pp. 71-74. For the same reason, the royal instruction of March 20 and 23, 1688, ordering the prosecution of cruel masters was repealed in February 23, 1689. See J. A. Goulart, *Da Palmatória ao Patíbulo*, pp. 186-87.

2. Freyre, *Casa Grande & Senzala*, 1:XXXI.

3. Franz Post was a Dutch painter who lived in Brazil from 1637-1644, and left several landscape paintings of the sugar areas of Pernambuco.

4. José Antônio Gonsalves de Mello, "Casa Grande," separata da *Revista do Museu do Açucar*, Vol. 1, No. 6 (Recife, 1971), p. 3.
5. Freyre, *Casa Grande & Senzala*, 1:XXXII; Mello, "Casa Grande," p. 4.
6. Cardim, *Tratado*, pp. 334-35.
7. Freyre, *Casa Grande & Senzala*, 1:41.
8. Soares de Sousa, *Tratado*, p. 29.
9. Members of the sugar aristocracy were intent on preserving their image and lifestyle even though in some cases, this led to financial ruin. Genovese found a similar attitude among wealthy planters of the American South: "The more economically debilitating their way of life, the more they clung to it." See *The Political Economy of Slavery*, p. 34.
10. "Informações e Fragmentos Históricos do Padre Joseph de Anchieta, S. J. (1584-1586)," in Materiais e Achegas para a História e Geografia por Ordem do Ministério da Fazenda, no. 1 (Rio de Janeiro, 1886), p. 34, cited in Freyre, Casa Grande & Senzala, 1:83. The great emphasis placed on the cultivation of sugar cane created a monoculture type of agriculture. The production of other foodstuffs was consequently neglected and these food items, because they had to be imported, were available only in small quantities and at very high prices.
11. Calado, *O Valeroso Lucideno*, 1:19.
12. *Diálogos das Grandezas do Brasil*, p. 90.
13. Cardim, *Tratado*, pp. 334-35.
14. Ernesto Ennes, *Os Primeiros Quilombos (Subsídios para a sua história)*, unpublished ms. at Arquivo Público do Estado de Pernambuco (Recife), p. 14; Diégues Junior, *O Banguê nas Alagoas*, p. 150.
15. *AGI*, Carta del Conse jo de Indias al Rey (9 de noviembre de 1627), Charcas, legajo 2.
16. Freyre, *Casa Grande & Senzala*, 2:465; As Genovese points out, "...there was more than despotic authority in this master-slave relationship.... The slaveholder commanded the products of another's labor, but by the same process was forced into dependence upon this other." See *The Political Economy of Slavery*, p. 32.
17. Mauro Mota, *Os bichos na fala da gente* (Recife: Instituto Joaquim Nabuco de Pesquisas Sociais - M.E.C., 1969), p. 217.
18. Freyre, *Casa Grande & Senzala*, 1:54.
19. Mello, *Tempo dos Flamengos*, p. 219.
20. There is no explanation for this fear, since traditionally slaves could only become free if they married a free person. To dispel it completely Father Manuel da Nóbrega asked the king to issue a decree stating that slaves would not become free when they married.

Manuel da Nóbrega to the King (Olinda, September 14, 1551) cited in Pereira da Costa, *Anais*, 1:293.

21. In 1638, the Dutch Ecclesiastical Council protested against the practice of separating a slave couple through the sale of either the husband or wife. See Mello, "A Situação do Negro," pp. 211-212.
22. Freyre, *Casa Grande & Senzala*, 2:475.
23. Nair de Andrade, "Musicalidade do Escravo Negro no Brasil," *Novos Estudos Afro-Brasileiros*, p. 198.
24. F. A. Pereira a Costa, *Folk-Lore Pernambucano*. 1a. edição autônoma (Recife: Arquivo Público Estadual, 1974), pp. 211-212.
25. Calado, *O Valeroso Lucideno*, 2:12.
26. Andrade, "Musicalidade do Escravo Negro no Brasil," p. 198.
27. Mello, "A Situação do Negro," p. 221.
28. Pereira da Costa, *Folk-Lore Pernambucano*, pp. 215-16.
29. *Ibid.*, p. 213.
30. A priest received from forty to fifty thousand reis in addition to having his meals provided by the planter at the casa grande. See Cardim, *Tratado*, p. 318; Verdonk, *Descrição das capitanias conquistadas*, p. 223.
31. Maria Dundas Graham, *Journal of a Voyage to Brazil* (New York: Frederick A. Praeger, 1969), p. 111.
32. Mello, "A Situação do Negro," pp. 211-12.
33. *Ibid.*, p. 226.
34. C. R. Boxer, "Negro Slavery in Brazil, a Portuguese Pamphlet (1764)," *Race*, vol. 5, no. 3 (London, January 1964), p. 42.
35. "Manuscritos da Igreja de Nossa Senhora do Rosário dos homens pretos do Recife," in *Arquivos*, Nos. 7-20 (Recife: Prefeitura Municipal, 1945-1951), p. 102.
36. A *confraria* or *irmandade* is a religious association or brotherhood.
37. Pereira da Costa, *Anais*, 2:467-68.
38. "Manuscritos da Igreja," p. 55.
39. Robert C. Smith, "Décadas do Rosário dos Pretos. Documentos da Irmandade," *Arquivos*, Nos. 7-20 (Recife: Prefeitura Municipal, 1945-1951), p. 144.
40. *AHU*, Resolução do Conselho Ultramarino (6 de março de 1703) cited in Flávio Guerra, *Alguns documentos de arquivos portugueses de interesse para a história de Pernambuco* (Recife: Arquivo Público Estadual, n.d.), p. 64.
41. Nina Rodrigues, *Os Africanos no Brasil*, p. 319.
42. *Orichá* was the god of all plagues and fevers but more particularly the god of smallpox. See Nina Rodrigues, *Os Africanos no Brasil*, p. 339.

43. Nieuhof, *Memorável Viagem*, p. 309.
44. Freyre, *Casa Grande & Senzala*, 2:351.
45. *AGN*, Inquisición, tomo 363 (1629), São Luis, no. 16.
46. AGN, Inquisicion, tomo 356 (1626) Tepeaca, 2ª parte, fol. 115.
47. Freyre, *Casa Grande & Senzala*, 2:350.
48. Nóbrega to the Fathers and Brothers of the Colegio de Lisboa (11 de agôsto de 1551), cited in Pereira da Costa, *Anais*, 1:289.
49. Calado, *O Valeroso Lucideno*, 1:85.
50. Antonil, *Cultura e Opulência do Brasil*, Livro I, p. 24.
51. Harley Ross Hammond, "Race, Social Mobility and Politics in Brazil," *Race*, Vol. 4, No. 2 (May, 1963), p. 4.
52. The best argument in defense of this thesis is found in Gilberto Freyre's *Casa Grande & Senzala*. For a more accurate evaluation of the racial attitudes of the Portuguese, see C. R. Boxer, *Race Relations in the Portuguese Colonial Empire 1415-1828* (Oxford: The Clarendon Press, 1963); Challenging Freyre's argument, Genovese contends that widespread miscegenation made life worse for field hands in the Brazilian plantations. Since runaways could easily mingle with the large free mulatto population "... planters took the precaution of locking up their allegedly well-treated slaves, including house slaves, every night.... In order to do so, the Brazilians had to build tight, often windowless, escape-proof cabins. Thus, Brazilian slave quarters were generally inferior to those in the United States." "The ease with which runaway slaves could pass for free men," Genovese concludes, "made necessary greater police control of the plantations." Genovese's point is well taken but does not rend Freyre's thesis meaningless. In racially mixed Brazil mulattoes and even Negroes were (particularly during the nineteenth century) usually thought to be free persons. This was no panacea but the predominance of this attitude affected slavery in at least two ways. First, it showed greater tolerance towards the growing number of free Negroes bestowing a certain dignity to the person of color. Second, it continually undermined the slave system by making it easier for the fugitive to move about and more difficult for masters to recover runaways. See Genovese, "The Treatment of Slaves in Different Countries: Problems in the Applications of the Comparative Method," in Laura Foner and Eugene D. Genovese, eds. *Slavery in the New World* (Eglewood Cliffs, N.J.: Prentice Hall, Inc., 1969) pp. 203-204.
53. Roger Bastide, "Dusky Venus, Black Apollo," *Race*, Vol. 3, No. 1 (November 1961), p. 12.
54. *Ibid.*, p. 10.
55. *Ibid.*, p. 11.
56. Antonil, *Cultura e Opulência do Brasil*, Livro I, p. 24.

57. "Livro do Tombo do Mosteiro de São Bento da Paraiba," *Revista do Arquivo Público* (Recife, Second Semester, 1946), p. 159. A *vintem* was a Portuguese coin worth twenty *reis*. See Sluiter, "Report on the State of Brazil, 1612," p. 534.

58. Benci, *Economia Cristã*, pp. 98-99.

59. Robert William Fogel and Stanley Engerman state that in the United States during the nineteenth century "Some skilled slaves were able to accumulate enough capital to purchase their freedom within a decade. For others the period extended to two decades or more." Unfortunately specific information on this topic is not available for Pernambuco during the sixteenth and seventeenth centuries. There is nothing to suggest, however, that slaves in Pernambuco could buy their freedom in less time than their counterparts in the United States. See *Time on the Cross* (Boston: Little, Brown and Company, 1974), p. 151.

60. Pereira da Costa, *Anais*, 1:347.

61. AHU, Consulta do Conselho Ultramarino (Lisboa, 9 de julho de 1659), Documentos referentes a Pernambuco, caixa 7;

62. Frank Tannenbaum, *Slave and Citizen, The Negro in the Americas* (New York: Vintage Books, 1946), p. 58.

63. Mello, *Tempo dos Flamengos*, p. 220.

64. "Traslado do Testamento com que faleceo Dona Maria de Albuquerque senhora do engenho da Moribeca Invocação de Santo Antonio," in Fernando Pio, ed. "Cinco documentos para a história dos engenhos de Pernambuco." Separata da *Revista do Museu do Açúcar*, No. 2 (Recife, 1969), p. 36.

65. *Ibid.*

66. Pereira da Costa, *Anais*, 4:229.

67. The best arguments on this topic are found in Freyre, *Casa Grande & Senzala*, and Tannenbaum, *Slave & Citizen*. For a divergent opinion on this subject see Carl N. Degler, *Neither Black nor White. Slavery and Race Relations in Brazil and the United States* (New York: The Macmillan Company, 1971); Genovese also disagrees. "Access to freedom and citizenship" is an important component of his three-category formula for studying treatment of slaves in different countries. He denies, however, any "organic connection" between this and the "general conditions of labor" under slavery and sees only an "indirect connection" between access to freedom and such things as "...family security, [and] opportunities for an independent social and religious life...." See "The Treatment of Slaves in Different Countries...," p. 203.

68. Benci, *Economia Cristã*, pp. 54-55, 61.

69. Boxer, "Negro Slavery in Brazil," p. 47n.
70. Rodrigues de Carvalho, "Aspectos da influencia africana," p. 30.
71. Edmund S. Morgan, *The Birth of the Nation 1763-1789* (Chicago: The University of Chicago Press, 1973) p. 97.

CHAPTER V

SLAVE RESISTANCE AND REBELLIONS

It was not lightly that the Jesuit Antonio Vieira in one of his sermons compared the sufferings of the Negro slave in the Brazilian *engenhos* to those of Christ. The harsh working conditions, the cruel punishments, the constant humiliation of being addressed, referred to, and counted as a mere beast of burden,[1] made Vieira's comparison rather appropriate. Under these conditions it is not surprising that many Negroes, instead of resigning themselves to their wretched lot, resorted to every conceivable method of resistance to ease or terminate their misery.

Perhaps the most subtle form of resistance was sabotage. In retaliation to the cruelty of their overseers and masters, it was not uncommon for the Negroes to set afire a cane field by dropping a piece of live charcoal from the fire, or to cause enough damage to the mill mechanism to paralyze it for many hours or even days. To prevent these "accidents" from happening, the overseers in the fields were always on the alert, the *feitor-da-moenda* and a guard kept constant watch at the mill house, and the head-overseer had strict orders to see that the cones in the purging house did not break, that the copper vessels did not burn and that the tools were not lost or stolen.[2] Since Negroes were thought to be lacking in intelligence, most acts of deliberate sabotage were thought to be accidents resulting from their stupidity or carelessness. The Ardras and Calabares, for example, were considered undesirable, because of their stupidity and negligence. Both of these characteristics, I suggest, were in many cases undetected forms of resistance since some of the Ardras when they wanted, "surpassed all the others [slaves] in vivacity and effort, in such way that it seems that the good and the bad [Ardras] belong to different nations."[3]

Among the more extreme forms of resistance practiced in the *engenhos* of Pernambuco, abortion, infanticide and suicides were the most common. To save their unborn and young children from the miseries of captivity, slave mothers sometimes committed self-inflicted abortions and infanticide. Adult slaves frequently sought to end their suffering by killing themselves. Many Negroes would go into a deep state of melancholy (*banzo*) and refused to eat or drink until they died. Others took to eating earth until they perished. Still others cut their throats or stabbed themselves to death.[4] Nieuhof wrote about a slave who having been sold to two or three masters in short succession was so exasperated that he ended his life by drowning himself while on a fishing trip.[5]

Less frequently, because of the obvious consequences, but by no means rarely, slaves resisted by attacking their overseers and masters. The Ardras, for instance, often attacked the overseers who made them work and gave them a severe beating.[6] Other Negroes went as far as killing the overseer who abused them. Occasionally a Negro in desperation even took the life of a cruel master himself. When this happened punishment was swift and merciless. On one occasion in Pernambuco a slave who confessed to having decapitated his master was crushed to death between the rollers of the mill.[7]

The most common and most successful form of resistance was to rebel against the master and escape into the forests. The frequency with which slaves escaped from the *engenhos* of Pernambuco during this period is sufficient evidence of the fact that the Africans were far from resigned to a lifetime of captivity, and that they would go to extremes to escape the miserable working conditions at the mill. In fact, slaves fled with such frequency that their loss (added to the number of Negroes who died) brought many of the planters to the brink of bankruptcy.[8]

Slave rebellions in Pernambuco began almost as soon as the institution of slavery was established. The Indians, the first to be

Slave Resistance and Rebellions

enslaved, unable to withstand the rigors of captivity, often fled into the woods where they built new villages. Negro slaves began escaping practically from the very moment they had a taste of their new life. As early as 1573, seven Negro slaves were hanged in Pernambuco "for being in rebellion [and for] assaulting many [people]."[9] By 1608, Negroes were escaping so frequently that the governor General Dom Diogo de Menezes e Sequeira estimated that planters in Pernambuco were losing at least half of their slaves in this fashion.[10]

In addition to the recurrent escapes of one or a few individuals, there were instances of mass desertions. During the war with the Dutch (1630-35), while some slaves either sided with their Portuguese and Brazilian masters or joined the invaders, a larger number refused obedience to both sides and fled into the forests. As a result, work at most of the sugar mills came to a standstill. A report by Dutch Councilman Schott on the situation of the mills located between the River da Jangada and River Una—the most prosperous sugar producing area—gives a clear picture of the problem.

> The only ones who had not escaped were old Negroes and young boys (*molequinhos*). Thus, in the engenho Maratapagipe were only found, João, Manuel, Mulemba, Maria Esperança, Catarina, Suzana and Adriana, 'three Negroes and four Negresses, all old and ailing.' Also in the engenho São José, a couple of old Negroes; in Utinga, 3 old Negresses and one moleque. In the engenho Sibiró de Riba, the Dutch Councilman found only 2 old Negroes and 2 old oxen. In the engenho Cocaú, the situation was better: there Schott found 4 large boilers, 4 new kettles and two old, 8 oxen, 2 cows, 2 calves and, in the slave quarters, Pedro Moleque, wife and two children, João, wife and son, Antonio Jacome with one moleque, Francisco Moleque with one Negress Manangona and two moleques. In N.S. da Palma were found... an old Negro and one Negress. All the others had escaped.[11]

The large number of fugitive slaves led to their organization in small villages where they could find safety and protection. These congregations of fugitive slaves were known individually as *mocambo* or *quilombo*.[12] In these rebel villages, the Negroes surrounded their huts with a fence or stockade and stockpiled as many provisions as they could lay their hands on, so that the hamlet took the character of a military outpost. The *quilombo* was more than a gathering point for fugitive slaves.

> Its internal organization had as [an] important element the tribal institutions which the Negroes brought from Africa and that here, as the slave rebelled, [turned from]... mere surviving elements [to open]... negation of the slavery system. The hierarchy which was established in the quilombos expressed a new value system created by the rebels, that is, it meant that the dichotomy master-slave ceased to exist [to give way to to the standards of control [set by]... the members of the quilombo themselves.[13]

But the *quilombo* did more than simply provide a refuge and a new social organization for the fugitive slaves. It was more than a form of passive resistance. An extension of the *quilombo* and its instrument of retaliation was the *guerrilha*. The *guerrilha* (guerrilla band) was a band of Negroes from a *quilombo*—or sometimes an independent group—who offered resistance through punitive action. They held up travelers on the highways, kidnapped slaves, attacked *engenhos* to steal victuals and weapons, and not infrequently killed overseers and masters.

These activities of the runaway Negroes became so widespread that they terrorized not only the inhabitants of the *engenhos* but also travelers and the populations of nearby towns. By 1612, it was almost impossible to travel in the backlands of Pernambuco without being harassed by Negro bands, and small towns did not dare expand into the interior. In 1640, the situation was so bad that the Dutch authorities agreed to return to the residents of the captaincy, weapons which had been confiscated so that they could protect themselves and their *engenhos* against raids by fugitive slaves.

To capture runaway slaves and to suppress the *guerrilhas*, militias were created under the command of a *capitão do mato* (bush captain). Usually the *capitão do mato* collected a certain sum from the planter upon the return of each fugitive slave.

During the Dutch occupation, there were bush captains who received a salary from the W.I.C. Even João Fernandes Vieira engaged in the pursuit and capture of fugitive slaves. He made a deal with the Dutch to bring all the Negroes he captured before the authorities and to buy them at "130 reais each *peça*".[14] Interestingly enough, there were Negroes who voluntarily went into the woods for the purpose of capturing rebel slaves. Henrique Dias, the Negro hero of the resistance against the Dutch, was one of those who served as *capitão do mato*.[15] Regular troops, sometimes assisted by dogs, were also used to destroy the quilombos but they, too, had little success. Later the task of fighting the rebel slaves fell to the *bandeirantes*, men from the São Paulo area, who had distinguished themselves as Indian slave hunters and in extending the Brazilian frontier. By 1741, a royal decree ordered that Negroes found in a *quilombo* for the first time were to be branded in the forehead with the letter "F." If found in a *quilombo* a second time, the Negro was to have one ear cut off. In 1759, the *bandeirante* Bartolomeu Bueno do Prado, after raiding the *quilombo* of Campo Grande in Minas Gerais, produced "3,900 pairs of ears from the Negroes he destroyed."[18]

Quilombos were not limited to any particular area of the country. They sprung up in the sugar areas of Pernambuco, Bahia, and Rio de Janeiro, and later in the mining districts of Minas Gerais and near the coffee *fazendas* in São Paulo, in Maranhão as wel as in Mato Grosso. In short, *quilombos* were a direct consequence of the cruelty of the slave system and appeared wherever slavery was established.

There were sizeable and important *quilombos* in Bahia, Rio de Janeiro and Minas Gerais. But by far the most important of these experiments, because of the size of the territorial area which it occupied, the number of Negroes it congregated, its peculiar political organization, and the length of time it survived—1630-1695—was the great *quilombo* of Palmares in the captaincy of Pernambuco.

The area known as Palmares extended roughly from the northern shore of the São Francisco river northward to the Cape of Santo Agostinho. It was a vast, mountainous area, with many forests and abounding with a variety of palm trees from which both the region and the *quilombo* derived their names.[19] Because of the nature of its terrain and vegetation, the region had always been a kind of sanctuary for runaway slaves. As early as 1612, fugitive Negroes were forming *quilombos* in that area.

Beginning with the Dutch invasion in 1630, large numbers of runaway slaves flocked into that region and began organizing what became known individually as the *"quilombo dos Palmares."* The forests of Palmares offered the Negroes practically everything they needed for their sustenance. At the same time, the woods protected the runaways from the incursions of the white men who were less adaptable and less familiar with the surroundings than the inhabitants of the *quilombo*.

The forests abounded with game such as jaguars, wild hogs, deer, foxes, ant-eaters, rabbits, and a variety of small animals which the Negroes captured with their primitive traps and used as food. The rivers provided an assortment of fishes and crabs. From the palm trees the Negroes extracted cooking oil, feasted on the hearts-of-palm, made butter out of the small coconuts, and from their large leaves they made covers for the roofs of their huts, and a number of small objects such as straw mats on which they slept, fans with which to fan the fire, and even hats.[20] In addition the Negroes raised chickens and planted corn, bananas, manioc, sweet potatoes, beans, and sugar cane. Even marijuana known then as *"fumo de Angola"* grew wild and was widely smoked by the Negroes in water pipes to help pass their moments of sadness or melancholy. Besides providing the Negroes with their food, the forest and the mountainous nature of the terrain protected them by making access by organized troops unfamiliar with the surroundings difficult and dangerous.

As their numbers grew, the runaway slaves or *quilombolas* began to organize on a more permanent basis. The *quilombo* of Palmares consisted of several *mocambos*, or hamlets each having a number of huts surrounded by a stockade. Each *mocambo* was under the leadership of a Negro of importance in the *quilombo*. By 1675, these *mocambos* were spread over a circular area of 60 leagues.

> At 16 leagues from Pôrto Calvo there was the mocambo of Zumbi: 5 leagues to the North, the mocambo of Acotirene; to the East of these, two mocambos called *das Tobocas*; 14 leagues to the Northwest of these mocambos, [there was] that of

Dambrabanga; 8 leagues further to the North, the "stockade" of Subupira; 6 leagues further to the North, the "royal stockade" of Macaco; 5 leagues to the West, the mocambo of Osenga; 9 leagues to the Northwest of Serinhaém, the "stockade" of Amaro; 25 leagues to the Northwest of Alagoas, the *"palmar"* of Andalaquituche, brother of Zumbi; 25 leagues Northwest of Pôrto Calvo, the mocambo of Aqualtune, mother of the king.[21]

By 1643, according to Barleu, six thousand Negroes lived in the small Palmares, the section located on the shore of the Gungouí River, and 5,000 others inhabited the so-called "great Palmares" located at the foot of the Barriga mountain range.[22] In the 1670s, the population of the entire *quilombo* was estimated at 20,000.[23]

To rule the growing *quilombo*, a system of government based on African custom was set up. A king, Ganga-Zumba, was chosen as the first ruler because of his valor and superior skill as a warrior in accordance with African tradition. Because the Negroes selected their ruler in this manner, and because the *quilombo* was organized on the lines of an African State, Palmares was also known as the "Republic of Palmares." Ganga Zumba ruled until 1678, when he was murdered for having concluded an unpopular peace with the white man, and was replaced by his nephew Zumbi. In addition to the king there was a council composed of the chiefs of the several *mocambos*. The council met only to discuss matters concerning the *quilombo* as a whole or to consider preparations for war. At the individual *mocambos*, the chiefs were the supreme local authorities.

The seat of the government and the capital of the *quilombo* was the "royal stockade" of Macaco where the king resided. According to Carneiro, the Macaco was located where today is found the city of União (Alagoas), and was the "Grande Palmares" (Great Palmares) mentioned by Barleu. The second most important village was the *mocambo* of Subupira. Heavily fortified and headed by Ganga-Zona, the king's brother, this *mocambo* was the military headquarters of the *quilombolas*.[24] The Negroes also had a fairly well organized army under the leadership of Commander-in-chief Ganga-Muíça. "Their weapons were bows, arrows, spears and fire-arms taken from punitive expeditions, from nearby residents, or purchased."[25]

In the *quilombo* the Negroes practiced a unique religion. It was a curious mixture of Catholicism, speckled with a variety of superstitions and complemented by some African rituals. In 1645, a Dutch expedition found in the Macaco, a chapel,[26] in which the Portuguese later identified "three statues, one of the Christ-child... another of Our Lady of the Conception, [and] another of São Brás."[27] The *quilombolas* also had their own priests, who performed the rituals of baptism and marriage, and possibly a service similar to the Catholic Mass. To serve as priest the *quilombolas* chose a *ladino* that is, a Negro more acculturated to the white man's ways and possibly better acquainted with their religion. Although weddings were performed more or less according to the Catholic tradition, the Negroes at the *quilombo* were free to marry as many wives as they wished. King Ganga-Zumba, for instance, had "three wives, two Negresses and one mulatto."[28] To the saints' statues and the priest, the Negroes added their own African rituals. Every evening after a head count to make sure that everyone was safe and present, the Negroes gathered and danced to the beating of their drums which could be heard until very late into the night. This was probably the religious *batuque* or some other African religious ritual such as the *xangô*.

While the Negroes were organizing in the forests they began making raids against the *engenhos* and nearby towns to kidnap slaves, women, and to obtain supplies and weapons. Some residents in nearby towns and *engenhos* in order to live in peace traded with the *quilombolas*, sold them weapons and ammunition, and even sold them information about punitive expeditions.[29] This, of course, made the Negroes more powerful and harder to defeat.

Some towns and *engenhos* fared better than others in their relations with the *quilombolas*.

> The Negroes having a particular aversion towards the residents of the villages of Alagoas, Penedo and Pôrto Calvo, [never] conceded them any truce and [being] always on open war against them attacked them continuously, plundering their homes and farms, carrying away their slaves, and particularly the women

and offering a safe abode to those who escape from the homes of their masters.[30]

The *quilombo* acted as a magnet attracting slaves from the *engenhos* nearby. Those who joined the *quilombo* voluntarily were received as free men. Those who were forcibly kidnapped were kept as slaves and forced to work in the fields until they could buy their freedom by kidnapping a replacement. In 1694, the problem was so acute that Governor Caetano de Melo e Castro decided to go to Palmares, because he feared that all slaves in the area would soon join the *quilombolas* and cause the complete ruin of their masters and consequently that of the local economy.

During the Nassau administration (1637-44), the situation was already serious, with the Negroes inflicting great losses to the rural population near Alagoas. In 1638, it was reported that the *quilombolas* had taken as many as 140 slaves from one parish alone.[31] To curb these attacks and to suppress the *quilombolas*, an expedition was sent to Palmares in 1644, under the command of Rudolf Baron. This expedition, however, had very little success since the *quilombolas*, warned in advance perhaps by slaves in nearby *engenhos* who often cooperated with them or by town merchants, abandoned their positions moving farther to the West. Following the unsuccessful attempt of Baron, another expedition was sent in 1645 under the command of Captain Jan Blaer. Fortunately more detailed information is available regarding this campaign because of the existence of a diary in which were registered the most important events of the march. The Blaer expedition left the town of Salgados on February 26. On March 2nd, Blaer fell ill and was taken back to Alagoas. The expedition however moved on, now under the command of Lieutenant Jurgens Rijbach. On the 18th, the Dutch reached what was known as "Old Palmares." This was an old *mocambo* abandoned by the Negroes three years earlier because

> the locale was very unwholesome and many of them had died there; this Palmares was half a mile long and [had] two entrances; the street was one *braça* wide having two water wells in the center;... the entrances of this Palmares were surrounded by two stockades

[one behind the other] connected by beams, but [they] were so covered by the vegetation that [only] with great difficulty we could get through.[32]

On the following day the expedition reached the "other Palmares." This was the one attacked and partially defeated by the Baron expedition the previous year.[33] Continuing their march the Dutch soldiers arrived at the "new Palmares," in reality the "royal stockade" of Macaco. This *mocambo*, according to the diary, had 220 houses and was surrounded by two strong stockades. To the frustration of the Dutch, only a few Negroes were inside when they brought down the door. The others, once again warned in advance, had fled farther into the woods.[34]

After these unsuccessful attempts by the Dutch there was a long moratorium on expeditions against the *quilombo*. The Dutch had to concentrate all their resources on the rebellion of Portuguese colonists which broke out in 1645 and could no longer spare the time and the soldiers to fight the runaway Negroes. After Pernambuco was retaken (1654), the Portuguese authorities began to send expeditions of their own to crush the *quilombolas*. At least fourteen Luzo-Brazilian expeditions were sent to Palmares before the *quilombo* was totally defeated.[35]

The first expedition of the post-Dutch period was sent in 1667 under the command of Zenóbio Accioly de Vasconcelos. This was merely a reconnaissance mission to survey the area of the *quilombo*. After the Vasconcelos mission, the Negroes were left alone for four years. As the raids and crimes committed by the Negroes intensified,[36] another expedition was sent in 1672 under the command of Jácome Bezerra. Although Bezerra had elaborate attack plans, his expedition was frustrated by the Negroes. In 1673, a force led by Cristovão Lins, Head-Captain of Pôrto Calvo also failed to crush the *quilombolas*.

The first significant victory against the *quilombolas* came in 1675. On September 23, an expedition of "280 men, whites, mulattoes and Indians" led by Head-Sergeant Manuel Lopes left Pôrto Calvo for Palmares. By December 22, they reached the Macaco, the capital of the *quilombo*. It was "a large city of more than 2,000 houses, fortified with a solid ... stockade and defended by three detachments and with a large number of defenders."[37] After a fierce combat the Negroes went into hiding some twenty-five leagues away while Lopes' troops pursued them. The *mocambo* was partially burned, and there were many dead and wounded among the *quilombolas*. In addition, seventy Negroes were taken prisoner. The Negro Zumbi, who later became the leader of the *quilombo*, was wounded in the conflict but managed to escape.[38]

Encouraged by Lopes' success, the Portuguese authorities concentrated on the complete submission of the *quilombo*. By 1677, "the campaign [against the *quilombo*] assumed the character of [a] struggle for the possession of the lands of Palmares—considered unanimously [as] the best in all the captaincy of Pernambuco."[39] Preparations were begun for another expedition. In 1676, Head-Captain Fernão Carrilho, famous for his successes in fighting against *quilombos* in Sergipe, was brought in to lead another march against Palmares. To pay for the war against the Negroes, a tax was levied on the residents of Pernambuco. Apparently, the measure was very unpopular and, in 1677, the residents of that captaincy petitioned the Crown not to contribute because they were already burdened and impoverished by so many other taxes.[40] Nevertheless, the war against Palmares continued as planned. Fernão Carrilho led two successful expeditions (1676-1677) against the *quilombo* killing many Negroes, including Ganga-Muíça. With his military headquarters destroyed and many of his warriors killed or imprisoned, the King Ganga-Zumba sued for peace in 1688.

While the details of the peace agreement were sent to Lisbon for approval, the younger generation of *quilombolas* repudiated the treaty with the Portuguese. They assassinated Ganga-Zumba, proclaimed his nephew Zumbi as their new leader, and resumed their raids against the *engenhos*. Zumbi was a brave warrior and led the resistance against the white man's attacks to the end. He became a legendary figure during his time and many of the Negroes thought he was immortal.

The Overseas Council at Lisbon having also repudiated the peace agreement with Ganga-Zumba, the campaigns agaist Palmares were resumed. From 1679 to 1686, six expeditions were sent to the *quilombo* without accomplishing the complete submission of the Negroes.[41] Determined to attain more conclusive results in his efforts to crush the *quilombo*, the Governor João da Cunha Souto Maior invited the *bandeirante* Domingos Jorge

Velho to take command of the campaign against Palmares. After all their demands were met and an official contract signed, the *bandeirantes* went to work. By December 1692, Domingos Jorge Velho and his troops arrived at the *quilombo*. A fierce attack was launched but the Negroes held out. Tired and running out of supplies, the *bandeirantes* retreated to Pôrto Calvo. While the *bandeirantes* recovered in Pôrto Calvo, Zumbi gathered his troops atop the Barriga mountains and prepared to meet the enemy.

In January 1694, the *bandeirantes* again confronted the runaways. Finding the Negroes well fortified behind their heavy stockade, Domingos Jorge Velho asked for reinforcements. When all had come, 3,000 men under the command of Domingos Jorge Velho and Head-Captain Bernardo Vieira de Melo faced the stockade.

After a prolonged siege during which the *bandeirantes* and Pernambucans could not reach the stockade without heavy losses, a new stratagem was tried. A diagonal fence was built connecting Jorge Velho's positions to a point in the Negroes' stockade not guarded because it ended at a precipice. Running short of ammunition and supplies, and noticing that the *bandeirantes'* fence was only seven or eight braças short of reaching his fortifications, Zumbi prepared to withdraw. In the middle of the night of the 5th to the 6th of February, the Negroes tried to escape by passing between the opening in the enemy's fence guarded by Vieira de Melo's troops and the precipice. Discovering the plan, the troops opened fire against the *quilombolas*. "It was dark, the battle took place on the edge of the precipice, and about two hundred Negroes fell off the cliff and an equal number were killed during the struggle." Another 519 *quilombolas* were taken prisoner.[42] On the morning of the 6th, some white troops entered the Macaco and captured those still inside, mostly the old, women and children. In the meantime, a contingent of *bandeirantes* destroyed the remaining *mocambos* and took 166 Negroes prisoner. For all practical purposes Palmares was finished.

Although the *quilombo* had been crushed, Zumbi and some of his top assistants could not be accounted for. At first, there were reports that Zumbi, in a dramatic action, had jumped off the cliff. But it seen became clear that the courageous Negro and some of his soldiers managed to escape and were still at large. For almost two years after the final attack on the Macaco, Zumbi and his followers were hounded by troops. Finally, on November 20, 1695, betrayed by a mulatto former member of the *quilombo*, Zumbi and some twenty of his men were surprised by *bandeirantes* under the command of André Furtado de Mendonça. Zumbi fought bravely but in vain. Only one of his men was taken alive.[43] Zumbi's head was taken to the Governor, who ordered it placed on a stake and displayed in a Recife square to intimidate the Negroes and as proof that he had indeed been captured and killed.[44]

Despite all the problems it created, Palmares was not a conspiracy to seize power, nor an armed insurrection to exterminate the white population. In fact, no examples of these more violent forms of resistance were recorded in Pernambuco during the sixteenth and seventeenth centuries. The significance of *quilombos* such as Palmares is that they represented not isolated acts of violence by separate small groups, but a continued struggle for freedom on the part of thousands of runaway slaves in every corner of the country where the institution of slavery existed. The large number of runaway slaves recorded in Pernambuco, and the continuity with which the Negroes escaped throughout this period is a clear indication of the cruel treatment they received and the best testimony of the Negro's refusal to resign himself to life in captivity at the *engenho*.

NOTES

1. Contrary to Roman legal tradition which recognized the slave as a person and gave him certain rights, Negroes in the *engenhos* of Pernambuco were frequently counted as beasts of burden and listed in correspondence and records under the category of *semoventes* together with cattle and horses. See AHU, Consulta do Conselho Ultramarino (Lisboa, 16 de dezembro de 1656) códice 15, fols. 260v-262.
2. Mello, "Um Regimento de Feitor-Mor," pp. 84.
3. van der Dussen, *Relatório sôbre as capitanias conquistadas*, p. 92.
4. Gilberto Freyre, "Deformações de corpo dos negros fugidos," *Novos Estudos Afro-Brasileiros* (Rio de Janeiro: Civilização Brasileira Editôra, 1937), p. 246.
5. Nieuhof, *Memorável Viagem*, p. 309.

6. "Breve Discurso Sôbre o Estado das Quatro Capitanias Conquistadas," pp. 171-72; van der Dussen, *Relatório sôbre as capitanias conquistadas*, p. 92.
7. AHU, Consulta de Partes do Conselho Ultramarino (Lisboa, 12 de novembro de 1683), códice 49, fols. 39v-40.
8. ANTT, Discurso sôbre gêneros para o comercio que há no Maranhão e Pará. Composto por Duarte Ribeiro de Macedo, 1633, cap. 2, Manuscritos do Brasil, no. 39; Carta de D. Diogo de Menezes a El-rey (Olinda, 23 de agôsto de 1608), Correspondencia do Governador D. Diogo de Menezes, 1608-1612, *ABNRJ*, Vol. 57 (1935), p. 39.
9. "Historia de la Fundación del collegio de la Capitania de Pernambuco," ABNRJ, Vol. 49 (1927), p. 23.
10. Carta de Dom Diogo de Menezes a El-Rey (Olinda, 23 de agôsto de 1608), Correspondencia do Governador D. Diogo de Menezes, 1608-1612, ABNRJ, Vol. 57 (1935), p. 39.
11. Mello, *Tempo dos Flamengos*, pp. 206-207.
12. A *quilombo* was officially defined as "every [place of] residence of more than five fugitive slaves in [a] remote area ... " See Clovis Moura, *Rebeliões da Senzala. Quilombos, Insurreições, Guerrilhas* (Rio de Janeiro: Coleção Temas Brasileiros, Conquista, 1972), p. 87.
13. *Ibid.*
14. Mello, *Tempo dor Flamengos*, p. 215.
15. José Antônio Gonsalves de Mello, *Henrique Dias, Governador dos Pretos, Crioulos e Mulatos do Estado do Brasil* (Recife: Universidade do Recife, 1954), p. 26.
16. In 1630, the Heeren XIX, notified the Dutch Political Council in Pernambuco of the shipment of 300 English bulldogs to help the Dutch capture Indians, Negroes and members of local resistance groups. See Mello, *Tempo dos Flamengos*, p. 185.
17. J. A. Goulart, *Da Palmatória ao Patíbulo*, pp. 68, 161.
18. Moura, *Rebeliões de Senzala*, p. 96.
19. Most of the Palmares territory is now located within the boundaries of the modern state of Alagoas.
20. "Diario da viagem do capitão João Blaer aos Palmares em 1645," trans. by Alfredo de Carvalho, RIAGP, No. 56 (Recife, 1902), pp. 88-90, 93, 95.
21. Edison Carneiro, *O Quilombo dos Palmares* (Rio de Janeiro: Editôra Civilização Brasileira, 1966), pp. 25-26.
22. Barleu, *História*, p. 253.
23. Moura, *Rebeliões da Senzala*, p. 181.
24. Carneiro, *O Quilombo dos Palmares*, p. 26.
25. Moura, *Rebeliões da Senzala*, p. 181.
26. "Diario da viagem do capitão João Blaer aos Palmares," p. 92.

27. Carneiro, *O Quilombo dos Palmares*, p. 27.
28. *Ibid.*
29. R. K. Kent, "Palmares: An African State in Brazil," *Journal of African History*, Vol. 6, No. 2 (1965), p. 171.
30. Pereira da Costa, *Anais*, 3:267. The towns of Alagoas, Penedo and Pôrto Calvo were located near Palmares within the boundaries of today's state of Alagoas.
31. Dagelijksche Notule, February 26, 1638, cited in Mello, *Tempo dos Flamengos*, p. 207.
32. Diario da viagem do capitão João Blaer aos Palmares," p. 91. A *braça* was a unit of length equivalent to 2.2 meters.
33. *Ibid.*
34. *Ibid.*, p. 92. 220 houses seem like a very conservative estimate since according to Barleu 5,000 Negroes lived in this *mocambo*.
35. Carneiro, *O Quilombo dos Palmares*, p. 13.
36. *AHU*, Carta do Governador Fernão de Sousa Coutinho ao Rei (1° de junho de 1671), Documentos referentes a Pernambuco, caixa 6.
37. Moura, *Rebeliões da Senzala*, p. 185.
38. *Ibid.*
39. Carneiro, *O Quilombo dos Palmares*, p. 8.
40. AHU, Consulta do Conselho Ultramarino (Lisboa, 28 de junho de 1677), Documentos referentes a Pernambuco, caixa 35.
41. According to Carneiro, these expeditions were led by the following men:
Gonçalo Moreira, 1679.
André Dias, 1680.
Manuel Lopes, 1682.
Fernão Carrilho, 1683.
João de Freitas da Cunha, 1684.
Fernão Carrilho, 1686.
See, *O Quilombo dos Palmares*, p. 313.
42. *Ibid.*, pp. 111-13.
43. *Ibid.*, p. 11.
44. *Ibid.*, p. 119.

PART III
CONCLUSION

CONCLUSION

During the sixteenth and seventeenth centuries the province of Veracruz and the captaincy of Pernambuco developed into important sugar producing areas. Because of the inhospitable climate, maize and wheat did not grow as well in Veracruz as in other parts of New Spain. Very early therefore, the province turned to tropical plantation-type agriculture and particularly to sugar cane as the most adaptable to its soil and climate. In the *várzeas* of Pernambuco, the *massapê* provided the ideal conditions for the growing of sugar cane, which gradually replaced brazilwood as the principal product of that region.

Although there is controversy as to exactly when sugar cane was introduced in Pernambuco, it is apparent that the plant was brought to that captaincy before it was introduced to Veracruz. Luis da Câmara Cascudo contends that sugar cane was brought to Pernambuco in 1503. Other historians state that the plant came to Brazil with the first expeditions. In any case, certainly by 1516, when the *Casa da India* was planning to build a sugar mill in Brazil, sugar cane must have been already available in the colony. In Veracruz the *sacharum officinarum* was introduced sometime later by Hernán Cortés who, by 1524 was growing sugar cane and building a sugar mill in Tuxtla.

Cortés' mill was in full operation by 1534 and therefore preceded the establishment of a similar refinery in Pernambuco by some eight years. Although sugar had been produced in Pernambuco as early as 1526, it was only in small quantities and probably by the primitive process of slashing the sugar cane with a machete and allowing the juice which ran out to crystallize by exposing it to the sun. The first bona fide sugar mill to be established in Duarte Coelho's captaincy was built in 1542 in the proximity of the city of Olinda. It was the "Engenho Nossa Senhora da Ajuda" and belonged, as we have seen, to Jerônimo de Albuquerque.

From this modest beginning the sugar industry expanded quite rapidly in both areas. In Veracruz, licenses for the building of sugar mills were sought and obtained by many, and soon several of these factories were springing up throughout the province. By 1550, the Crown, realizing the potential of the new industry, ordered the Viceroy of New Spain to encourage its development by making grants of land to those who wanted to plant cane or build sugar mills. By the end of the century the province had at least forty-six mills in operation varying in size from small animal-driven *trapiches* to the great *ingenios* Orizaba-Tequila and Santísima Trinidad which, according to Chevalier, was the largest sugar refinery in the country at that time. The production of sugar was the first processing industry in New Spain and by the first half of the seventeenth century it had established itself as the single most important economic activity in Veracruz.

In Pernambuco, the sugar industry did not really develop until the establishment of the captaincy system and the coming of Duarte Coelho, the first *donatário*. With the encouragement of the Crown, Duarte Coelho and his successors granted *sesmarias* in the lowlands along the rivers and streams to those willing and capable of establishing sugar plantations. Soon the rich *massapê* of Pernambuco was covered with sugar cane and Iguaraçu, Olinda, Beberibe, Casa-Forte, and Várzea became important centers of cultivation. After the establishment of the first mill in 1542, the number of *engenhos* multiplied rapidly. By the end of the year, at least two mills were in full production. By 1550, five *engenhos* were in operation. Twenty years later the captaincy had twenty-three mills. During the last quarter of the sixteenth and through most of the seventeenth centuries, sugar exports from Pernambuco experienced a

Conclusion

remarkable increase which coincided with the great expansion in the sugar industry itself. During this period, the number of mills jumped from fifty in 1587 to ninety in 1612, to 150 in 1629 reaching 246 by 1710.

Despite similarities in their early development, the sugar industries in Veracruz and Pernambuco experienced different rates of expansion and attained different levels of importance. While Veracruz at the end of the sixteenth century had some forty-six mills, Pernambuco by 1600 boasted 120 *engenhos*. At this time although the sugar industry of Veracruz was probably the most important in New Spain, it was already surpassed in stature and significance by its counterpart in the captaincy of Pernambuco. By the first half of the seventeenth century sugar and Pernambuco were synonymous, and that captaincy was already the leading sugar producer in the world.

Like other types of plantation agriculture, sugar cane required the labor of large numbers of workers. In Veracruz and in Pernambuco the European colonizers first resorted to the enslavement of the Amerindians to obtain the necessary labor force to man their plantations and to operate their sugar mills. In both areas, however, overwork and close contact with the white man brought about the near complete obliteration of the Indian population.

In Veracruz, the destruction of the natives began with the wars of conquest, increased with the enslavement of the Indians and was made more rapid and severe by the spread of fevers and epidemics. Beginning with the first settlements Indians were distributed in *encomienda* and forced to work for the Spaniards in their mines and sugar mills. Although the Indians of Veracruz were accustomed to some forms of labor, they proved unfit to withstand the long hours of hard work at the mill and the punishments to which they were subjected. They died in large numbers. Yet an even more devastating loss of life resulted from the spread of fevers and epidemics. With the first wave of settlers a number of European diseases were introduced to the Spanish colony. Smallpox, yellow fever, measles and other plagues found sanctuary in the hot and humid areas of Veracruz and were quickly spread by the large number of mosquitoes which infested the region. Unprotected against these diseases and weakened by the strenuous work at the mill,

Indians died by the tens of thousands until many areas of the province were almost depopulated.

In Pernambuco because of the peaceful nature of the early occupation, Indians were spared the devastation of wars of conquest. In the beginning, Indians were friendly towards the Portuguese and cut Brazilwood for them in exchange for beads and trinkets. Their devastation started with the development of plantation agriculture which brought about their enslavement and closer contact with the Europeans. As the natives were needed for the sugar plantations, raids to enslave them became frequent. Many were killed in these campaigns while others were driven farther into the less hospitable interior. Those who were captured were condemned to a life of captivity at the *engenhos*. At the plantations and the mills, closer contact with the white man made the Indian more susceptible to European diseases. Syphilis was common. Fevers and epidemics, though they never reached the deadly proportions of those which plagued New Spain in 1545 and 1576, often carried away large numbers of Indians and occasionally decimated entire villages of natives. Equally, if not more deadly, was hard labor at the sugar plantation and sugar mills. Tossed from their simple and nomadic life into a sedentary and arduous situation, the Indians could not adapt. Many perished from exhaustion and maltreatment, others starved or died from eating sand, still others died of melancholy. In the case of Pernambuco, therefore, perhaps more than war and disease, though they were certainly byproducts of the industry, it was the work at the sugar operations that killed the Indian.

In both Spanish and Portuguese America, however, the exploitation and decimation of the Indian population did not go unnoticed. In the Spanish possessions members of the religious orders such as Bartolomé de Las Casas, Juan de Zumárraga and Vasco de Quiroga vehemently condemned the exploitation of the Indians by the Spaniards and took steps to improve the condition of the natives. In Brazil, the Jesuits led by Fathers Manuel da Nóbrega and José de Anchieta became the champions of the Indians. They denounced the hatred which characterized the settlers' attitudes towards the Indians and began to gather those who were free in *reduções* to save them from life in captivity in the *engenhos* and to facilitate their conversion to Christianity.

Conclusion

In their efforts to save the Indians from slavery and destruction, the religious orders in Spanish America were more successful than the Jesuits in Portuguese Brazil. Largely due to the efforts of Las Casas, the New Laws which prohibited the future enslavement of the Indians were instituted in 1542-1543. Following the New Laws and continued pressure by the religious orders, a number of royal decrees outlawed the use of Indians in occupations considered dangerous to their health and welfare. Finally in 1601, Philip III expressly prohibited the use of Indians in textile and sugar mills because of the high fatality rate associated with these occupations. A system of *veedores* or inspectors and the watchful eyes of the friars helped to make sure that the Indians were not employed in the arduous tasks of the mills.

In Brazil, although the Jesuits helped to bring about a number of decrees prohibiting the enslavement of the Indians, these measures were for the most part rather vague and went unheeded by the sugar planters. In fact despite the efforts of the Jesuits, the enslavement of the Indians did not end until well into the eighteenth century when this practice rather than being terminated by royal decrees simply became an unprofitable business venture.

In Veracruz the decline of the Indian population and the enforcement of protective measures created a severe labor shortage in the sugar industry. In Pernambuco a similar shortage occurred, but in the absence of effective protective laws, it was largely due to the increasing decline in the number of natives. Faced with such a shortage, sugar planters in Veracruz and in Pernambuco began to look for alternatives and more reliable sources of labor. In both cases the importation of African slaves provided the answer. African slaves were no strangers to the Spanish and Portuguese as they had been coming to America since the first expeditions. However it was not until Indian labor proved unsuitable or scarce that Negroes were introduced in large numbers to provide the labor for the sugar plantations.

In Veracruz the substitution of Indians for African slaves began much earlier than in Pernambuco. The introduction of Negroes into the Spanish colonies in America had been authorized since 1501. By the 1520s the traffic was in full swing, with the Negroes being introduced under import licenses granted by the Crown. By the end of the century the Reynel *asiento* had opened the door for the massive importation of Negroes into Spanish America under monopoly contracts. So when the need for African labor became apparent in New Spain, the existence of established channels greatly facilitated the importation of Negroes. As early as 1535, Rodrigo de Albornoz received a license to import one hundred slaves for his sugar mills and other properties. Others followed suit, and by 1537 the slave traffic was well established with large numbers of Africans being brought in through Veracruz. By 1553, the number of slaves brought in under these licenses was already large enough to worry the authorities. In the beginning these Negroes were brought from the Caribbean islands or entrepôts in southern Spain. By 1585, slaves were already being introduced to New Spain directly from Africa under licenses granted to individuals. In 1592 a shipment of 140 *piezas de esclavos* brought directly from Cape Verde arrived in Veracruz under a license given to the Jaureguis of Seville. As the need for Negroes continued to grow after the plague of 1576, the great asientos were sent up to provide a larger and steadier flow of Negroes into the Spanish colonies. By the terms of these *asientos* one fourth of the Negroes brought each year to Spanish America were to be unloaded at Veracruz.

In Pernambuco the importation of large numbers of Africans began much later and for the most part it was done in an irregular fashion. Although there were several requests for Negroes during the first half of the sixteenth century, the slave traffic from Africa was not officially established until 1559, when the Crown authorized each person owning a sugar operation to import up to 120 *peças de escravos* from the Congo. Because Portuguese traders were more interested in the trade with the Spanish colonies, most of the Negroes brought to Pernambuco during the period we are studying were imported under a number of licenses given by the Crown to individual planters. Shipments were relatively small and consigned to many different importers, lacking the regularity and other advantages of the *asiento* system. The exception to this rule was during the Dutch occupation when the West India Company had the monopoly over the slave trade.

While the flow of Africans to Pernambuco started later than the importation of Negroes to Veracruz, it grew rapidly during the years 1576-1600, and during the seventeenth century, clearly surpassed in volume the influx of Negroes to the Mexican province. As the sugar industry in Pernambuco grew considerably larger than its counterpart in Veracruz it required a proportionally higher number of slaves. As a result, the total number of Negroes brought to Pernambuco was substantially larger than the quantity imported for the sugar plantations of Veracruz. Although reliable figures are not available for Veracruz, it is known that Pernambuco alone imorted no less than 250,000 Negroes during the period we are studying, a total substantially larger than the 130,000 Africans brought to all of New Spain between 1519 and 1650.

Since Portuguese factories in Africa supplied most of the slaves brought to Spanish and Portuguese America, Negroes brought to Veracruz and Pernambuco often shared a common origin. From time to time, however, a number of factors affected the flow of Negroes from a particular area in Africa to both of the two American markets. In the early years of the traffic most slaves brought to both areas came from Guinea, Cape Verde, and São Tomé. With the capture of São Tomé by the Dutch in 1599, the center of the trade moved south and established itself in Angola. While the slave trade from Angola to Pernambuco flourished, the importation of Negroes from that African region to Veracruz encountered some difficulties. The distance from Angola to Veracruz was much greater than from Angola to Pernambuco. As a result, slaves shipped to the Spanish colony suffered a higher incidence of deaths than those sent to the much closer shores of the Portuguese captaincy. When Dutch forces sent from Pernambuco captured Angola in 1641, Negroes brought to the captaincy came almost exclusively from that African region. On the other hand, the taking of Angola by the Dutch brought to a halt the importation of Negroes from that region to the sugar mills of Veracruz. While the Dutch controlled Angola and the Portuguese revolted against Spain (1640), Negroes brought to Veracruz were imported under individual licenses and were supposedly obtained in areas not controlled by the Dutch or Portuguese. This situation continued until 1622 when the *asiento* was resumed and holders of the monopoly bought Negroes from whoever could supply them. In 1680, the *asiento* passed to Juan Barroso del Pozo. From that time until 1696 when the *asiento* went to the *Companhia Portuguesa de Cabo Verde, Cacheu e Negócios dos Pretos*, Negroes brought to Veracruz came almost exclusively from Curaçao and other Caribbean islands through Dutch middlemen.

Because of the simultaneous occupation of Pernambuco and Angola by the Dutch, the Brazilian captaincy imported a larger number of Negroes from the Congo and Angola regions than Veracruz. Nevertheless, practically all tribal groups which came to Pernambuco were also represented in Veracruz. Thus, in varying numbers the Berbers, Wolofs, Ardras, Minas, Angolas, Congos and Negroes from São Tomé, Calabar, Sierra Leone, Cape Verde and the Sudan constituted the great bulk of the slave population of both Veracruz and Pernambuco during this period.

The work performed by Negro slaves in the sugar plantations of Veracruz and Pernambuco was very similar. In both regions slaves worked long hours and were allowed very little free time. Work was particularly arduous during the grinding season which lasted in both areas from late August or September until February and sometimes May. During this period the mills were in operation seven days a week, twenty-four hours a day.

In both regions the typical work day for field hands started at dawn and lasted until dark. Field hands were usually divided into male and female gangs, with children eight to fourteen usually working with the women. Adult males cut cane while women and children were usually engaged in tying the cane in bundles and weeding and watering the fields. Each gang worked under the supervision of an overseer. In Veracruz, male overseers supervised the male gangs while female overseers directed the female slaves. In Pernambuco as a general rule male overseers supervised both male and female gangs.

Work in the mill also started at dawn but during the grinding season it continued into the night and around the clock seven days a week. Slaves toiling in the mills worked in rotation twenty-four hours a day. Owing to the more strenuous work required by most phases of the manufacturing process, fewer women were employed at the mill. It seems, however, that the *engenhos* of Pernambuco employed a larger number of females in the lighter tasks of the mill than did the refineries of Veracruz.

Conclusion 175

In addition to unskilled laborers, the sugar mills of Veracruz and Pernambuco employed a number of skilled workers. These included brickmakers, ironsmiths, carpenters and herdsmen. Although these men were often white or mulatto workers who received a salary, in many cases they were Negro slaves who had learned the trade. Among the skilled workers the most important was the sugar master known in Veracruz as *maestro de azúcar* and as *mestre de açúcar* in Pernambuco. The sugar master was an expert in the making of sugar on whose knowhow depended the quality and quantity of sugar produced by each mill. Some of the sugar masters were white men, but many experienced slaves also learned the trade and served in that capacity. It was only rarely that young slaves were trained to be craftsmen or sugar masters. Usually slaves being considered for skilled jobs were older. Robert W. Fogel and Stanley L. Engerman found a similar pattern in their study of slavery in the American South. They argue that as a general rule "... this would be an uneconomical policy, since the earlier an investment is made in occupational training, the more years there are to reap the returns on that investment." In the context of slavery in Veracruz and Pernambuco, this was, instead, a sound precautionary measure not entirely uneconomical. To protect their investment against sabotage masters wanted to be sure of the slave's loyalty before entrusting him with tools and equipment and in the case of the sugar master with almost complete control over the most crucial steps in the sugar making operation.[1]

Besides those engaged in field work or connected with the prodution of sugar, the larger plantations of Veracruz and Pernambuco had a number of slaves employed as domestic servants. Among these domestic slaves, some of the females worked in the kitchen cooking and baking, or cleaning the plantation house. Others served as nannies and wet nurses to the children of their white masters, or as companions to their mistresses. The males usually handled the heavier chores around the house, served as valets or footmen, or simply served as companions to their masters. The number of domestic slaves varied according to the status and financial situation of the plantatin owner. In the larger more prestigious plantations many of these domestic slaves were really superfluous, mere hangers-on without specific duties to perform and retained mainly as status symbols.

Since the large planters of Pernambuco attained a higher measure of prestige and social status they kept a larger number of domestic slaves than their counterparts in Veracruz. Because of their large numbers and close contact with their masters and mistresses these domestic slaves played a significant role in the sociological development of the rural family in Pernambuco, and left a more lasting mark on the language, culture and folklore of the region than their brothers and sisters in Veracruz.

Because they were indispensable for the operation of the sugar plantations, African slaves were a very expensive commodity during the second half of the sixteenth and particularly during the seventeenth century. In the Veracruz and Pernambuco markets prices varied according to supply and demand. On account of the growing need for Negroes, however, prices during this period reflect an almost constant upward trend. In Veracruz in 1550, an average Negro sold for 200 pesos. Ten years later, planters were paying as much as 500 pesos for an African slave despite attempts by the Spanish Crown to set a maximum price of first 120 and later 140 ducats a head. The Crown's attempts to curb prices led slave traders to stop the shipment of new Negroes from Africa. This had the effect of reducing the supply of slaves on hand and increasing the illegal sale of Negroes at whatever price the market would bear. This situation persisted until the great *asientos* starting at the end of the century reestablished the flow of Negroes from Africa to New Spain. Despite the *asientos*, however, slaves continued to be expensive throughout the seventeenth century. In 1619, for instance, a thirty-year-old woman and four-month-old son were sold for 475 pesos, and, in 1653 an eighteen-year-old male sold for 415 pesos.

In the case of Pernambuco the upward trend in the price of Negroes is even more clearly discernible. In the last decade of the sixteenth century the price of an African slave ranged from 13 thousand reis to 40 thousand reis. In 1642, a *peça* from Angola sold for 96 thousand reis. Later that year some Negroes were sold at 100 thousand reis. During the Dutch occupation, particularly between 1637 and 1645, an average Negro went for

200 to 300 florins, while a strong, well built African commanded as much as 600 and even 800 florins.

In addition to supply and demand other factors influenced the price of slaves in both markets. Among these, age, physical condition, tribal origin and special skills were the most important. In Veracruz as well as in Pernambuco, healthy male Negroes between the ages of eighteen and twenty-five, or what was known as a *pieza* or *peça*, sold for the highest prices. In both markets single women and older males were less in demand and went for lower prices. In Veracruz a woman with an infant sold at a higher price than a woman alone. In Pernambuco on the other hand, infants did not count and when sold with their mothers apparently did not add anything to the price of the woman.

In both markets preferences for Negroes from certain African regions or tribal groups also affected the price. In 1561, for instance, Negroes from the Cape Verde islands commanded the highest prices in Veracruz. In the seventeenth century this preference, and consequently the high prices, shifted to slaves from Angola because they were humble and docile. Also in Pernambuco the Angolas commanded the highest prices during the seventeenth century on account of their docility and physical strength. On the other hand, the Ardras and Negroes from Calabar sold at lower prices because they were rebellious and supposedly lazy and negligent. In Pernambuco during the seventeenth century, Negroes from Guinea, Sierra Leone and Cape Verde were not considered suitable for hard work and therefore commanded a lesser price than the Angolas. But because they were clean and good-looking, these Negroes were preferred by the Portuguese as domestic servants.

Negroes who had mastered a trade were very much in demand. Thus, those who were carpenters, ironsmiths or artisans often carried a higher price tag. Slaves who had learned the language of the colonists and were more accustomed to European ways, usually sold for more than those just arrived from Africa. The most valuable skill a Negro could master, however, was to learn the job of sugar master. A slave with this qualification would normally sell for the highest price the market would bear. In Veracruz as early as 1576, a Negro with excellent knowledge of the sugar master trade was valued at eight hundred "pesos de oro de minas."[2]

It would be difficult to determine with any degree of accuracy whether the price of Negroes was higher in one region or the other by reducing the different currencies to a common denominator. There is little doubt, however, that as a general rule planters in Pernambuco had a much larger investment in slaves than planters in Veracruz. During the seventeenth century the high price of Negroes and the high incidence of deaths among them became, as the records indicate, a major problem for the *senhores de engenho* of Pernambuco. Because Negroes were very expensive, planters in Pernambuco bought them on credit from traders and later from the W.I.C. A large number of these slaves escaped or died before they were paid for. To continue in business a planter had to replace them with new slaves. This, of course, meant buying more Negroes on credit and consequently increasing the planter's debts. Eventually, these debts became so large that the revenue from the *engenho* was no longer sufficient to repay them. Whenever creditors insisted in collecting their money, the entire industry was threatened with bankruptcy. Although planters in Veracruz faced similar difficulties with fugitive slaves and the high incidence of deaths, these problems apparently did not burden the local sugar industry to the extent that they did in Pernambuco. While credit must certainly have been used for the purchase of Negroes in Veracruz there are no indications that it developed into a form of subsidy indispensable for the survival of the sugar industry, as was the case in Pernambuco. When all these things are considered the evidence suggests that owing to a number of factors (see Chapter III, Part II), the cost of maintaining an adequate supply of slave labor was a much heavier burden to the sugar planters of Pernambuco than to their counterparts in Veracruz.

Although Negroes were very expensive and were required to work very hard, they were fed an inadequate diet. In Veracruz and in Pernambuco, slave diets varied according to the habits of the land and with the nature of the victuals available in the immediate area. In Veracruz the main staple of the slave's diet was maize consumed in the form of the Indian tortilla. In Pernambuco, on the other hand, the basis of the slave diet was manioc flour consumed dry or in the form of a gruel. As with maize in Veracruz, manioc in Pernambuco was an important item in the diet of the natives.

In both regions the basic diet was sometimes supplemented by other items such as salt, molasses, beef and beans in Veracruz, and molasses, dried meat and dried fish in Pernambuco. In addition, Negroes tried to improve their diet by fishing, hunting and gathering. The extent to which they were successful in doing so depended, of course, on the amount of time they had and on the quantity of foodstuffs available in the immediate surroundings. Although fish was abundant in the rivers of both regions, it seems that Pernambuco offered a larger variety of fruits than Veracruz. Because Negroes in Pernambuco frequently enjoyed a number of these native fruits, it may be concluded that as a rule, they slave diet in that captaincy, although by no means more adequate than in the plantations of Veracruz, might have been at least somewhat more varied.

Regarding the treatment of slaves, it has been argued that slavery in Brazil was considerably milder than in the United States and in the Spanish-American colonies. A discussion of slavery in the United States does not lie within the scope of this work. Let us therefore confine ourselves to the Spanish and Portuguese experiences with the "peculiar institution" as it existed in the sugar plantations of Veracruz and Pernambuco.

It is undoubtedly true that laws regulating slavery in the Spanish colonies were considerably harsher than those devised by the Portuguese for application in Brazil. In New Spain for instance, the death penalty was at one time, prescribed by law for fugitive slaves who were absent from their masters for six months or more. During the first half of the sixteenth century, a Negro carrying a knife or any other weapon without specific authorization was punished with castration. Later the legal punishment for this offense was reduced to 100 lashes in the public square for the first time and 200 lashes plus having one hand nailed to the flogging pole at the square for the second offense.

It is indeed to the credit of the Portuguese monarchs that in their decrees pertaining to slavery they did not go as far as to prescribe such extreme measures. On the other hand, it would be a great mistake to assume that because the penalties called for in the Portuguese decrees were relatively milder, slaves were spared the miseries of more cruel punishments. In practice, within the confines of the *engenhos* of Pernambuco, neither overseers nor masters needed or waited for the encouragement or the support of the law to avenge themselves on slaves who had incurred their anger. The records of the period, as we have seen, abound with instances of slaves being castrated or murdered by their masters, whipped to death, or burned alive in the furnaces of the mill.

In Pernambuco as in Veracruz, punishment was frequent and severe. Every known instrument used in the plantations of Veracruz to punish and torture slaves was also used in the *engenhos* of Pernambuco. The whip, iron chains and collars, the hot branding iron, and the *tronco*, were no less familiar to slaves in Pernambuco than they were to Negroes in the plantations of Veracruz. In addition to using all of these devices, Portuguese masters did not lag behind their Spanish counterparts in devising more bizarre ways of punishing their slaves. Thus the Spanish slave owner who kept a private jail in his property, or who dragged a nude slave through the streets, or who castrated a Negro with his own hands, was no harsher than Portuguese masters and mistresses who cut their slaves' ears or noses, burned their Negroes with drops of sealing wax, or had a slave's eyes gouged out in a fit of jealousy. There were, of course, masters in Veracruz and in Pernambuco who were kind and who treated their slaves in a humane way. As a general rule, however, the evidence (for the period we are studying) overwhelmingly suggests that the life of the Negro slave in the sugar mills of Veracruz and Pernambuco, as well as in other parts of Brazil, was a continuing nightmare, a life filled with suffering, compared, not lightly, by Father Antonio Vieira to the sufferings of Christ as the Calvary, and by Antonil to the agony of eternal damnation.

The larger sugar plantations of Veracruz and Pernambuco were self-sufficient, self-contained, economic, social, and cultural entities. In both regions the large sugar plantation was a separate community, a separate world in which life rotated around the triangle formed by the mill, the plantation house, and the chapel. Within the boundaries of his property the plantation owner was the sole dispenser of justice and the arbiter of

Conclusion 181

social order. In both regions each plantation had its own mores and standards of conduct. Penalties for those who violated the rules were also determined locally regardless of royal decrees and often in direct conflict with them. At the plantation, sugar was king, and the will of the master was at one and the same time both the gospel and the law.

In Veracruz, the master's house was the heart of the plantation and the center of all authority. In Pernambuco, the casa grande was all that and more. It was the cornerstone of the slave system and the very symbol of the Brazilian sugar aristocracy. Often an imposing structure, the casa grande remains to this day an integral part of the rural scenery of Pernambuco, a vivid remembrance of a graceful life style, a grim reminder of centuries of fear and oppression.

The style of life inside the large plantation houses was ostentatious. At Santísima Trinidad, for instance, the plantation owner and his family lived and enjoyed themselves as aristocrats surrounded by a large number of servants. On holidays extravagant celebrations were held at the plantation. On these occasions the planter's family and their guests wore fine clothes and enjoyed a variety of activities including tournaments and bullfights. Even though the life style of the rich planters of Veracruz was luxurious, it was not as lavish as that of the small coterie which formed the cream of the sugar aristocracy in Pernambuco. In the large *engenhos* of Pernambuco banquets, parties and celebrations were frequent. On special occasions such as birthdays and weddings, festivities were even more elaborate. There were bullfights, tournaments, and games, all very expensive and ornate. Music was provided by hired musicians or sometimes by Negro slaves. During these occasions women dressed in the finest taffetas, silks, and velvets imported from Portugal and, during the Dutch period, from Holland. As for the men, they spared no expense to sport the best swords and accessories as well as the most fashionable clothes. Such elegance was displayed by the planters and their families that it was remarked, in the early part of the seventeenth century, that not even at the court in Madrid did people dress better than the Brazilian sugar mill owners and their families.

In violent contrast to the opulence of the plantation house were the slave huts. In Veracruz, these were mostly round structures with conical roofs usually made of straw. They were grouped in a small area and enclosed by a fence with a single entrance. In the Mexican province this village-like grouping was known as "*el real de negros.*" In Pernambuco the slave hut was usually a small one-room rectangular structure built of lath and plaster and covered with straw or palm leaves. Each hut had one door and a small opening high up in the wall close to the roof which served as a window. Some were windowless. Several of these huts were grouped in a small area forming a little community within the *engenho*. In Pernambuco the individual hut as well as the community of huts were known as "*senzala.*"

In the *real* as in the *senzala*, slaves had no comfort or privacy. They lived in a communal manner, four or five to a hut regardless of family ties, age or sex. Few slaves were married. In Veracruz most Negroes seemed to have preferred common law relationships. In Pernambuco even though masters permitted cohabitation, many prevented their slaves from getting married. In both regions even those Negroes who were married were seldom assured of a lasting family relationship. In Veracruz as well as in Pernambuco, no consideration was given to the marital status of slaves at the time they were sold. Children were taken away from their parents and sold. And, despite legal provisions to the contrary in Veracruz, and sporadic remonstrations by members of religious organizations in Pernambuco, married couples were frequently separated by the sale of either the husband or wife. Again, there were exceptions to this rule. In both regions domestic slaves in particular, having earned the confidence and affection of their masters and mistresses were sometimes encouraged to marry, and when they did so, were permitted to keep their families together.

Despite the rigors of slavery, Negroes in the plantations of Veracruz and Pernambuco managed not only to preserve part of their African heritage, religion and traditions, but to make a lasting contribution to the folklore of both regions. The strongest influences were in music, popular dances and religion. Musical instruments still in use in Veracruz such as the marimba and the artesa are of African origin. Some of the dances still popular in Veracruz such as the "chuchumbe" and the "sacamandú" were also introduced by African slaves. In Pernam-

Conclusion

buco because of the larger number of Negroes, African influences on the culture and folklore of the region were more pervasive than in Veracruz. Among the African dances the best known in Pernambuco were the *batuque* and the *maracatu*. The *batuque* has gradually disappeared but the *maracatu* remains an important part of the folklore of Pernambuco and is still danced by several groups during the annual festivities of carnaval.

To the extent that it was possible, African slaves in Veracruz and in Pernambuco continued to practice their own religions. In both places most of these cults centered around witchcraft, animism, and fetishism. In both places, African superstitions were quickly taken up not only by the Indians who had similar methods of worship, but by a large number of white masters and mistresses. In the plantations of Veracruz and Pernambuco it was quite common for white masters and mistresses to resort—sometimes secretly, sometimes openly—to African sorcerers or to witchcraft to help cure their infirmities or to solve their amorous problems.

In Pernambuco, however, the superstitions of the slaves and the religious practices of their fetishism, were better preserved than in Veracruz. To this day, many superstitions of African origin are still faithfully observed by a sizeable portion of the population. In addition, the African cult of voodoo, or *xangô* is still widely practiced in the state and attended by persons of practically all walks of life.

Although the declared reason for enslaving the Africans was to save their souls by instructing them in the Catholic faith, little was done in the plantations of Veracruz and Pernambuco to attain that objective. In the two regions both masters and the Church neglected the spiritual needs of the Negro. Although many plantations, particularly in Pernambuco, had a chapel and a priest paid by the planters, few slaves received religious instruction. Many died without baptism and the last sacraments of the Church. In both regions when this happened, Negroes were denied a Christian burial and were simply dumped into the rivers or the sea. The Crown's attempts to remedy the situation, in the few instances when they were made, were only half-hearted measures which went unheeded by both planters and the Church.

As in everything, there were, of course, exceptions. A number of Negroes were baptized and received religious instruction. In most cases, these were Negroes owned by religious orders and domestic slaves who lived in the cities. They learned the catechism, attended Mass on Sundays and even had their own religious associations or brotherhoods (*cofradías* in Veracruz, and *confrarias* or *irmandades* in Pernambuco). In Veracruz for fear of conspiracy, the activities of the *cofradías* were somewhat restricted and could only be conducted under the supervision of a white prelate, or other responsible person. In Pernambuco the *confrarías* or *irmandades* enjoyed a greater degree of freedom and some of them became well-known and respected organizations. The brotherhoods of Our Lady of Guadalupe and Our Lady of the Rosary of the Black Men, both established during the seventeenth century, had sizeable memberships and even owned their own churches.

The nature of relations between masters and slaves differed from plantation to plantation. In almost all cases, however, domestic slaves in Veracruz and in Pernambuco had closer relations with their owners than Negroes who worked as field hands or at the mill. Owing in part to the closer contact required by the duties they performed, a number of these domestic slaves won the trust and affection of their masters and their mistresses. This confidence, affection, and even physical love which sometimes developed between masters and slaves, however, was less due to the flexibility and racial tolerance of the Spanish or Portuguese colonizers than to the capacity of the slaves to imitate their owners, to learn the white man's ways, in short to become more like whites than Africans.

In Veracruz and even more clearly in Pernambuco, the African chosen as friend, confidante, or lover was not the brute their masters sent to the boiler house. In the Mexican province he was the Negro *ladino* who spoke Spanish and was familiar with European customs. In most cases he was born in New Spain and often was an *Afro-mestizo*. In Pernambuco, those chosen for domestic service were mostly Negroes from Guinea, Sierra Leone, and Cape Verde, selected for the purpose because they were more attractive, cleaner and had more delicate features. All, of course, was determined according to the masters' preference and prejudices.

Conclusion

Negroes taken as servants in the plantation houses of Veracruz and Pernambuco usually dressed in a manner similar to their masters and mistresses, unlike slaves outside who went around naked or in rags. The young often grew up with their masters in the plantation houses. In most cases they did not speak any African idioms. Their language was that of the master; their customs and manners had little that could be traced to their African heritage and were usually those of the master. Often in Veracruz, and probably more frequently in Pernambuco, the young Negro and the white boy shared the same father. In short, tolerance and affection, as well as sexual attraction, increased as the slave gradually lost more and more of his African characteristics and became more and more like the white man.

Sexual relations between the Spanish or Portuguese master and first generation African women resulted primarily from the absence of European women rather than from a lack of a color bar or a preference for women of darker color on the part of the colonizers. Since in Pernambuco the scarcity of European women lasted longer than in Veracruz, relations of this type were more frequent in the Portuguese captaincy than in the Mexican province. Amorous relations between the European master and pitch-black African women, however, were of an impulsive nature and short duration. The type chosen by planters in both regions for longer affairs or for their concubines, was the mulatto woman. It was the mulatto slave, the second or third generation of a mixed union, who awakened the passions of their masters. Not because black was beautiful, but precisely because they were no longer really black and had acquired many of the features and manners of the dominant race. But even though the white master sought his mulatto slave for the pleasures of the bed, only rarely were these mixed unions accorded the respectability of matrimony. In Veracruz and in Pernambuco the Negro woman could serve as a sexual outlet for the white male but was not considered good enough to be his wife.

In Veracruz children of illicit unions between masters and slaves usually followed the mother into slavery. Children of an interracial marriage—in the few instances when they occurred—were usually given their freedom. In this respect the *senhores de engenho* of Pernambuco had, apparently, a more liberal attitude. Masters who had illicit relations with their slaves sometimes freed the children they sired even though few acknowledge their paternity. Children of interracial marriages were automatically freed by their fathers.

Considering the absence of legal restrictions, instances of voluntary manumission for humanitarian reasons were not many, although in Pernambuco they might have been somewhat more numerous than in Veracruz. In both regions domestic slaves were more frequently freed by their masters. Domestic slaves had closer relations with their owners who sometimes freed them in gratitude for their services, and domestic slaves in many cases did not engage in any work on a full-time basis. In Pernambuco more than in Veracruz, many were hangers-on kept by their owners as a status symbol; but, most importantly, in the large plantations domestic slaves were not connected with the production of sugar. Negroes who worked in the fields and in the mill were the best suited for hard work and consequently indispensable. So, in most cases when they were freed, it was not for humanitarian reasons but in the owners' self interest. This occurred most often when these slaves were too sick or too old to work and became a burden to the master. This, in many cases, was the same as sentencing the Negro to death since he was in no condition to earn his livelihood in the outside world. Although this practice must also have been used in Veracruz it was more common in the *engenhos* of Pernambuco.

Condemned to a life of captivity and having few opportunities for manumission, slaves resorted to many forms of resistance to save themselves and their offspring from their deplorable condition. In Veracruz and in Pernambuco, abortion, infanticide, and suicide were the most common avenues chosen by the Africans to terminate their misery. The most successful form of resistance, however, was to rebel against the master and escape. In Veracruz as well as in Pernambuco these instances of rebellion were very frequent. In both places Negroes began escaping practically from the very moment they had a taste of their new life. In Veracruz, the records refer to the problem of fugitive slaves since the time the first Negroes were brought to New Spain and the first attempt to organize a sizeable revolt was discovered as early as 1537. In that year a

Conclusion

number of Negroes accused of plotting to take over the land and exterminate the Spaniards were killed and quartered on orders from the Viceroy. This incident created an almost paranoid fear of slave rebellions among the Spanish population, that was to last throughout the period we are studying. Also in Pernambuco, slaves began escaping almost as soon as they realized the nature of their condition. As early as 1573, seven Negroes were hanged in that captaincy for acts of rebellion and for attacking several people.

In Veracruz as in Pernambuco, the topography of the areas near the sugar mills offered a real haven for fugitive slaves. In Veracruz they fled to the rugged mountains nearby. In Pernambuco Negroes found sanctuary in the region known as Palmares, also a mountainous area, with many forests. In the Mexican province by the end of the sixteenth century, fugitive slaves had established a number of small settlements on and near the mountains between Orizaba and Veracruz. By 1570, fugitive slave activity had spread to practically every corner of the province. In Pernambuco, fugitive slaves were forming small *quilombos* in the Palmares region as early as 1612. While a large number of Negroes fled to the mountains in Veracruz, they did so in small groups and in many separate occasions. In Pernambuco in addition to the many escapes by individuals or small groups, there were instances of mass desertions. These were caused by the wars with the Dutch (1630-35) when, taking advantage of the existing confusion, thousands of Negroes fled to the forests of Palmares.

From their hideouts in the mountains near Orizaba, and in Palmares, fugitive slaves attacked travellers on the roads and raided nearby plantations. In both places these activities presented considerable danger to the residents and to the economy, and there was fear that Negroes at the mills were conspiring to unite with the runaways and stage large revolts to exterminate the white population. In Veracruz, however, this fear was much more intense and widespread than in Pernambuco. In three occasions (1609, 1612, and 1670) intensified attacks or rumors of attacks by *cimarrones* in Veracruz, brought the white population to the verge of despair.

In Veracruz and in Pernambuco runaway slaves organized themselves in small villages or groups of villages, and established societies modeled after African lines. In Cofre de Perote in the mountains near Orizaba, for instance, a large group of Negroes lived in a small village surrounded by a stockade. They were well organized and self-sufficient, raising their own cattle and a variety of crops. They had their own king, whom they called Yanga, and militarily they were well prepared to face any attack. And in Pernambuco thousands of fugitive Negroes organized themselves into what was known as the "*Quilombo dos Palmares*," a large settlement which was an almost perfect replica of an African state. To dislodge these Negroes from their hideouts elaborate military campaigns were undertaken. At Cofre de Perote, the white troops failed. An agreement was reached, the Negroes were set free and allowed to have their own town, San Lorenzo de Los Negros. At Palmares the runaways lost. After numerous expeditions the *quilombo* was disbanded and the leaders of the Negroes killed.

As frequent and important as they were, *cimarron* activities in Veracruz never reached the epic proportions of the *Quilombo dos Palmares*. At Palmares thousands of fugitive slaves congregated to live in accordance with their own customs and their own laws. For well over half a century these Negroes fought for their freedom and for the preservation of their way of life in what was to be the longest period of resistance by a group of runaway slaves in the Western Hemisphere.

Although runaway slaves in Veracruz and in Pernambuco sometimes killed their overseers or masters in the process of escaping or during raids, there is not (despite allegations to the contrary in Veracruz) sufficient evidence that a conspiracy to seize power and kill the white residents was organized in either region during this period. In Veracruz and in Pernambuco Negroes ran away not to plot against their masters but to escape the humiliations, the misery and the harsh punishments of the slave system. and the frequency with which they fled is the strongest indictment against the cruel nature of slavery under the Spanish and the Portuguese.

Slavery in the sugar plantations of Veracruz and Pernambuco was an inhuman and odious institution. Differences in the slave system as it existed in the two regions were, as we have seen, numerous. But, as a general rule they were dictated by the exigencies of differing local conditions. In principle, slavery in

Veracruz was similar to slavery in Pernambuco as well as to slavery in other parts of the hemisphere. It thrived on the continued debasement and humiliation of the slave for the benefit of his white master; it required for its survival the constant reassurance of the supremacy of the master over the slave, of the white over the black race; and last, but not least, it gloried in the elevation of an unproductive and useless aristocracy while reducing the Negro to the level of a beast.

NOTES
1. See *Time on the Cross*, p. 150.
2. Sandoval, *La Industria del Azúcar*, p. 157.

BIBLIOGRAPHY

I. PRIMARY SOURCES

A. ARCHIVES

Algemeen Rijksarchief, The Hague, Netherlands.
Archivo General de Indias, Seville, Spain.
Archivo General de la Nación, Mexico City, Mexico.
Arquivo Histórico Ultramarino, Lisbon, Portugal.
Arquivo Nacional da Tôrre do Tombo, Lisbon, Portugal.
Arquivo Público Estadual, Recife, Brazil.
Biblioteca Nacional do Rio de Janeiro, Rio de Janeiro, Brazil.

B. PUBLISHED DOCUMENTS

Anais da Biblioteca Nacional do Rio de Janeiro. Rio de Janeiro: Biblioteca Nacional.
Bentura Beleña, Don Eusebio. *Recopilación Sumaria de todos los Autos acordados de la real audiencia y sala del crimen de esta Nueva España, y providencias de su superior Gobierno; de varias Reales Cédulas y Ordenes que después de publicada la Recopilación de Indias han podido recogerse asi de las dirigidas á la misma Audiencia ó Gobierno, como de algunas otras que por sus notables decisiones convendrá no*

ignorar. Mexico: Don Felipe de Zuniga y Outiveros, año 1787.
Boletín del Archivo General de la Nación. Mexico City.
Coelho, Duarte. *Cartas de Duarte Coelho a El-Rey.* Reprodução facsimilar, leitura paleográfica e versão moderna anotada por José Antônio Gonsalves de Mello e Cleonir Xavier de Albuquerque. Recife: Universidade Federal de Pernambuco, Imprensa Universitaria, 1967.
Colección de documentos inéditos para la historia de Hispano-América—Catálogo de los Fondos Americanos del Archivo de Protocolos de Sevilla. Sevilla.
Colección de Documentos Inéditos, relativos al descubrimiento, conquista y organización de las antiguas posesiones Españolas de América y Oceanía sacados de los Archivos del Reino y muy especialmente del de Indias. 42 vols. Madrid, 1867. Reprinted at Nedelin, Liechtenstein: Kraus Reprint Ltd., 1966.
Documentos Históricos, Biblioteca Nacional do Rio de Janeiro. Rio de Janeiro: Biblioteca Nacional.
Konetzke, Richard. *Colección de documentos para la historia de la formación social de Hispanoamérica 1493-1810.* 3 vols. Madrid: Consejo Superior de Investigaciones Científicas, 1953-1962.
Livro Primeiro do Govêrno do Brasil 1607-1633. Rio de Janeiro: Ministério das Relações Exteriores, 1958.
Paso y Troncoso, Francisco del. *Epistolario de Nueva España 1505-1818.* 8 vols. Mexico: Antigua Librería Robredo, de José Porrúa e Hijos, 1940.
———— *Papeles de Nueva España, Segunda Serie.* 7 vols. Madrid: Geografía y Estadística, 1905.
Pereira da Costa, F. A. *Anais Pernambucanos*, 10 vols. Recife: Arquivo Público Estadual, 1958-1965.

II. SECONDARY ACCOUNTS

MONOGRAPHS, GENERAL STUDIES, AND SPECIAL ACCOUNTS

Aguirre Beltrán, Gonzalo. *La Población Negra de México 1519-1810.* Mexico: Ediciones Frente Cultural, 1946.

―――― "The Slave Trade in Mexico," *Hispanic American Historical Review*, vol. 24 (August, 1944), pp. 412-431.
―――― "El trabajo del indio comparado con el del Negro en Nueva España," *México Agrario*, vol. 4, pp. 203-207.
―――― "The Tribal Origins of Slaves in Mexico," *Journal of Negro History*, vol. 31 (July, 1946), pp. 269-351.
Alegre, S. J., Francisco Javier. *Historia de la Compañia de Jesus de Nueva España*, 6 vols. Roma: Institutum Historicum, S. J., 1956.
Andrade, Nair de. "Musicalidade do Escravo Negro no Brasil," in *Novos Estudos Afro-Brasileiros*. Rio de Janeiro: Civilização Brasileira, 1937, pp. 192-200.
Antonil, André João [pseudonym of Giovanni Antonio andreoni, S. J.]. *Cultura e opulencia do Brasil por suas drogas, e minas, com varias noticias curiosas do modo de fazer o assucar; plantar, & beneficiar o Tabaco; tirar ouro das minas; & descubrir as da Prata; E dos grandes emolumentos, que esta conquista da America Meridional dá ao Reyno de Portugal com estes, & outros generos, & Contractos Reaes*. Lisboa: Officina Real Deslandesiana, 1711.
Azevedo, J. Lúcio de. *Épocas de Portugal Economico. Esboços de História*. 3a edição. Lisboa: Livraria Classica Editôra, 1973.
Barbot, John. "A Description of the coast of North and South Guinea written for the most part in 1682," in *Churchill's Voyages*. 3rd edition, 6 vols., vol. 5, London: n. p., 1744-1746.
Barléu, Gaspar. *História dos feitos recentemente praticados durante oito anos no Brasil e noutras partes sob o govêrno do illustríssimo João Maurício Conde de Nassau*. Rio de Janeiro: Serviço Gráfico do Ministério da Educação, 1940.
Barrett, Ward. *The Sugar Hacienda of the Marquesses del Valle*. Minneapolis: University of Minnesota Press, 1970.
Basauri, Carlos. "La Población Negroide Mexicana," *Estadística*, vol. 1 (Mexico: December, 1943), pp. 96-107.
Bastide, Roger. "Dusky Venus, Black Apollo," *Race*, vol. 3, no. 1 (London, November, 1961), pp. 10-18.
Benci, S. J., Jorge. *Economia Cristã dos Senhores no Governo dos Escravos (Livro Brasileiro de 1700)*. 2a edição preparada

e prefaciada por Serafim Leite, S. J. Pôrto: Livraria Apostolado da Imprensa, 1954.

Berthe, Jean-Pierre. "Xochimancas: Les travaux et les jours dans une hacienda sucrière de Nouvelle-Espagne au XVIIe siècle," *Jahrbuch für Geschichte von Staat, Wirtschaft und Gesellschaft Lateinamerikas,* vol. 3 (Cologne, 1966), pp. 88-117.

"A Bolsa do Brasil." Trans. by José Higyno Duarte Pereira. *Revista do Instituto Archeologico e Geographico Pernambucano,* vol. 4, no. 28 (Recife, January-March, 1883) pp. 127-167.

Borah, Woodrow. *New Spain's Century of Depression.* Berkeley and Los Angeles: The University of California Press, 1951.

Borah, Woodrow and Sherburne F. Cook. *The Aboriginal Population of Central Mexico on the Eve of the Spanish Conquest.* Berkeley and Los Angeles: The University of California Press, 1963.

Bowser, Frederick P. *The African Slave in Colonial Peru, 1524-1650.* Stanford, California: Stanford University Press, 1974.

Boxer, C. R. *The Dutch in Brazil, 1624-1654.* New York and Oxford: Clarendon Press, 1957.

———— *The Golden Age of Brazil, 1695-1750. Growing Pains of a Colonial Society.* Berkeley and Los Angeles: The University of California Press, 1969.

————. "Negro Slavery in Brazil, a Portuguese Pamphlet (1764)," *Race,* vol. 5, no. 3 (London, January, 1964), pp. 38-47.

———— *The Portuguese Seaborne Empire 1415-1825.* New York: Alfred P. Knopf, 1969.

———— *Race Relations in the Portuguese Colonial Empire 1415-1828.* Oxford: The Clarendon Press, 1963.

———— *Salvador de Sá and the Struggle for Brazil and Angola 1602-1686.* London: The Athlone Press, 1952.

"Breve Discurso Sôbre o Estado das Quatro Capitanias Conquistadas de Pernambuco, Itamaracá, Parahyba e Rio Grande Situadas na Parte Septentrional do Brasil." Trans. by José Higyno Duarte Pereira. *Revista do Instituto Archeologico e Geographico Pernambucano,* no. 34 (Recife, December, 1884), pp. 139-194.

Burns, E. Bradford. *A Documentary History of Brazil.* New York: Alfred P. Knopf, 1966.

Cabañas, Joaquín Ramirez. *La Ciudad de Veracruz en el siglo XVI*. Mexico: Imprenta Universitaria, 1943.
Calado, Frei Manoel. *O Valeroso Lucideno e Triunfo da Liberdade*. 2 vols., Recife: Edição da Cooperativa Editôra de Cultura Intelectual de Pernambuco, 1942.
Calmon, Pedro. *História da Civilização Brasileira*. 5ª edição aumentada. São Paulo: Companhia Editôra Nacional, 1945.
Câmara Cascudo, Luis da. *Geografia do Brasil Holandês*. Rio de Janeiro: Livraria José Olympio Editôra, 1956.
———. "Universalidade do Sabor da Sacarose da Cana de Açúcar," in *Sociologia do Açúcar*. Recife: Instituto do Açúcar e de Alcool, Museu do Açucar, 1971, pp. 23-27.
Cardim, Fernão. *Tratados da Terra e Gente do Brasil*. Introdução e notas de Baptista Caetano, Capistrano de Abreu e Rodolpho Garcia. Rio de Janeiro: Editôres J. Leite & Cia, 1925.
Cardozo, Joaquim. "Observações em tôrno da história da cidade do Recife, no periodo holandês," *Revista do Serviço Histórico e Artístico Nacional*, no. 4 (Rio de Janeiro, 1940), pp. 383-406.
Carneiro, Edison. *O Quilombo dos Palmares*. Rio de Janeiro: Civilização Brasileira, 1966.
Cavo, P. Andres. *Historia de México*. Mexico: Editorial Patria S. A., 1949.
"Certidão de 7 de dezembro de 1847 da escritura de compra e venda do engenho Apipucos lavrada em 5 de dezembro de 1577," *Revista do Museu do Açúcar*, vol. 1, no. 7 (Recife, 1972), pp. 85-88.
Chaunu, Pierre. "Pour une 'Geopolitique' de l'espace Américain," *Jahrbuch für Geschichte von Staat, Wirtschaft, und Gesellschaft Lateinamerikas*, vol. 1 (Cologne, 1964), pp. 3-26.
Chaunu, Huguette and Pierre. *Séville et L'Atlantique (1504-1650)*. 8 vols. Paris: Librarie Armand Colin, 1955.
Chávez Orozco, Luis and Enrique Florescano. *Agricultura y Industria Textil de Veracruz Siglo XIX*. Xalapa: Universidad Veracruzana, 1965.
Chevalier, François. *Land and Society in colonial Mexico: the Great Hacienda*. Trans. by Alvin Eustis. Ed. by Lesley Byrd Simpson. Berkeley and Los Angeles: The University of California Press, 1963.

Cook, Sherburne F. and Lesley Byrd Simpson. *The Population of Central Mexico in the Sixteenth Century.* Ibero-Americana 31. Berkeley and Los Angeles: The University of California Press, 1948.

Corro R., Octaviano. *Los cimarrones en Veracruz y la fundación de Amapá.* Veracruz: Imprenta Comercial, 1951.

Curtin, Philip D. *The Atlantic Slave Trade, A Census.* Madison: The University of Wisconsin Press, 1970.

Davidson, David M. "Negro Slave Control and Resistance in Colonial Mexico, 1519-1650," *Hispanic American Historical Review*, vol. 46 (August, 1946), pp. 235-253.

Davis, David Brion. "The Comparative Approach to American History: Slavery," in Laura Foner and Eugene D. Genovese, eds., *Slavery in the New World.* Englewood Cliffs, N. J.: Prentice Hall, Inc. 1969, pp. 60-68.

―――――. *The Problem of Slavery in Western Culture.* Ithaca, New York: Cornell University Press, 1966.

Deerr, Noel. *The History of Sugar.* 2 vols. London: Chapman and Hall, 1949-1950.

Degler, Carl N. *Neither Black nor White, Slavery and Race Relations in Brazil and the United States.* New York: The Macmillan Company, 1971.

Diálogos das Grandezas do Brasil. 2a edição integral, segundo o apógrafo de Leiden, aumentada por José Antônio Gonsalves de Mello. Recife: Universidade Federal de Pernambuco, Imprensa Universitaria, 1966.

"Diario da viagem do capitão João Blaer aos Palmares." Trans. by Alfredo de Carvalho. *Revista do Instituto Archeologico e Geographico Pernambucano*, no. 56 (Recife, 1902), pp. 87-96.

Diégues Júnior, Manuel. *O Banguê nas Alagoas; traços da influência do sistema econômico do engenho de açúcar na vida e na cultura regional.* Rio de Janeiro: Edição do Instituto do Açúcar e do Álcool, 1949.

Ellis, Myriam. "The Bandeiras in the Geographical Expansion of Brazil," in Richard Morse, ed., *The Bandeirantes. The Historical Role of the Brazilian Pathfinders.* New York: Alfred P. Knopf, 1965, pp. 48-63.

Engerman, Stanley L. "Comments on the Study of Race and Slavery," in Stanley L. Engerman and Eugene D. Genovese, eds., *Race and Slavery in the Western Hemisphere: Quantitative Studies.* Princeton, N. J.: Princeton University Press, 1975, pp. 495-530.

Ennes, Ernesto. "Os Primeiros Quilombos (Subsídios para a sua história)." Unpublished manuscript at *Arquivo Público Estadual,* Recife, Brazil.

Fernandes, Florestan. "Antecedentes Indígenas: Organização Social das Tribos Tupis," in Sérgio Buarque de Holanda, ed., *História Geral da Civilização Brasileira,* 3rd. edition. 7 vols. São Paulo: Difusão Europeia do Livro, 1968. Tomo I, vol. I, pp. 72-86.

Florencia, S. J., Francisco. "La Peste de 1575," in Ernesto de La Torre Villar, *Lecturas Históricas Mexicanas.* 5 vols. Mexico: Empresas Editoriales, 1966. I:573-579.

Fogel, Robert William and Stanley L. Engerman. *Time on the Cross.* Boston: Little, Brown and Company, 1974.

Freyre, Gilberto. *Casa Grande & Senzala. Formação da Familia Brasileira sob o Regime de Economia Patriarcal.* 14ª edição brasileira, 2 vols. Recife: Imprensa Oficial, 1966-1970.

―――. "Deformações de corpo dos negros fugidos," in *Novos Estudos Afro-Brasileiros.* Rio de Janeiro: Civilização Brasileira Editôra, 1937, pp. 243-248.

―――. *Nordeste, aspectos da influência da cana sôbre a vida e a paisagem do Nordeste do Brasil.* 4ª edição. Rio de Janeiro: Livraria José Olympio Editôra, 1967.

Gandavo, Pêro de Magalhães. "Historia da Provincia de Santa Cruz a que vulgarmente chamamos Brasil," in *The Histories of Brazil.* Translated and annotated by John B. Stetson, Jr. Boston: Milford House, 1972.

Gemelli Carreri, Juan F. *Viaje a la Nueva España México a fines del Siglo XVII.* 2 vols. Mexico: Ediciones Libro-Mex, 1955.

Genovese, Eugene D. *The Political Economy of Slavery. Studies in the Economy and Society of the Slave South.* New York: Pantheon Books, 1965.

―――. "The Treatment of Slaves in Different Countries: Problems in the Applications of the Comparative Method," in Laura Foner and Eugene D. Genovese, eds., *Slavery in the New World.* Englewood Cliffs, N. J.: Prentice Hall, Inc., 1969, pp. 202-210.

Goulart, José Alipio. *Da Palmatória ao Patíbulo (Castigos de Escravos no Brasil)*. Rio de Janeiro: Coleção Temas Brasileiros, Conquista, 1971.

Goulart, Mauricio. "O Problema da Mão-de-Obra: O Escravo Africano," in Sérgio Buarque de Holanda, ed., *História Geral da Civilização Brasileira*. 3rd edition, 7 vols. São Paulo: Difusão Europeia do Livro, 1968. Tomo I, vol. II, pp. 183-191.

Graham, Maria Dundas. *Journal of a voyage to Brazil*. New York: Frederick A. Praeger, 1969.

Guerra, Flávio. *Alguns documentos de arquivos portugueses de interesse para a história de Pernambuco*. Recife: Arquivo Público Estadual, n. d.

Hanke, Lewis. *Aristotle and the American Indians; a study in race prejudice in the modern world*. London: Hollis & Carter, 1959.

Harley, Ross Hammond. "Race, Social Mobility and Politics in Brazil," *Race*, vol. 4, no. 2 (London, May 1963), pp. 3-13.

Harris, Marvin. *Patterns of Race in the Americas*. New York: Walker and Co., 1964.

Herskovitz, Melville J. *The Myth of the Negro Past*. Boston: Beacon Press, 1968.

Israel, J. I., *Race, Class and Politics in Colonial Mexico 1610-1670*. London: Oxford University Press, 1975.

Kent, R. K. "Palmares: An African State in Brazil," *Journal of African History*, vol. 6, no. 2 (1965), pp. 161-175.

Kiemen, Mathias C. *The Indian Policy of Portugal in the Amazon Region, 1614-1693*. Washington, D. C.: Catholic University of America Press, 1954.

Konetzke, Richard. "La esclavitud de los indios como elemento de la estructuración social de Hispanoamérica," in *Estudios de historia social de España*. 4 vols. Madrid: Consejo Superior de Investigaciones Científicas, 1949. I:441-479.

Kubler, George. "Population Movements in Mexico, 1520-1600," *Hispanic American Historical Review*, vol. 22 (November, 1942), pp. 606-643.

Laet, Joannes de. *História ou Annaes dos Feitos da Companhia Privilegiada das Indias Occidentais desde o seu começo até o fim do anno de 1636*. Trans. by José Higyno Duarte Pereira and Pedro Souto Maior. 2 vols. Rio de Janeiro: Officinas Gráficas da Bibliotheca Nacional, 1916-1925.

León Nicolás. *Las Castas de México Colonial o Nueva España. Noticias Etno-Antropológicas.* Mexico: Talleres Gráficos del Museo Nacional de Arqueología, Historia y Etnografía, 1924.

Leonard, Irving A. *Baroque Times in Old Mexico.* Ann Arbor: The University of Michigan Press, 1971.

Léry, Jean de. *Le Voyage au Brésil de Jean de Léry 1556-1558.* Avec une introduction par Charly Clerc. Paris: Payot, 1927.

"Livro do Tombo do Mosteiro de São Bento da Paraíba," *Revista do Arquivo Público* (Recife: Second Semester, 1946), pp. 141-354.

López de Velasco, Juan. *Geografía y Descripción Universal de las Indias.* Madrid: Establecimiento Tipográfico de Fortanet, 1894.

"O Machadão do Brasil," Trans. by A. Souto Maior. *Revista do Instituto Archeologico e Geographico Pernambucano* (Recife, March, 1908), pp. 125-170.

Magalhães, Basilio de. *O Açúcar nos primórdios do Brasil Colonial.* Rio de Janeiro: Edição do Instituto do Açúcar e do Alcool, 1953.

"Manuscritos da Igreja de Nossa Senhora do Rosário dos Homens Pretos do Recife," *Arquivos,* nos. 7-20 (Recife: Prefeitura Municipal, 1945-1951), pp. 52-120.

Marchant, Alexander. *From Barter to Slavery. The Economic Relations of Portuguese and Indians in the Settlement of Brazil, 1500-1580.* Baltimore: The Johns Hopkins Press, 1942.

Mauro, Frédéric. *L'Expansion Européenne 1600-1870.* Paris: Presses Universitaires de France, 1964.

―――. "México y Brasil dos Economías Coloniales Comparadas," *Historia Mexicana* (Mexico: April-June, 1961), pp. 571-587.

―――. *Le Portugal et L'Atlantique aux XVIIe Siècle 1570-1670.* Paris: Ecole Pratique des Hautes Etudes, 1960.

Mello, José Antônio Gonsalves de. "Casa Grande." Separata da *Revista do Museu do Açúcar.* Vol. 1, no. 6 (Recife, 1971).

———. ed. *Confissões de Pernambuco 1594-1595; primeira visitação do Santo Oficio às partes do Brasil*. Recife: Universidade Federal de Pernambuco, 1970.

———. *Henrique Dias, Governador dos Pretos, Crioulos e Mulatos do Estado do Brasil*. Recife: Universidade do Recife, 1954.

———. "Um Regimento de Feitor-Mor de Engenho de 1663," *Boletim do Instituto Joaquim Nabuco de Pesquisas Sociais*. Vol. 2 (Recife, 1953), pp. 80-87.

———. "A Situação do Negro sob o Dominio Hollandez," in *Novos Estudos Afro-Brasileiros*. Rio de Janeiro: Civilização Brasileira Editôra, 1937, pp. 201-221.

———. *Tempo dos Flamengos. Influência da Ocupação Holandesa na Vida e na Cultura do Norte do Brasil*. Rio de Janeiro: Livraria José Olympio Editôra, 1947.

Montaigne, Michel de. "Essais," in Albert Thibaudet and Maurice Rat, ed. *Montaigne Œuvres Complètes*. Bruges: Bibliothèque de la Pléiade, Editions Gallimard, 1967, pp. 1-1097.

Morgan, Edmund S. *The Birth of the Nation 1763-1789*. Chicago: The University of Chicago Press, 1973.

Mota, Mauro. *Os bichos na fala da gente*. Recife: Instituto Joaquim Nabuco de Pesquisas Sociais - M.E.C., 1969.

Moura, Clovis. *Rebeliões de Senzala. Quilombos, Insurreições, Guerrilhas*. Rio de Janeiro: Coleção Temas Brasileiros, Conquista, 1972.

Nieuhof, Joan. *Memorável Viagem Marítima e Terrestre ao Brasil*. Tradução do Inglês por Moacir N. Vasconcellos, confronto com a edição holandesa de 1682, introdução, notas, crítica bibliográfica e bibliografia por José Honório Rodrigues. São Paulo: Livraria Martins, 1942.

Nina Rodrigues, Raymundo. *Os Africanos no Brasil*. São Paulo: Companhia Editôra Nacional, 1932.

Palmer, Colin Alphonsous. "Negro Slavery in Mexico, 1570-1650." Unpublished Ph.D. dissertation, Department of History, The University of Wisconsin, 1970.

Parry, J. H. *The Spanish Theory of Empire in the Sixteenth Century*. Cambridge: The University Press, 1940.

Perdigão Malheiros, Agostinho Marques. *A Escravidão no Brasil. Ensaio Histórico-Jurídico-Social*. 2 vols. São Paulo: Edições Cultura, 1944.

Pereira da Costa, F.A. *Folk-Lore Pernambucano*. 1ª edição autónoma. Recife: Arquivo Público Estadual, 1974.

———. "Origens Históricas da Industria Assucareira em Pernambuco," *Arquivos*, nos. 7-20 (Recife: Prefeitura Municipal, 1945-1951), pp. 257-329.

Pi-Sunyer, Oriol. "Historical Background to the Negro in Mexico," *Journal of Negro History*, vol. 42, no. 4 (October, 1957), pp. 237-246.

Pike, Ruth. *Aristocrats and Traders: Sevillian Society in the Sixteenth Century*. Ithaca, New York: Cornell University Press, 1972.

———. *Enterprise and Adventure: the Genoese in Seville and the Opening of the New World*. Ithaca, New York: Cornell University Press, 1966.

Ramos, Arthur. *The Negro in Brazil*. Trans. by Richard Pattee. Washington, D.C.: The Associated Publishers, Inc., 1951.

Rawley, James A. *The Transatlantic Slave Trade: A History*. New York: W.W. Norton & Company, 1981.

Rodney, Walter. "Portuguese Attempts at Monopoly on the Upper Guinea Coast," *Journal of African History*, vol. 6 (1965), pp. 307-322.

Rodrigues, José Honório. *Brasil: Periodo Colonial*. Mexico: Instituto Panamericano de Geografia e Historia, 1953.

Rodrigues de Carvalho. "Aspectos da influência africana na formação social do Brasil," in *Novos Estudos Afro-Brasileiros*. Rio de Janeiro: Civilização Brasileira Editôra, 1937, pp. 16-74.

Saco, José Antonio. *Historia de la Esclavitud de la Raza Africana en el Nuevo Mundo y en especial en los Paises Américo-Hispanos*. 4 vols. Habana: Cultural, S.A., 1938.

Salvador, Frei Vicente do. *História do Brasil 1500-1627*. 5ª edição. São Paulo: Edições Melhoramentos, 1965.

Sandoval, Alonso de. *De Instauranda Aethiopium Salute; El Mundo de la Esclavitud Negra en América*. Bogotá: Biblioteca de la Presidencia de Colombia, 1956.

Sandoval, Fernando B. *La Industria del Azúcar en Nueva España*. Mexico: Universidad Nacional Autónoma de Mexico. Instituto de Historia, 1951.

Scelle, Georges. "The Slave Trade in the Spanish Colonies of America: The Assiento," *The American Journal of International Law*, vol. 4, no. 3 (July, 1910), pp.612-661.

———. *La Traite Négrière aux Indes de Castille.* 2 vols. Paris: Larose and Tenin, 1906.

Sluiter, Engel. "Report on the State of Brazil, 1612," *Hispanic American Historical Review*, vol. 29 (November, 1949), pp. 518-562.

Silva Rêgo, A. da. *Portuguese Colonization in the Sixteenth Century: A Study of the Royal Ordinances (Regimentos).* Johannesburg: Witwatersrand University Press, 1965.

Smith, Robert C. "Décadas do Rosário dos Pretos. Documentos da Irmandade," *Arquivos*, nos. 7-20 (Recife: Prefeitura Municipal, 1945-1951), pp. 143-170.

Southey, Robert. *History of Brazil.* 3 vols. London: Longman, Hurst, Rees, Orme, and Brown, 1817-1822.

Souto Maior, A. *História do Brasil*, 9ª edição. São Paulo: Companhia Editôra Nacional, 1971.

Tannenbaum, Frank. *Slave and Citizen: The Negro in the Americas.* New York: Vintage Books, 1946.

Taunay, Affonso de Escaragnolle. *Subsídios para a História do Tráfico Africano no Brasil Colonial.* Rio de Janeiro: Instituto Histórico, Imprensa Nacional, 1941.

"Traslado do Testamento com que faleceo Dona Maria de Alburquerque senhora do engenho da Moribeca Invocação de Santo Antonio," in Fernando Pio (ed.), "Cinco documentos para a história dos engenhos de Pernambuco." Separata da *Revista do Museu do Açúcar*, no. 2, Recife, 1969, pp. 35-43.

Trens, Manuel B. *Historia de Veracruz.* 6 vols. Jalapa-Enríquez, Veracruz, n. p., 1944-1950.

Valente, Waldemar. "Tratamento do escravo africano no Brasil," in *Antropologia do Açúcar*. Recife: Museu do Açúcar, 1972, pp. 71-100.

van der Dussen, Adriaen. *Relatório sôbre as capitanias conquistadas pelos holandeses (1639), suas condições econômicas e sociais.* Tradução, introdução e notas de José António Gonsalves de Mello, neto. Rio de Janeiro: Instituto do Açúcar e do Álcool, 1947.

Verdonk, Adriano. "Descrição das Capitanias de Pernambuco, Itamaracá, Parahyba e Rio Grande," *Revista do Instituto Archeologico e Geographico Pernambucano*, no. 55 (Recife, 1901), pp. 215-227.

Villaseñor y Sanchez, J. Antonio de. *Theatro Americano. Descripción general de los reynos y provincias de las Nueva España y sus jurisdicciones.* 2 vols. Mexico: Ed. Nacional, 1952.
von Lippmann, Edmund O. *História do Açúcar.* Trans. by Rodolfo Coutinho. 2 vols. Rio de Janeiro: n. p., 1941.
Wätjen, Hermann. *O Dominio Colonial Hollandez no Brasil. Um Capítulo da História Colonial do Século XVII.* Trans. by Pedro Celso Uchoa Cavalcanti. Recife: Edição especial da Companhia Editôra Nacional para o Govêrno do Estado de Pernambuco, 1938.
Zavala, Silvio. *Los Esclavos Indios en Nueva España.* Mexico: El Colegio Nacional, 1968.
Zelinsky, Wilbur. "The Historical Geography of the Negro Population of Latin America," *Journal of Negro History*, vol. 34 (April, 1949), pp. 153-221.
Zorita, Alonso de. *Breve y summaria relación de los señores y maneras y diferencias que habia de ellos en Nueva España*, in Joaquin Garcia Icazbalceta (ed.), Nueva Colecćion de documentos para la historia de México. 8 vols. Mexico: Andrade y Norales, 1891, vol. 3.
Zurara, Gomes Eanes da. *Crónica de Guiné.* Segundo o ms. de Paris. Introdução, notas, novas considerações e glossário de José de Bragança. Lisboa; Livraria Civilização Editôra, 1973.

INDEX

Aberraza, Melcora de, 24
Abreu, Thomás de, 134
Aculzingo, 24
African Slave Trade: asientos, 12-19, 23, 29, 172, 176; contraband, 13, 15, 17; import duties, 10, 13, 76-77; import licenses, 10-11, 15-17, 75, 85, 171-173
Afro-mestizos, 47, 184
Aguilar, Francisco de, 19
Aguirre Beltrán, Gonzalo, 11, 12, 15, 19
Albornoz, Rodrigo de, 11, 25, 172
Albuquerque, Jerônimo de, 76, 90, 168
Albuquerque, Maria de, 141
Alçaprema, 91
Alegre, Francisco Javier, 55, 60
Alforria, 139-140
Alvarado, town of, 53
Amsterdam, 75
Anchieta, José de, 77, 125, 170
Andrade, Agostinho Cesar de, 78
Anginho, 103
Angola, 12, 14, 16, 19-20, 44, 60, 78-80, 82, 87, 100, 116, 118, 126, 132, 173-174, 176

Angolas, 174, 177
Antonil, André João, 93, 102, 138-139, 180
Aragão, Baltazar de, 126
Arana, Diego de, 11
Ardra, 79, 100, 150, 174, 177
Arguim, 73
Armenta, Juan de, 11
Artesa, 44
Asientista, 12-15, 58
Asoleadero, 25
Audiencia of New Spain, 15
Azevedo, João Lucio de, 69
Azores, 90

Bacalhau, 94
Bahena, Alvaro de, 54
Bandeirantes, 153, 159-160
Bantu, 79, 100
Barbados, 82
Barléu, Gaspar, 155
Baron, Rudolf, 157
Barreiros, Antonio Ribeiro, 134
Barros Cristovão de, 141
Barros, Francisco, 134
Barroso del Pozo, Juan, 16-17, 173
Batuque, 130-131, 135, 156, 183

205

Beberibe, 90, 168
Benci, Jorge, 105
Berbers, 174
Berbesies, 30
Bezerra, Jácome, 158
Bixorda, Jorge Lopes, 84
Blaer, Jan, 157
Bôlo, 104
Borah, Woodrow, 4
Bowser, Frederick P., 19
Boxer, Charles R., 79, 142
Brandão, Francisco Lopes, 115
Brazilwood, 66-67, 75, 167, 170
Bretoa, 74

Cabral, Pedro Álvares, 74
Cacatepec, 55
Cadena, Jerônimo, 109, 121
Caetés, 67
Café mandingueiro, 136
Caja de Negros, 31
Calabar, 79, 100, 117, 150, 174, 177
Calabar, Domingos Fernandes, 119
Calado, Manoel, 129, 138
Câmara Cascudo, Luis da, 89, 167
Camarão, Antonio Felipe, 107
Camino Real, 53, 58
Canaries, 12, 111
Cape of Good Hope, 79
Cape of Santo Agostinho, 153
Cape Verde, 12, 19, 25, 30, 79, 90, 100, 111, 137, 172-174, 177, 184
Capico, Pêro, 90
Capitão de Aldeia, 70
Capitão do Mato, 152-153
Cardim, Fernão, 77, 98, 125
Carneiro, Edison, 155
Caminha, Pêro Vaz de, 71
Carrilho, Fernão, 159, 163
Carrion, Melchor de, 11
Carta de doação, 83, 111
Cartagena de Indias, 13-15, 23
Carvalho, Agostinho, 134
Casa da India, 74, 77, 89, 90, 167
Casa da Mina, 73
Casa de Contratación, 10, 12-14
Casa de Guiné, 73

Casa de ingenio, 25
Casa Forte, 90, 168
Cataro, Maria, 24
Cempoala, 5, 24-25
Charles V, 10, 35
Chaunu, Pierre, 12, 87
Chevalier, François, 24, 42
Chiapas, 4, 6
Chietla, 24
Chuchumbe, 44, 182
Cimarron, 52-59, 187-188
Coatzacoalcos, 6
Coelho, Duarte, 75-76, 83, 91, 111, 168
Cofradía, 46, 184
Cofre de Perote, 56, 188
Companhia de Lagos, 73
Companhia Portuguesa de Cabo Verde, Cacheu e Negócio dos Pretos, 17, 174
Concubinage, 47, 68, 138, 185
Confraria, 134, 184
Congo, 79, 118, 172, 174
Conquistadores, 10
Consulado y Comercio de Sevilla, 16
Cook, Sherburne, 4
Córdoba, 24-25, 58, 61
Correa, Manoel Gonçalves, 134
Cortés, Hernán, 11, 23-25, 42, 167
Cortés, Juan, 11
Costa, João Esteves da, 134
Cotastla, 5
Coun, Albert, 11
Council of Portugal, 20
Council of the Indies, 10, 12, 46
Coutinho, Francisco Pereira, 83-84
Coutinho, Gonzalo Vaes, 14-15
Coutinho, João Rodrigues, 14
Cruz, Manuel Fernandes, 97, 109
Cuernavaca, 24, 36-37, 42, 53
Cunha, João de Freitas da, 163
Curaçao, 17

Davidson, David M., 47
Davis, David Brion, 39
Deerr, Nöel, 87
Degler, Carl N., 146

Index

Dias, André, 163
Dias, Henrique, 78, 153
Dias Matoso, Juan, 25

Elmina (see also São Jorge da Mina), 80, 131
Encomienda, 3
Engenho Real, 92, 95
Engerman, Stanley L., 175
Enríquez de Almanza, Martín, 30, 54
Española, 10, 30
Espiche, 5
Etna, 97
Etthmeyer, Mrs. Otto, 128
Eynger, Heinrich, 10-11

Feitoria, 65, 75
Ferdinand (of Aragón), 10
Fernandes, Florestan, 66
Fernandes d'Elvas, Antonio, 15
Fogel, Robert W., 175
Foral, 83
Fragoso, Francisco, 140
Francês, João Lourenço, 109
Freyre, Gilberto, 68, 92, 123, 125, 127, 136, 145
Fula, 30
Fumo de Angola, 154

Gandavo, Pêro de Magalhães, 77
Ganga-Muíça, 155, 159
Ganga-Zona, 155
Ganga-Zumba, 155-156, 159
García, Antonio, 16
Garrido, Juan, 11
Gemelli Carreri, Juan F., 57
Genovese, Eugene D., 114, 143, 145-146
Goa, 142
Goes, Pêro de, 76
Gold Coast, 80
Gómez Angel, Melchor, 16
Gonçalves, Antão, 9, 73
González de Herrera, Pedro, 55-57
Goulart, Mauricio, 76-77
Graham, Maria Dundas, 132
Grillo, Domingo, 16

Guanajuato, 6, 32, 53
Gueguetlán, 24
Guinea, 19, 30, 82, 100, 137, 173, 184
Gulf of Guinea, 9
Gumenot, Lorenzo de, 10

Haecx, Hendrick, 141
Henry, the Navigator, 73-74
Holland, 126, 128, 181
Huatusco, 53, 58

Igarassú, 76, 118
India, 90, 111
Indian: cultures in Brazil, 66; deaths, 3-4, 11, 26, 67-68; decrees and laws protecting, 7, 26, 27, 69-70, 72, 142, 170, 171; depopulation, 3-5, 7, 17, 25, 29, 67, 69, 70, 73, 169-170; enslavement of, 3, 5, 67-69, 169-171; punishment of, 69; resistance, 4; tribute, 3, 5; working conditions, 4
Indios de socorro, 7, 26
Ingenio, 25
Inquisition (Holy Office of the), 32, 44, 131
Ipojuca, 91
Irmandade, 134, 184
Isthmus of Tehuantepec, 6
Itamaracá, 78, 90, 91, 111
Izcalpan, 26

Jaboatão, 91-92
Jalapa, 5, 24-26, 53
Jalisco, 6
Jaques, Cristovão, 75
Jews, 117
João III, 75, 84
João VI, 118, 130

Kubler, George, 5

La Antigua, 26
La Rinconada, 24, 53
Labor: shortage of, 5, 7, 9, 17, 26, 79, 171
Laet, Joannes, 78

Lagos, 73
Laguna de Términos, 6
Lamego, Manuel Rodrigues, 16
Las Casas, Bartolomé de, 3, 7, 170-171
Las Siete Partidas, 35, 51
Laurencio, Juan, 55, 57
Laval, François Pyrard de, 126
Lima, 19
Lisbon, 9, 12, 56, 73-74, 76, 90, 138, 159
Lins, Cristovão, 158
Lomelín, Augustín, 16, 58
Lomelín, Ambrosio, 16
Lomelín, Franco, 16
Lomelín, Leonardo, 25
Lopes, Manuel, 158-159, 163
López Montalvan, Diego, 31

Macumbeiro, 135-136
Madeira, 90
Madrid, 126, 181
Maestro de azúcar, 28, 30, 31, 175, 177-178
Mamposteiro, 140
Mandadoras, 28
Mandinga, 30
Mandingueiro, 135
Manumission, 35, 39, 47, 139-142, 186
Maracatu, 130-131, 135, 183
Marfil, Pedro, 32
Marijuana, 154
Marquesado del Valle, 31
Massapê, 111, 167-168
Martínez, Francisco, 24
Matlala, 24
Matosa, Francisco de la, 60
Mauro, Frédéric, 42
Measles, 4, 169
Medellín, 24, 53
Melo e Castro, Caetano de, 157
Mendes, Francisco, 77
Mendez de Sossa, Cristóbal, 16
Mendonça, André Furtado, 161
Mendoza, Antonio de, 11, 24, 52
Menezes e Sequeira, Diogo de, 151
Mestre de açucar, 97, 101, 175

Mexico City, 19, 44, 52-55, 57-58
Michoacan, 24, 37
Mina, 12, 79, 117, 174
Misantla, 53
Miscegenation, 47, 137-139, 145, 185-186
Mocambo, 152, 154-155, 157, 160, 163
Montaigne, Michel de, 66
Moreira, Gonçalo, 163
Morocco, 90
Mozambique, 132
Muribeca, 91

Naples, 116
Narváez, Panfilo de, 11
Nassau, Johan Maurits, Count of, 77, 80, 82, 107, 117, 157
Navarro, Moysés, 110
Nayarit, 6
Negra do pote, 74
Negro de banda forra, 93
Negro de ganho, 139
Negroes: alleged superior strength of, 27, 31, 36; characteristics of, 17, 30, 100, 150, 177
New Laws (of 1542-43), 5, 7, 171
New Spain, 10-12, 14, 17, 25, 29-30, 51-52, 167-170, 172, 179, 184, 186
Nina Rodriques, Raymundo, 79, 135
Nieuhof, Joan, 135, 150
Nóbrega, Manuel da, 68, 138, 143, 170
Noronha, Pedro de, 77

Oaxaca, 24, 37
Olinda, 76-78, 80, 90-91, 104, 132, 168
Orichá, 135, 144
Orizaba-Tequila, 24-26, 41, 56, 168
Orizaba, town of, 24, 53-54, 187-188
Ovando, Nicolás, 9
Overseas Council (of Portugal), 159

Pachuca, 53
Páez, Hernando, 11
Palmatoria, 104
Pánuco, 6, 26

Index

Papaloapan, 26
Parada, Antón de la, 54
Paraiba, 78, 91
Peça de Indias, 84, 117
Peças de escravos, 76-77, 84-85, 100, 153, 172, 176-177
Perdigão Malheiros, Agostinho Marques, 10, 85
Peru, 65
Philip II, 5, 69
Philip III, 5, 27, 171
Piezas de esclavos, 172, 177
Piezas de India, 12-13, 18-20
Pinto, Jorge Homem, 109
Plagues and epidemics, 3-4, 12, 38, 68, 102, 120, 169-170
Pompeii, 116
Pôrto Calvo, 138, 154-56, 158, 160
Portugal, 73-74, 90, 125-126, 140
Post, Frans, 125, 142
Potí, Pêro, 107
Prado, Bartolomeu Bueno, 153
Principe, Island of, 90
Puebla de los Angeles, 57
Punta de Antón Lizardo, 53

Querétaro, 6
Quilombo, 103, 152, 162, 187
Quilombo dos Palmares, 54, 60, 153-154, 156-161, 188
Quiroga, Vasco de, 7, 170

Ramos, Arthur, 87
Rawley, James, 10
Real de negros, 43-44, 182
Rebolasco, Joan Bautista de, 19
Recife, 14, 77, 79-82, 100, 107, 117, 127-128, 132, 161
Redução, 68-69, 170
Rego, André de Barros, 112
Reynel, Pedro Gómez, 12-15, 18-20, 23, 172
Rijbach, Jurgens, 157
Río Blanco, 53
Rio de Janeiro, 80, 153
Rio de Ouro, 9

Rio Grande, 78
Rodrigues, José Honorio, 115

Sacamandú, 44, 182
Sacharum officinarum, 89, 167
Saco, José Antonio, 15
Salvador, 14, 76, 84
San Cristobal, 19
San Juan de la Punta, 57
San Juan de Ulloa, 19, 23, 30
San Lorenzo de Cerralvo, 57
San Lorenzo de los Negros, 57, 188
Sandoval, Alonso de, 25
Santa Hermandad, 52
Santísima Trinidad, 24-26, 41-43, 168, 181
Santo Antônio do Cabo, 91
Santo Domingo, 10
São Jorge da Mina, 16, 73
São Tomé, 12, 14, 19, 77, 80, 90, 173
São Vincente, 75, 90, 111
Sardinha, Pêro Fernandes, 67
Sayller, Hieronymus, 10
Scelle, Georges, 18
Schetz, Erasmus, 111
Sebastião (King of Portugal), 69
Sedeño, Juan, 11
Senhores de engenho, 43, 185-186, 178
Senzala, 95-96, 124-125, 128, 130, 135, 182
Sesmaria, 90, 111, 168
Seville, 9, 12, 74, 172
Sicily, 90, 116
Sierra Leone, 79, 100, 137, 174, 177, 184
Siliceo, Sebastián de, 16
Simonsen, Roberto, 87
Sinaloa, 6
Slavery: profitability of, 108-109, 120, 178
Slaves: clothing of, 35, 105-106, 137-138, 185; as concubines, 47, 106, 138, 185; cruelty towards, 31, 33-34, 52, 58, 100-105, 142, 153, 179-180; deaths during crossing, 14, 81; decrees and laws protecting, 33, 35,

105, 118, 133; demand for, 10-12, 29, 76, 79, 82, 86, 92, 169, 173; desire for freedom, 35-36, 51, 143, 161, 186; diet of 27-28, 81, 94, 154, 178-179; domestic, 29, 46-47, 74, 99, 101, 104, 116, 127-128, 136-138, 141, 175-177, 181-182, 184-185; entertainment among, 44-45, 126, 129-130, 181; family life of, 43-44, 124, 128, 144, 156, 182, housing of, 43, 124-125, 128, 130, 135, 145, 181-182; importation of, 9-11, 25, 74; in cities and towns, 74; labor in sugar plantations, 27-28, 93-94, 96-97, 114, 116, 149, 174; legal position of, 35, 161; mortality of, 31, 33, 38, 94, 108, 118, 120; number of, 11-12, 14, 16-17, 19, 25-26, 74, 77-78, 81-85, 87, 114, 163, 173; overworking of, 27, 31, 96-97, 102, 174; prices of, 10, 13, 15, 17, 29-30, 80, 99-100, 108, 117, 176-178; as prostitutes, 106, 138-139; punishment of, 31-34, 51-52, 54, 60, 94, 97, 102-105, 108, 118, 179-181; purchasing own freedom, 93, 139-140, 146; religion among, 33, 44-45, 129-136, 156, 183-184; resistance and rebellions by, 11, 51-54, 57, 60, 86, 104, 118, 149-154, 156-162, 186-188; runaways, 32, 35, 52-53, 57-58, 60, 78-79, 103, 118, 145, 150, 152-162, 178, 186-188; as skilled workers, 28, 30, 98-99, 101, 175, 177
Smallpox, 4, 11, 120, 169
Soares, Diogo, 91
Soares, Fernão, 91
Sobrino, Gaspar, 126
Sousa, Martim Afonso de, 90, 111
Sousa, Tomé de, 84, 91, 125
Souto Maior, João da Cunha, 159
Spain 7, 10-11, 15, 172-173
Sudan, 79, 174
Sugar mills, 11, 24, 41, 75-76, 82, 90-91, 123-124; capital requirements of, 92, 113; income from, 25, 91, 125

Tabocas, Battle of, 129
Tacamachalco, 4
Tamaulipas, 6
Taunay, Affonso de Escaragnolle, 10
Tenochtitlán, 43, 66
Tigre, 127
Tlacotalpan, 53
Toledo, Maria de, 11
Tordesillas, 83
Trapiche, 25, 91
Trapichillos a mano, 25
Tronco, 103, 180
Tumbeiros, 81
Tupi, 66
Tupinambá, 83
Tuxpan, 24
Tuxtla, 24, 26, 31, 42, 167
Valle de Ostotipac, 24
Valencia, 90, 111
Valley of Orizaba, 25-26
Várzea, 90, 167
Várzea do Capibaribe, 90, 168
Vasconcelos, Zenóbio Accioly de, 158
Veedores, 26, 171
Velasco I, Luis de, 12, 52, 55
Velho, Domingos Jorge, 159-160
Venice, 90
Veracruz, City of, 5, 11, 13-15, 23, 34, 53, 55, 172, 187
Vesuvius, 97
Viceroy, 11, 12, 15, 24, 30, 52, 54, 168
Vieira, Antonio, 79, 107, 149, 180
Vieira, João Fernandes, 86, 93, 95, 102, 110, 153
Vieira de Melo, Bernardo, 160
Vilhena, Luis dos Santos, 118
Vivero y Velasco, Juán de, 24

Wagner, Zacharias, 118
Wätjen, Hermann, 80-81
West India Company, 80, 106, 108-110, 116-117, 119, 128, 141, 153, 172, 178
Witchcraft, 45, 131-132, 135-136, 156, 183
Wolof, 30, 79, 174

Index

Xamloluco, 5
Xangô, 132, 135, 156

Yanga, 54-57, 60, 188
Yebra, Pedro de, 54
Yellow fever, 4-5, 169

Zacatecas, 6
Zorita, Alonso de, 3
Zumárraga, Juan de, 7, 170
Zumbi, 154-155, 159-161